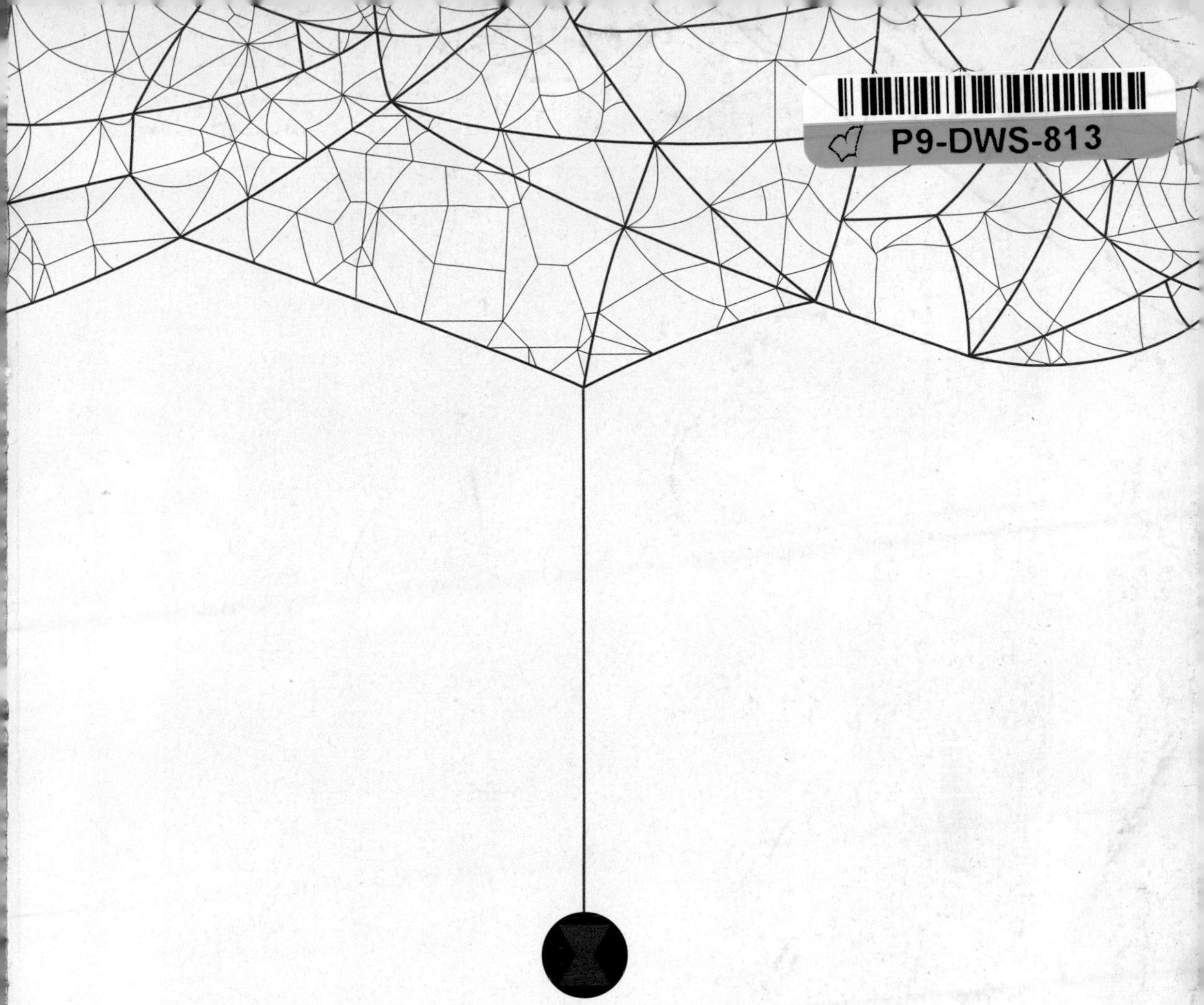

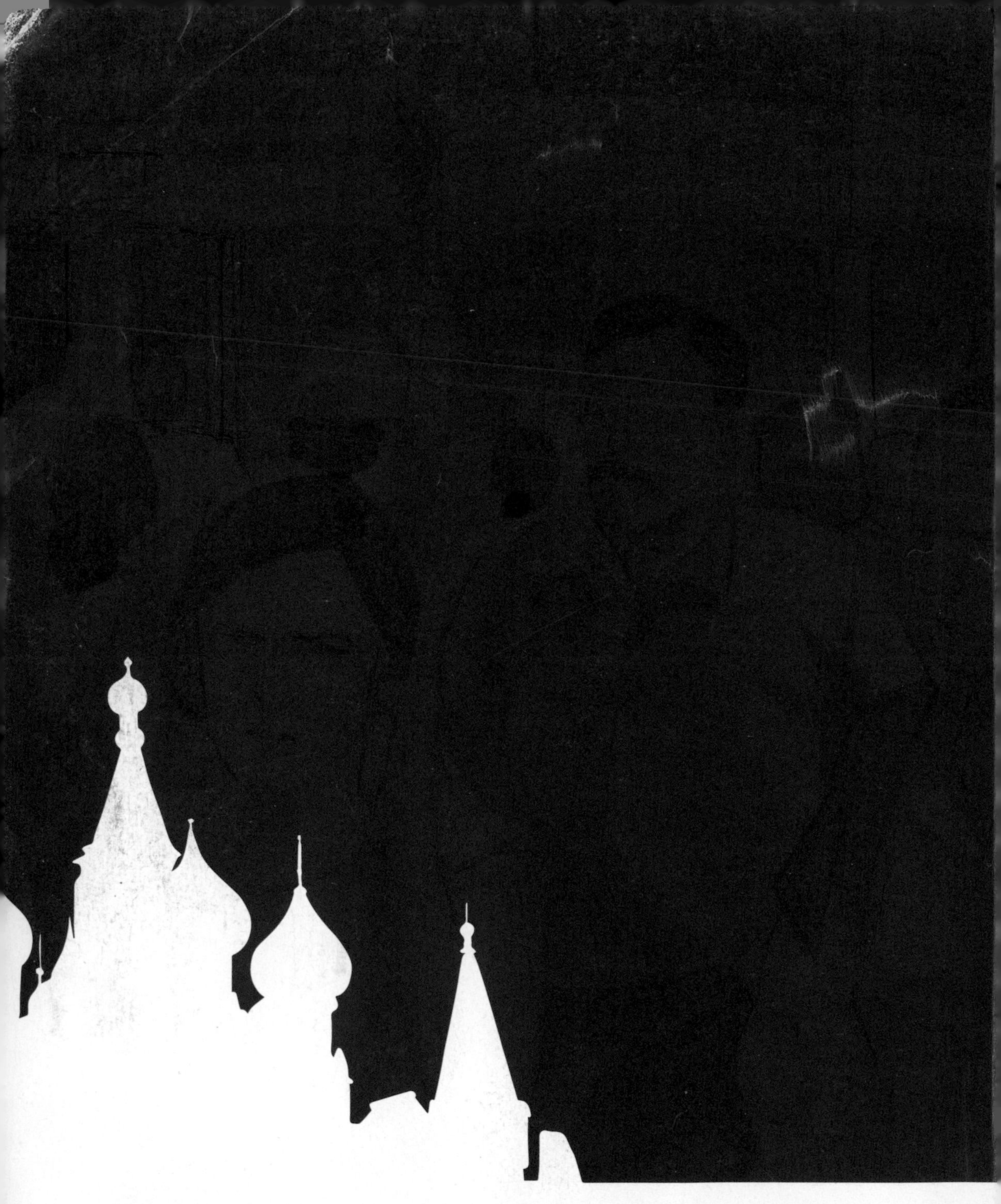

Collection Editor: Jennifer Grünwald • Assistant Editor: Sarah Brunstad • Associate Managing Editor: Alex Starbuck • Editor, Special Projects: Mark D. Beazley
Senior Editor, Special Projects: Jeff Youngquist • SVP Print, Sales & Marketing: David Gabriel • Book Design: Jeff Powell

Editor in Chief: Axel Alonso • Chief Creative Officer: Joe Quesada • Publisher: Dan Buckley • Executive Producer: Alan Fine

BLACK WIDOW VOL. 2: THE TIGHTLY TANGLED WEB. Contains material originally published in magazine form as BLACK WIDOW #7-12 and PUNISHER #9. First printing 2015. ISBN# 978-0-7851-8820-9. Published by MARVEL WORLDWIDE, INC., a subsidiary of MARVEL ENTERTAINMENT, LLC. OFFICE OF PUBLICATION: 135 West 50th Street, New York, NY 10020. Printed in the U.S.A. ALAN FINE, EVP - Office of the President, Marvel Worldwide, Inc. and EVP & CMO Marvel Characters B.V.; DAN BUCKLEY, Publisher & President - Print, Animation & Digital Divisions; JOE QUESADA, Chief Creative Officer; TOM BREVOORT, SVP of Publishing; DAVID BOGART, SVP of Operations & Procurement, Publishing; C.B. CEBULSKI, SVP of Creator & Content Development; DAVID GABRIEL, SVP Print, Sales & Marketing; JIM O'KEEFE, VP of Operations & Logistics; DAN CARR, Executive Director of Publishing Technology; SUSAN CRESPI, Editorial Operations Manager; ALEX MORALES, Publishing Operations Manager; STAN LEE, Chairman Emeritus. For information regarding advertising in Marvel Comics or on Marvel.com, please contact Niza Disla, Director of Marvel Partnerships, at ndisla@marvel.com. For Marvel subscription inquiries, please call 800-217-9158. **Manufactured between 11/28/2014 and 1/5/2015 by R.R. DONNELLEY, INC., SALEM, VA, USA.**

10 9 8 7 6 5 4 3 2 1

BLACK WIDOW
THE TIGHTLY TANGLED WEB

WRITER
NATHAN EDMONDSON

ARTIST/COVER ART
PHIL NOTO

LETTERER
VC'S CLAYTON COWLES

EDITOR
ELLIE PYLE

PUNISHER #9

ARTIST/COVER ART **MITCH GERADS**

LETTERER **VC'S CORY PETIT**

EDITOR **JAKE THOMAS**

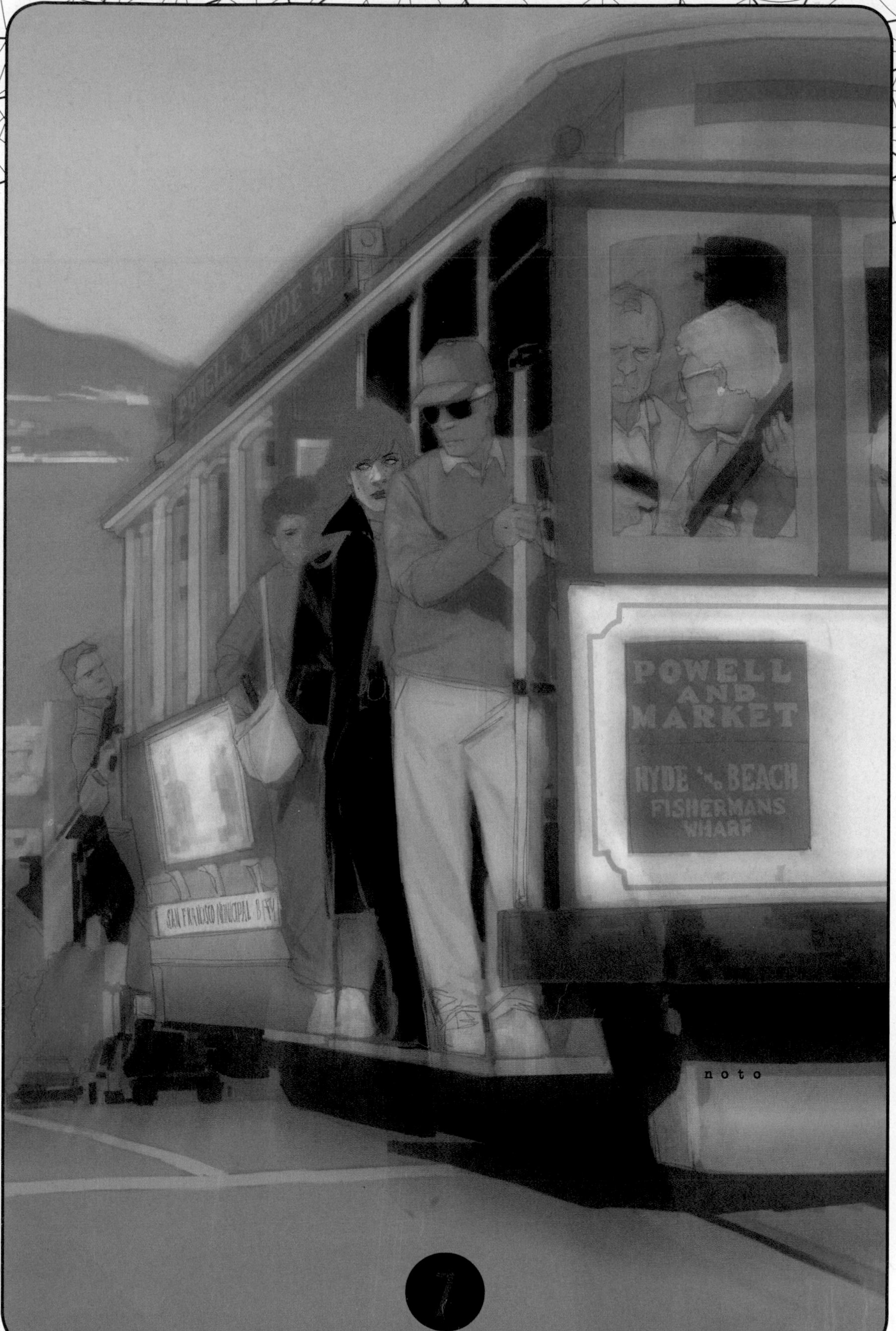
POWELL & HYDE ST.
SAN FRANCISCO MUNICIPAL RY
POWELL AND MARKET
HYDE AND BEACH
FISHERMANS WHARF
noto
7

FOG OF WAR

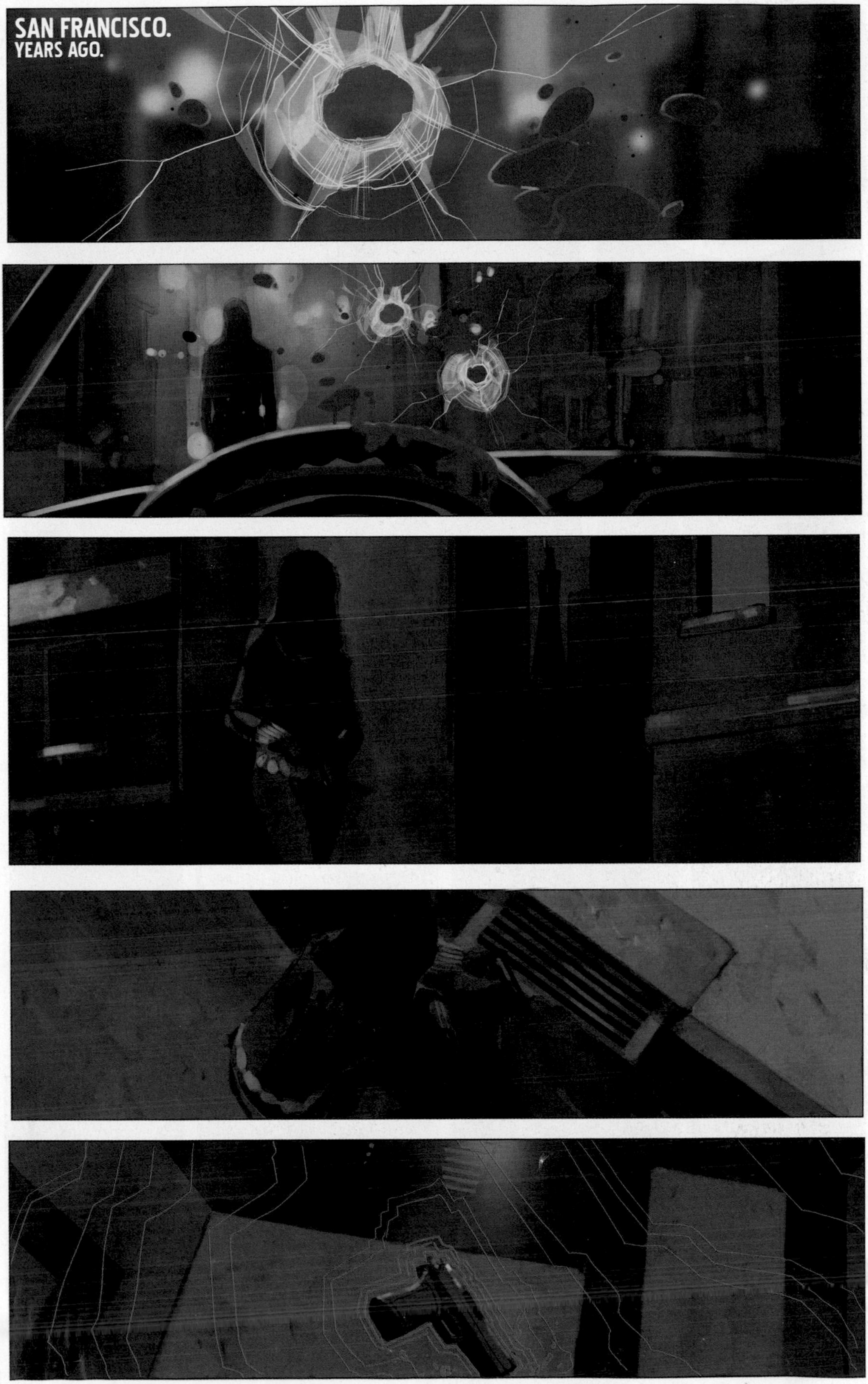
SAN FRANCISCO.
YEARS AGO.

FAST BREATHING. ELEVATED HEART RATE...

...AND WITHOUT ME?

HAVEN'T YOU GOT CRIMES TO FIGHT, PAJAMA BOY?

SO WHAT *ARE* YOU DOING?

I'M LOOKING INTO SOMETHING FOR *FURY*.

WHY ARE YOU LYING TO ME?

WHAT DID YOU DO, NAT?

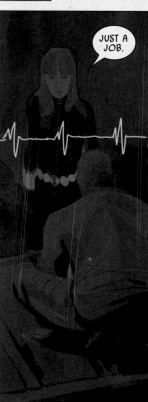

JUST A JOB.

AND IS FURY TELLING YOU TO HURT PEOPLE?

OR IS THAT NOT SOMETHING YOU DRAW THE LINE AT ANYMORE...

I DON'T NEED A LECTURE, MATT. I'M ONE OF THE GOOD GUYS.

I DON'T KNOW WHAT YOU DID TONIGHT, NAT.
BUT YOUR HEART ISN'T ALL THAT SURE ABOUT IT. MAYBE YOU SHOULD RECONSIDER THE JOBS YOU'RE--
I KNOW WHAT RIGHT LOOKS LIKE, MATT.
I KNOW.

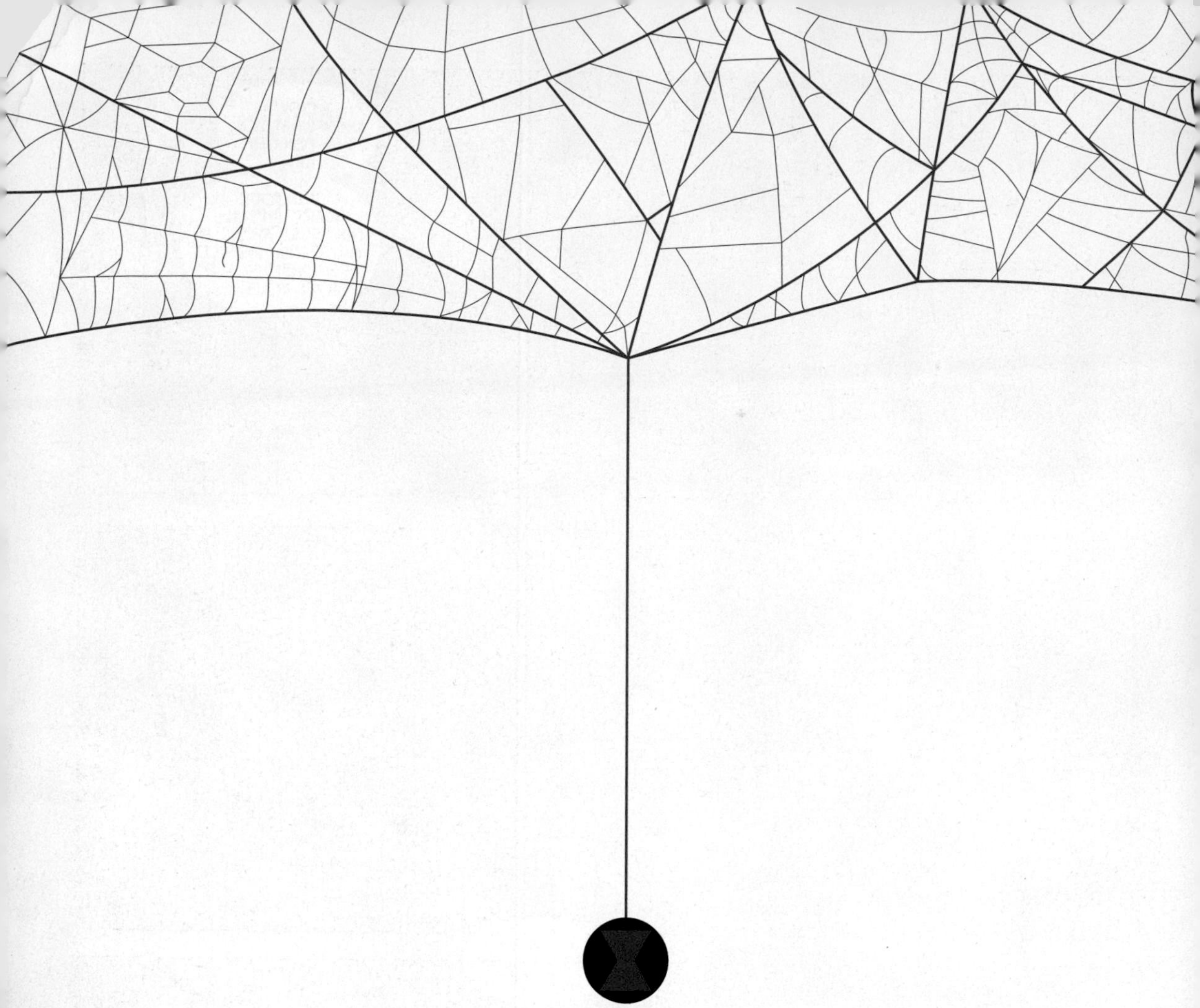

Natasha Romanova is an Avenger, an agent of S.H.I.E.L.D. and an ex-KGB assassin, but on her own time, she uses her unique skill set to atone for her past. She is:

BLACK WIDOW

Years ago, Natasha lived in San Francisco with a man she loved, Matt Murdock, the blind super hero known as Daredevil. Recently, Daredevil moved back to San Francisco after his identity and heightened senses (including a kind of radar sense and the ability to tell whether someone is lying by listening to their heartbeat) were revealed to the world. Now, business has brought Natasha back to town.

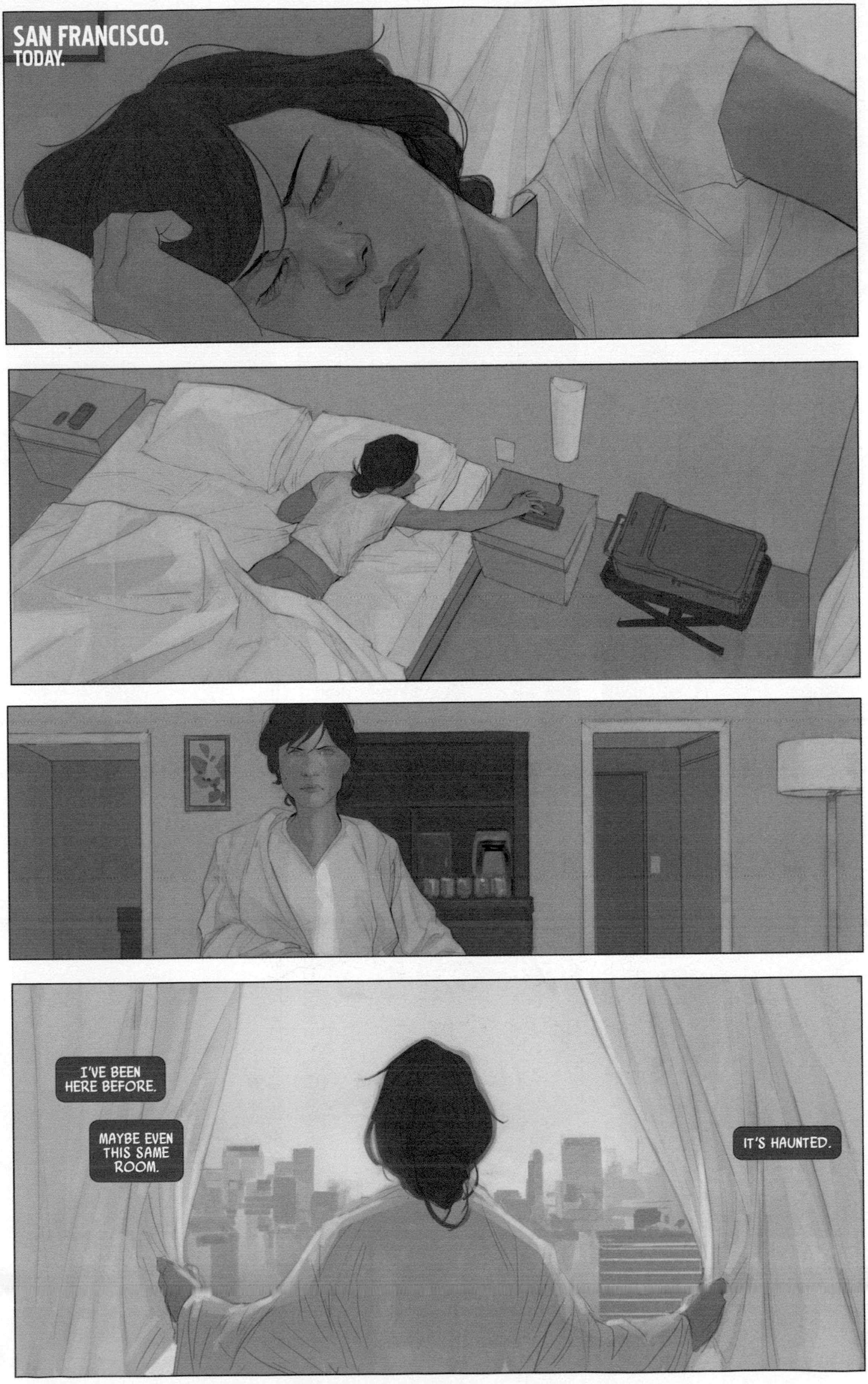
SAN FRANCISCO.
TODAY.
I'VE BEEN HERE BEFORE.
MAYBE EVEN THIS SAME ROOM.
IT'S HAUNTED.

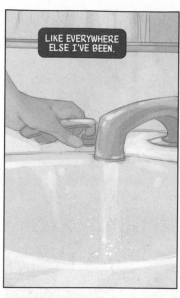

LIKE EVERYWHERE ELSE I'VE BEEN.

I'D TAKE DRUGS TO HELP ME SLEEP, BUT I CAN'T RISK GROGGY MORNINGS.

SOMETIMES I WISH I HAD SOME CAPTAIN AMERICA SUPER-STRENGTH TO GET THROUGH TIRED DAYS.

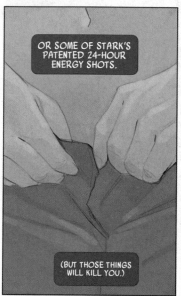

OR SOME OF STARK'S PATENTED 24-HOUR ENERGY SHOTS.

(BUT THOSE THINGS WILL KILL YOU.)

NOT SURE WHY HE NEEDS THEM. THE GUY'S GOT A GENERATOR STUCK IN HIS CHEST.

DON'T EVEN GET ME STARTED ON THOR--

BEEP BEEP

TALK TO ME, ISAIAH.

THE BUY IS SET TO GO.

DO YOU HAVE WHAT YOU NEED?

I HAVE THE BUYER'S ENCODED THUMB DRIVE. I'LL BE IN POSITION TO POSE AS THE SELLER.

GOOD. CALL ME WHEN IT'S DONE. I'M GOING TO GO FEED YOUR CAT. I'D THINK AGAIN ABOUT GOING THIS ALONE, THOUGH.

HAVE YOU CONSIDERED CALLING DAREDEVIL FOR... BACKUP?

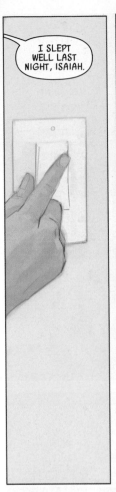

I SLEPT WELL LAST NIGHT, ISAIAH.

I'M FINE ON MY OWN.

...AND NOW WE'LL SEE IF I CAN POSE AS AN IDENTITY-STEALING VIRUS PROGRAMMER...

...TO INFILTRATE SOME CYBERTERRORISTS.

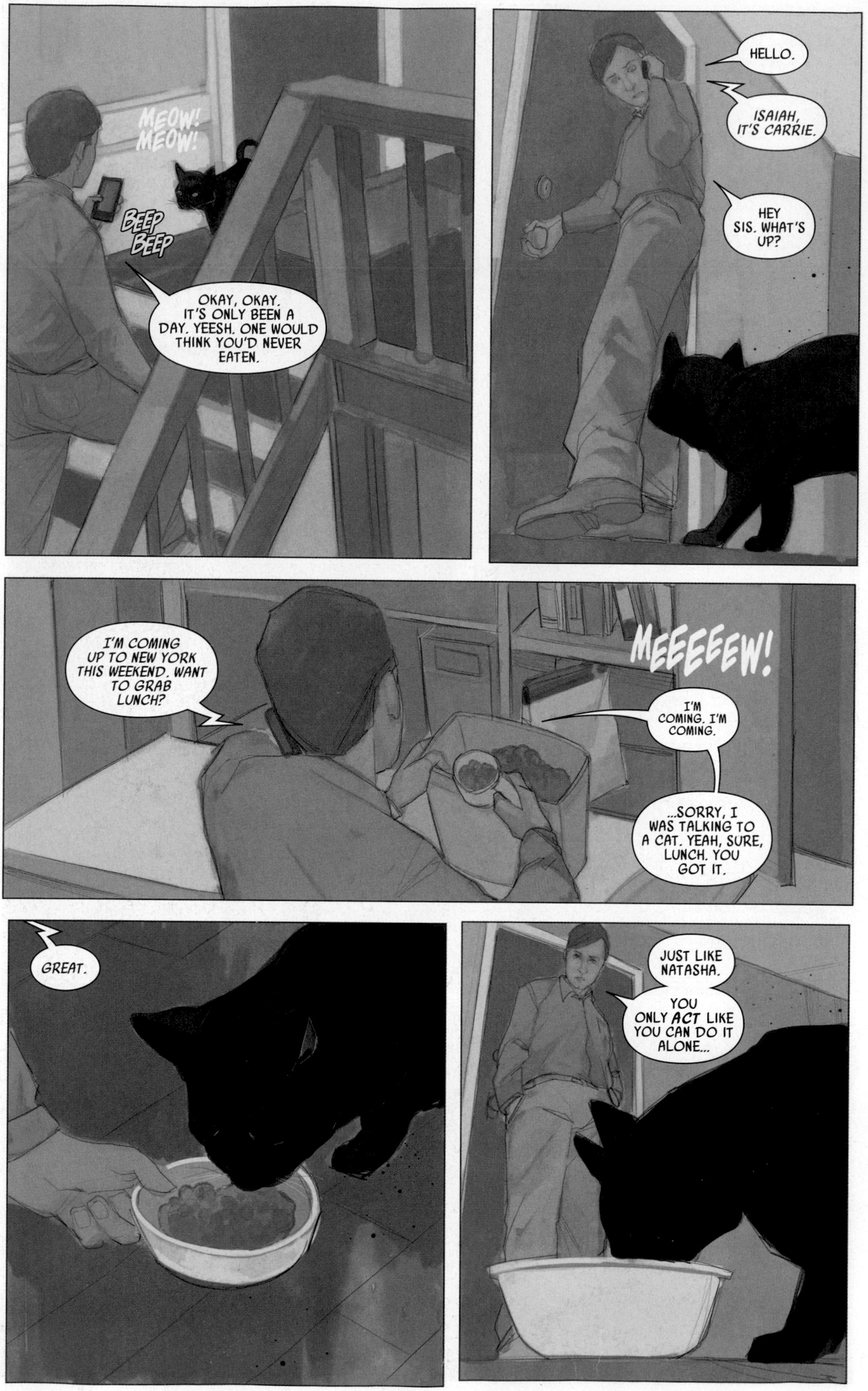
MEOW! MEOW!
BEEP BEEP
OKAY, OKAY. IT'S ONLY BEEN A DAY. YEESH. ONE WOULD THINK YOU'D NEVER EATEN.
HELLO.
ISAIAH, IT'S CARRIE.
HEY SIS. WHAT'S UP?
I'M COMING UP TO NEW YORK THIS WEEKEND. WANT TO GRAB LUNCH?
MEEEEEW!
I'M COMING. I'M COMING.
...SORRY, I WAS TALKING TO A CAT. YEAH, SURE, LUNCH. YOU GOT IT.
GREAT.
JUST LIKE NATASHA.
YOU ONLY ACT LIKE YOU CAN DO IT ALONE...

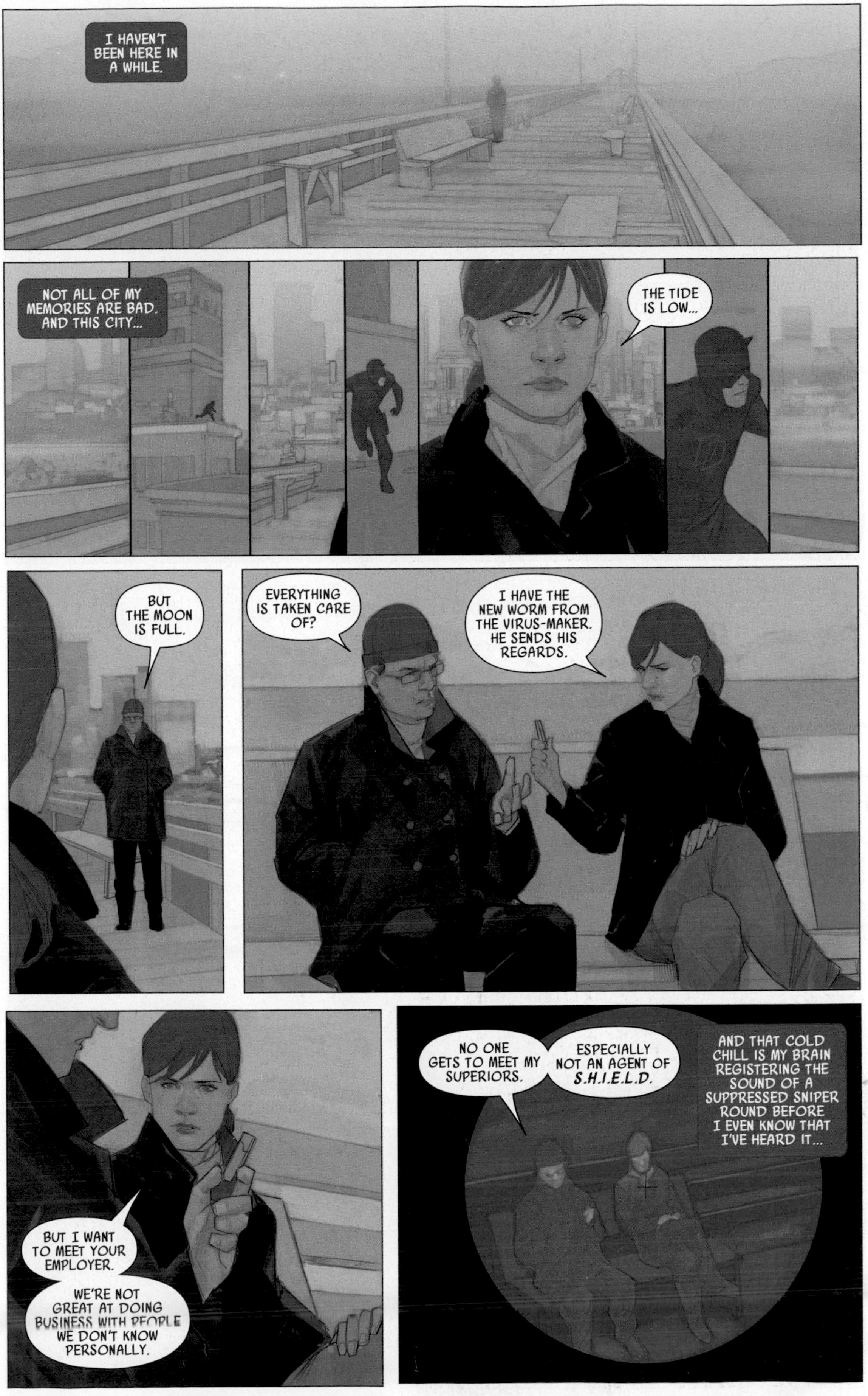
I HAVEN'T BEEN HERE IN A WHILE.
NOT ALL OF MY MEMORIES ARE BAD. AND THIS CITY...
THE TIDE IS LOW...
BUT THE MOON IS FULL.
EVERYTHING IS TAKEN CARE OF?
I HAVE THE NEW WORM FROM THE VIRUS-MAKER. HE SENDS HIS REGARDS.
BUT I WANT TO MEET YOUR EMPLOYER.
WE'RE NOT GREAT AT DOING BUSINESS WITH PEOPLE WE DON'T KNOW PERSONALLY.
NO ONE GETS TO MEET MY SUPERIORS.
ESPECIALLY NOT AN AGENT OF S.H.I.E.L.D.
AND THAT COLD CHILL IS MY BRAIN REGISTERING THE SOUND OF A SUPPRESSED SNIPER ROUND BEFORE I EVEN KNOW THAT I'VE HEARD IT...

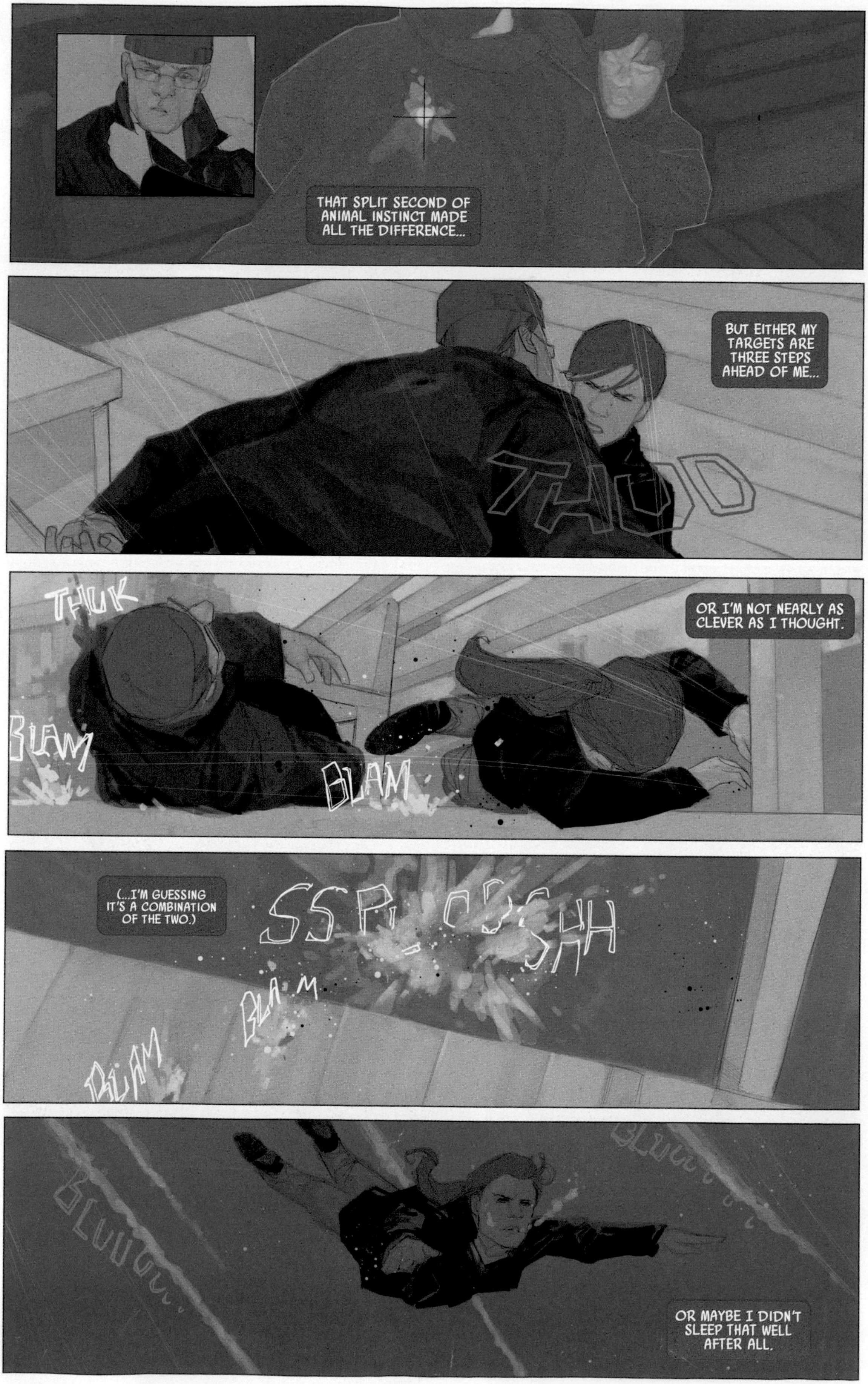
THAT SPLIT SECOND OF ANIMAL INSTINCT MADE ALL THE DIFFERENCE...
BUT EITHER MY TARGETS ARE THREE STEPS AHEAD OF ME...
THUD
THUK
OR I'M NOT NEARLY AS CLEVER AS I THOUGHT.
BLAM
BLAM
(...I'M GUESSING IT'S A COMBINATION OF THE TWO.)
BLAM
BLAM
OR MAYBE I DIDN'T SLEEP THAT WELL AFTER ALL.

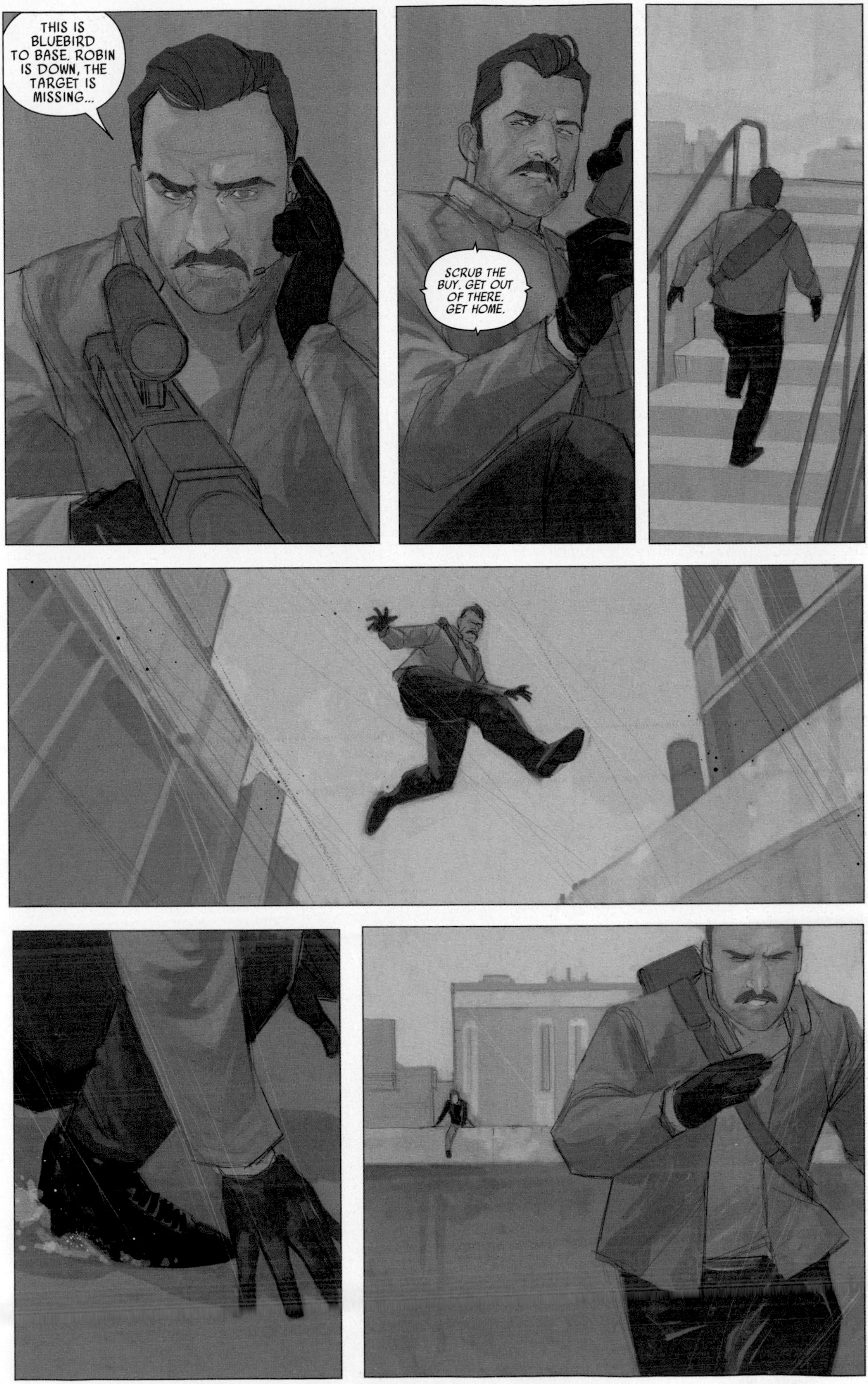
THIS IS BLUEBIRD TO BASE. ROBIN IS DOWN, THE TARGET IS MISSING...
SCRUB THE BUY. GET OUT OF THERE. GET HOME.

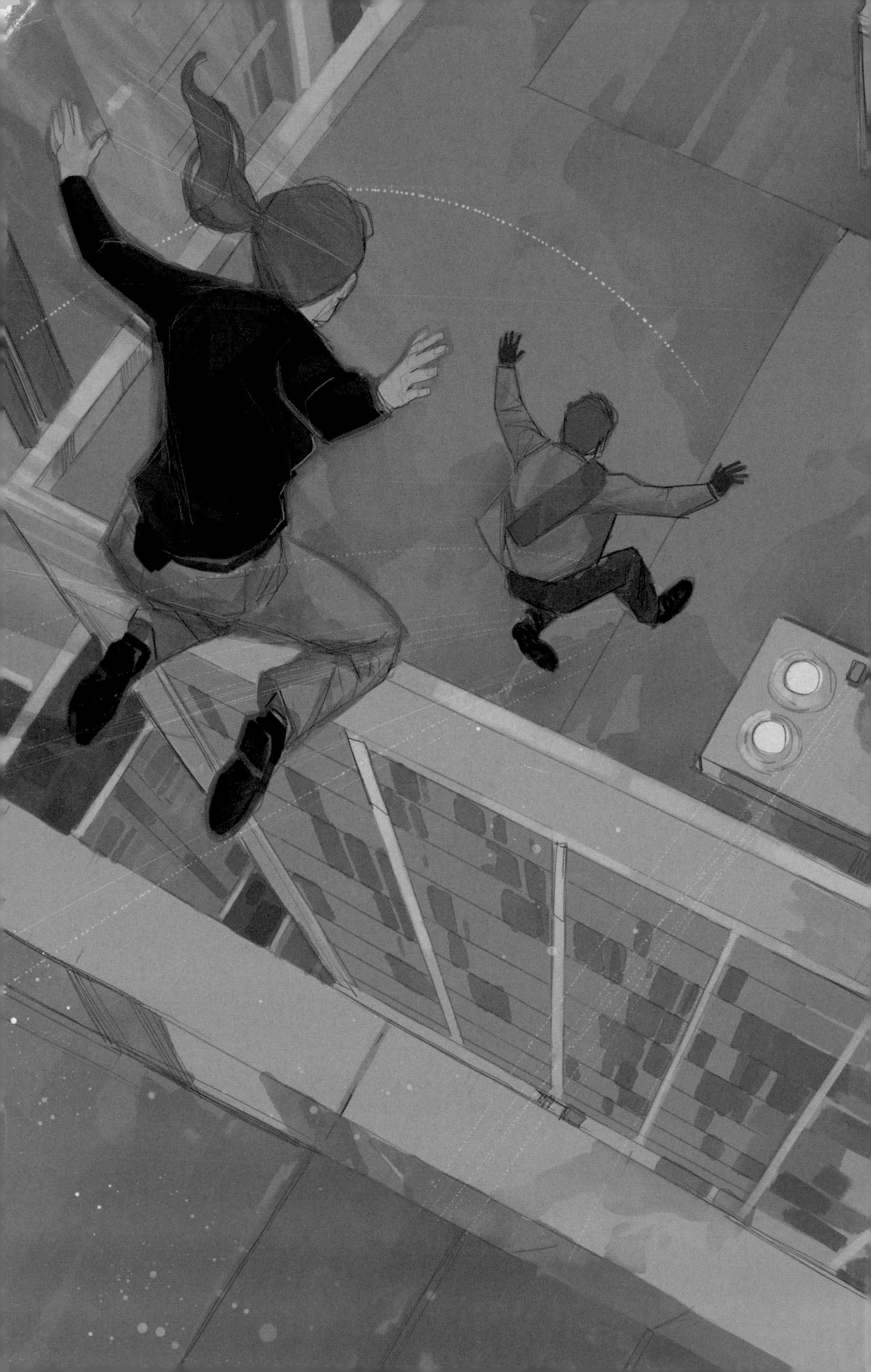

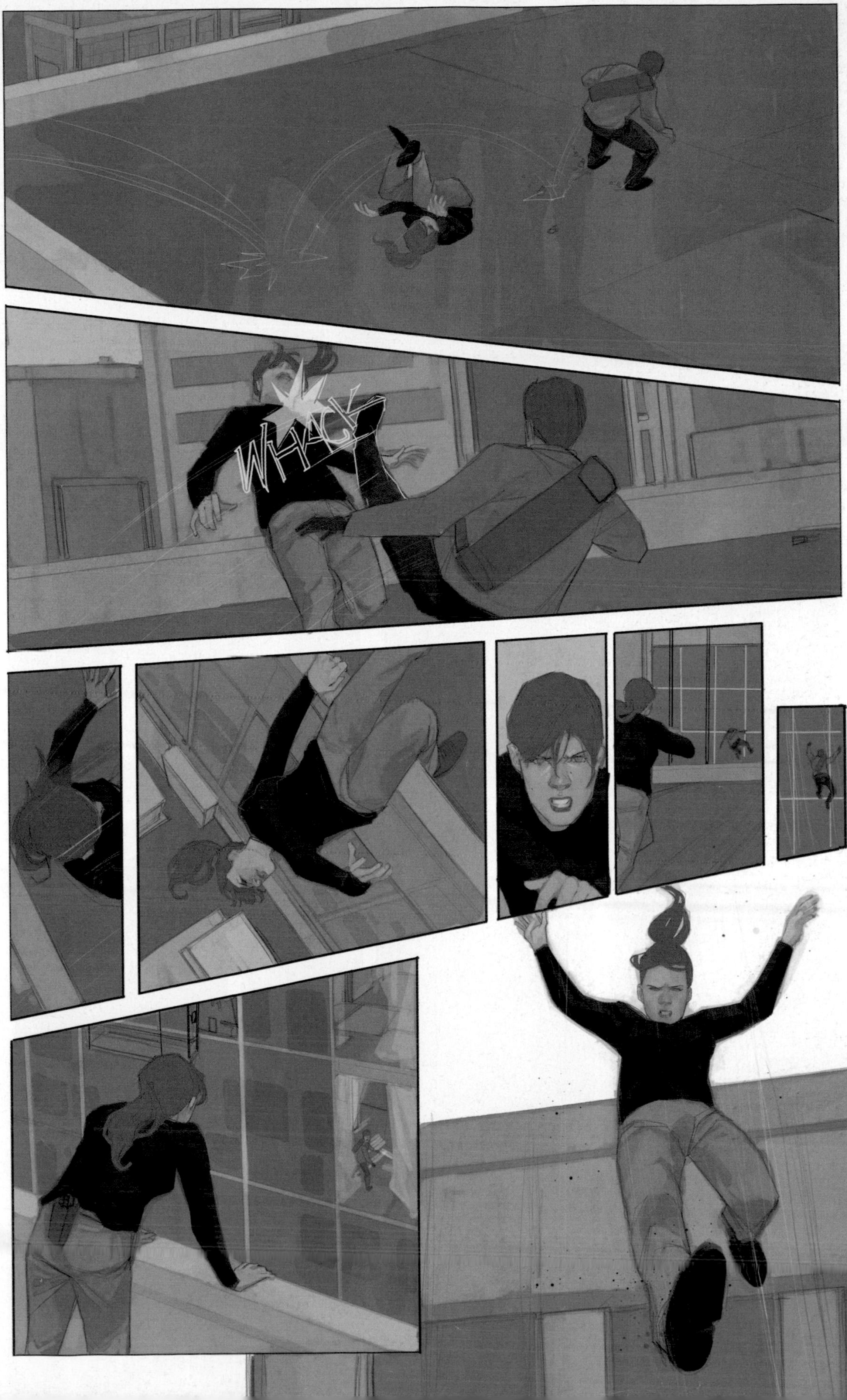
WHACK

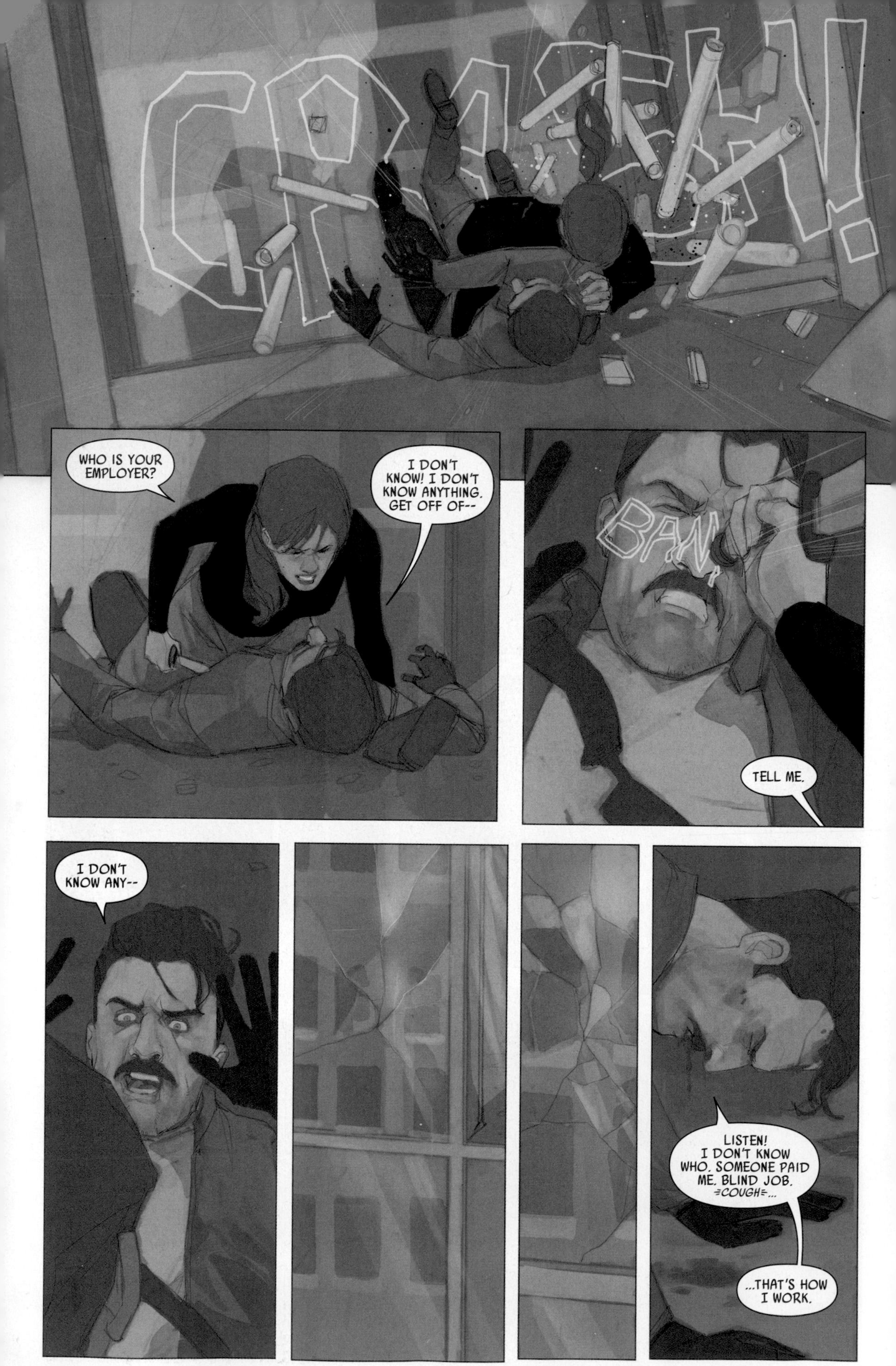
CRASH!
WHO IS YOUR EMPLOYER?
I DON'T KNOW! I DON'T KNOW ANYTHING. GET OFF OF--
BAM
TELL ME.
I DON'T KNOW ANY--
LISTEN! I DON'T KNOW WHO. SOMEONE PAID ME. BLIND JOB. =COUGH=...
...THAT'S HOW I WORK.

WHO PAID YOU?

THEN THEY WILL KNOW THAT YOUV'E FAILED.

WHICH MEANS YOU'RE ALREADY SCREWED.

I--I ONLY GOT CASH BY MAIL. I WAS TO PROTECT THE MIDDLEMEN!

I WANT THE PHONE NUMBER.

THEY GAVE ME THIS PHONE. BUT THEY WON'T CALL AGAIN.

WHERE DID YOU MEET THEM? WHERE DID THEY GIVE IT TO YOU?

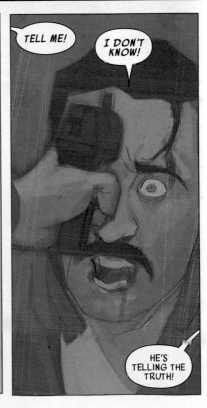

TELL ME!

I DON'T KNOW!

HE'S TELLING THE TRUTH!

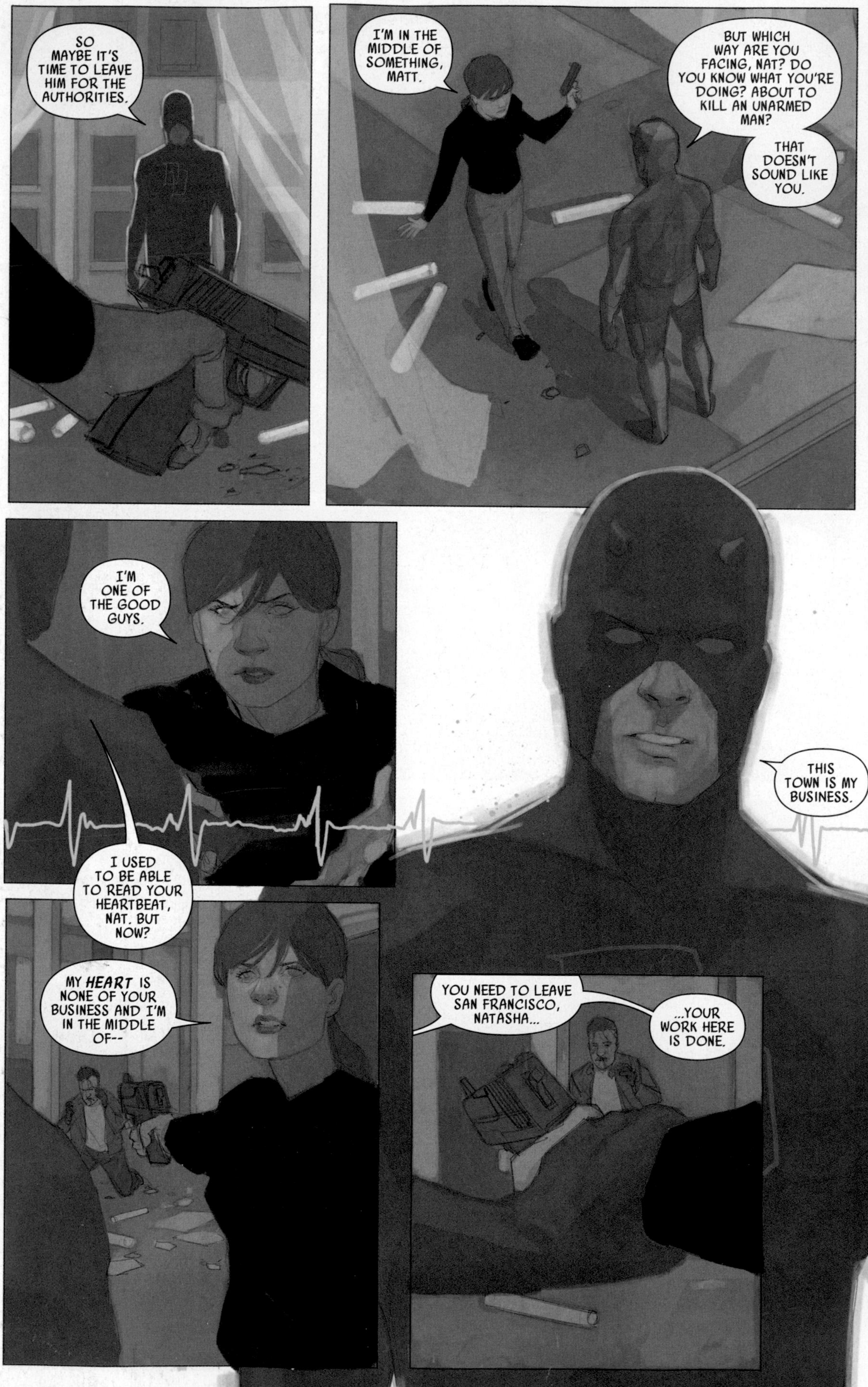
SO MAYBE IT'S TIME TO LEAVE HIM FOR THE AUTHORITIES.
I'M IN THE MIDDLE OF SOMETHING, MATT.
BUT WHICH WAY ARE YOU FACING, NAT? DO YOU KNOW WHAT YOU'RE DOING? ABOUT TO KILL AN UNARMED MAN?
THAT DOESN'T SOUND LIKE YOU.
I'M ONE OF THE GOOD GUYS.
I USED TO BE ABLE TO READ YOUR HEARTBEAT, NAT. BUT NOW?
MY HEART IS NONE OF YOUR BUSINESS AND I'M IN THE MIDDLE OF--
THIS TOWN IS MY BUSINESS.
YOU NEED TO LEAVE SAN FRANCISCO, NATASHA...
...YOUR WORK HERE IS DONE.

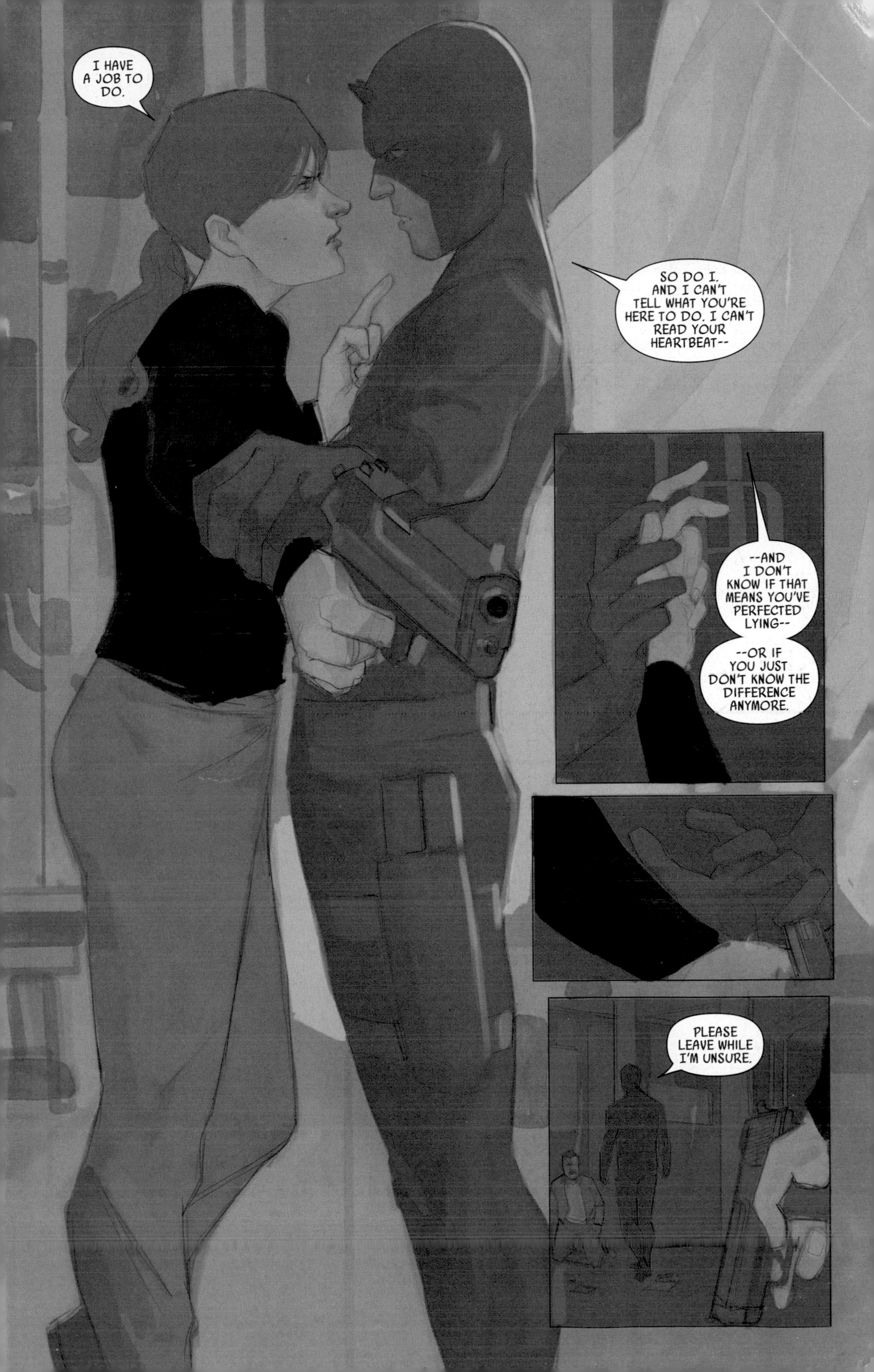
I HAVE A JOB TO DO.
SO DO I. AND I CAN'T TELL WHAT YOU'RE HERE TO DO. I CAN'T READ YOUR HEARTBEAT--
--AND I DON'T KNOW IF THAT MEANS YOU'VE PERFECTED LYING--
--OR IF YOU JUST DON'T KNOW THE DIFFERENCE ANYMORE.
PLEASE LEAVE WHILE I'M UNSURE.

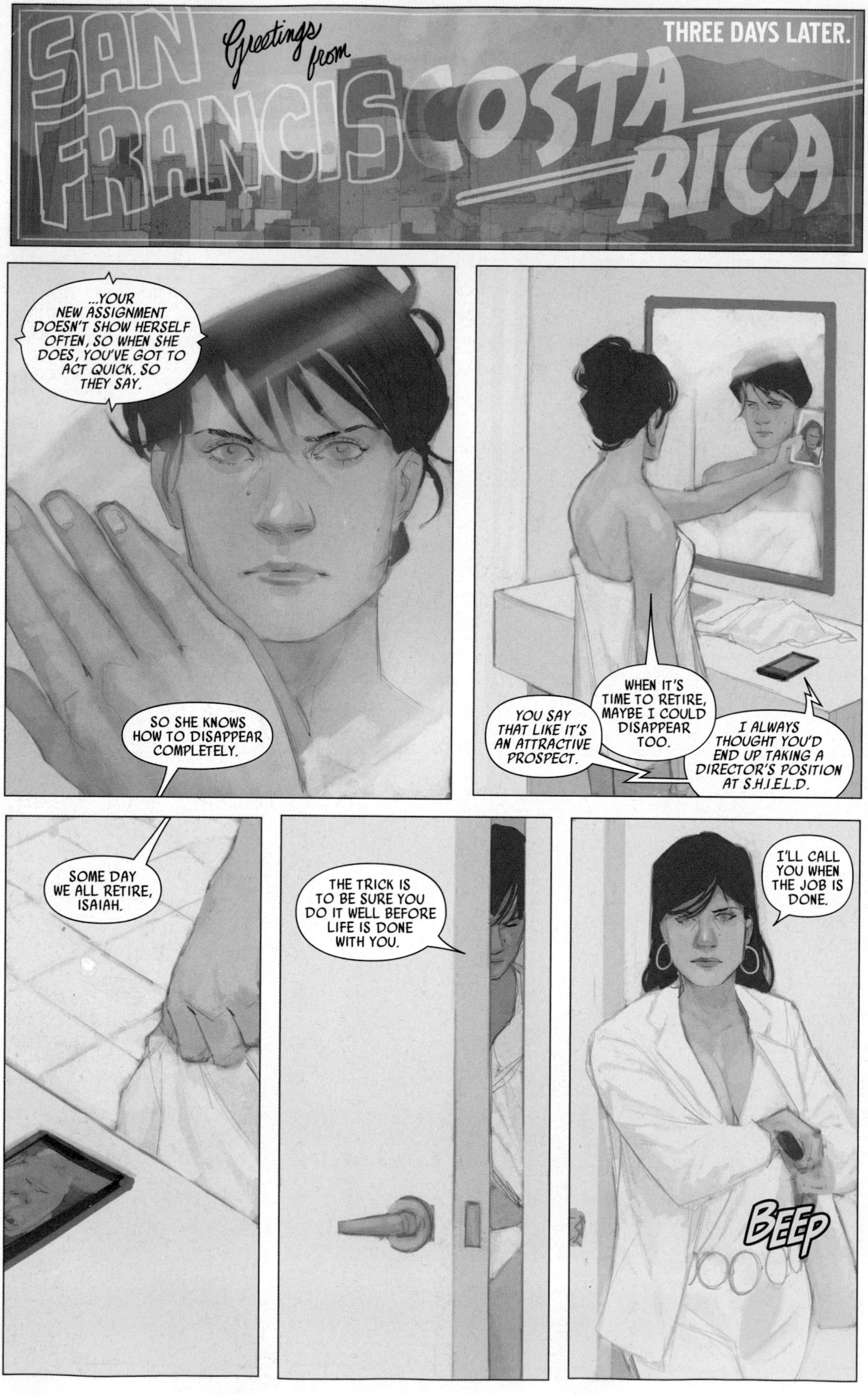
SAN FRANCISCO
Greetings from
COSTA RICA
THREE DAYS LATER.
...YOUR NEW ASSIGNMENT DOESN'T SHOW HERSELF OFTEN, SO WHEN SHE DOES, YOU'VE GOT TO ACT QUICK. SO THEY SAY.
SO SHE KNOWS HOW TO DISAPPEAR COMPLETELY.
WHEN IT'S TIME TO RETIRE, MAYBE I COULD DISAPPEAR TOO.
YOU SAY THAT LIKE IT'S AN ATTRACTIVE PROSPECT.
I ALWAYS THOUGHT YOU'D END UP TAKING A DIRECTOR'S POSITION AT S.H.I.E.L.D.
SOME DAY WE ALL RETIRE, ISAIAH.
THE TRICK IS TO BE SURE YOU DO IT WELL BEFORE LIFE IS DONE WITH YOU.
I'LL CALL YOU WHEN THE JOB IS DONE.
BEEP

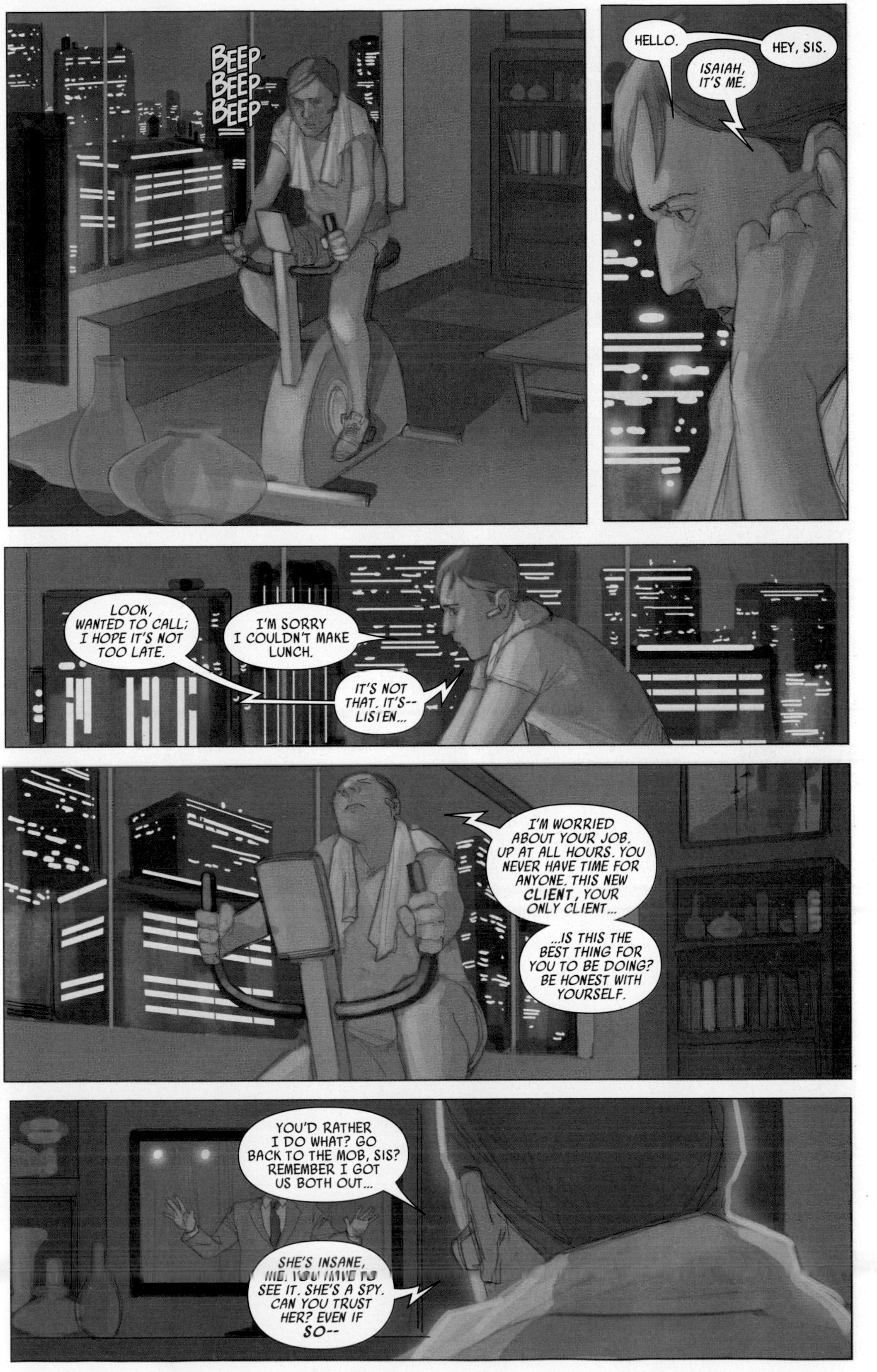
BEEP BEEP BEEP
HELLO.
ISAIAH, IT'S ME.
HEY, SIS.
LOOK, WANTED TO CALL; I HOPE IT'S NOT TOO LATE.
I'M SORRY I COULDN'T MAKE LUNCH.
IT'S NOT THAT. IT'S-- LISTEN...
I'M WORRIED ABOUT YOUR JOB. UP AT ALL HOURS. YOU NEVER HAVE TIME FOR ANYONE. THIS NEW CLIENT, YOUR ONLY CLIENT...
...IS THIS THE BEST THING FOR YOU TO BE DOING? BE HONEST WITH YOURSELF.
YOU'D RATHER I DO WHAT? GO BACK TO THE MOB, SIS? REMEMBER I GOT US BOTH OUT...
SHE'S INSANE,
SEE IT. SHE'S A SPY. CAN YOU TRUST HER? EVEN IF SO--

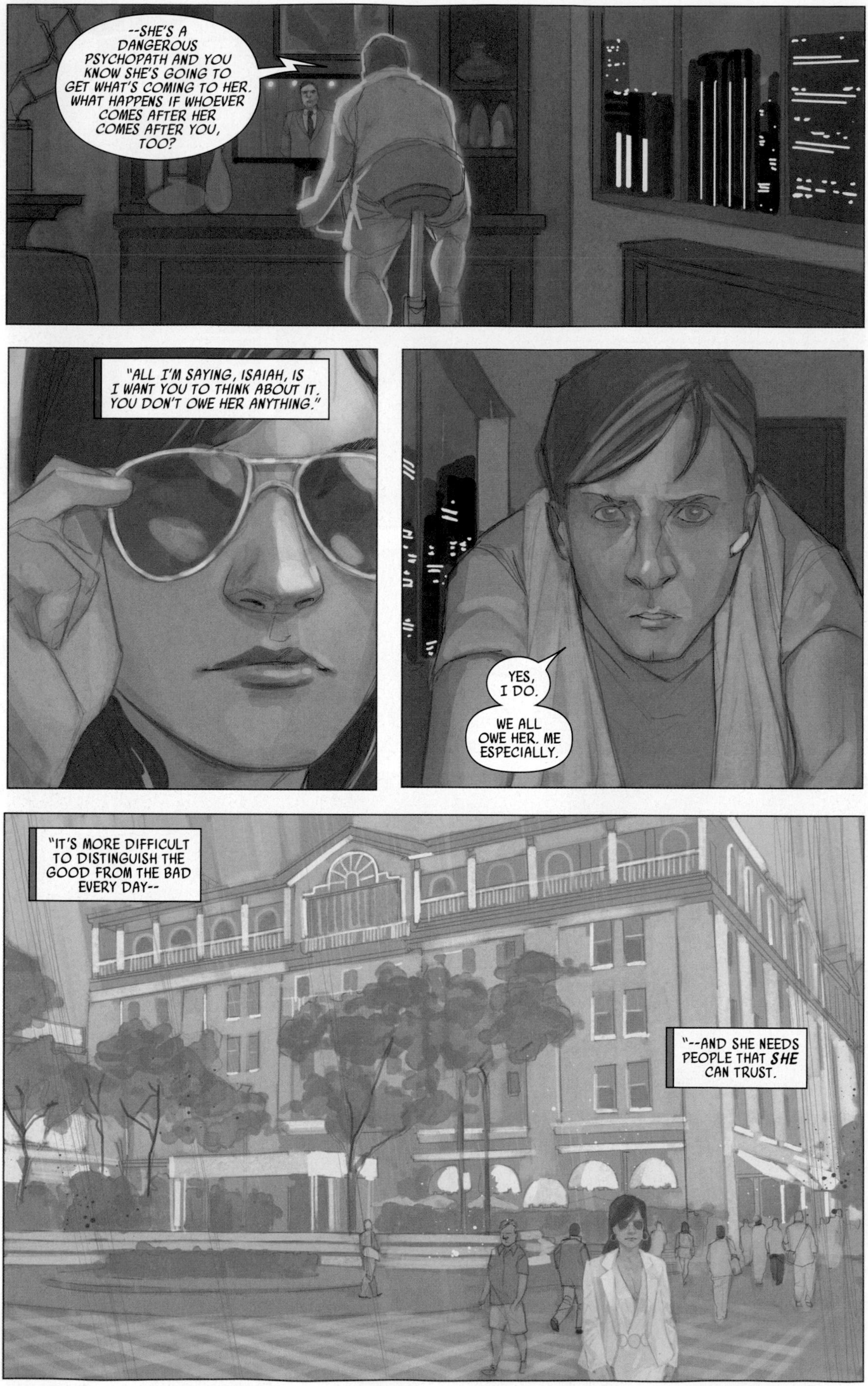
--SHE'S A DANGEROUS PSYCHOPATH AND YOU KNOW SHE'S GOING TO GET WHAT'S COMING TO HER. WHAT HAPPENS IF WHOEVER COMES AFTER HER COMES AFTER YOU, TOO?
"ALL I'M SAYING, ISAIAH, IS I WANT YOU TO THINK ABOUT IT. YOU DON'T OWE HER ANYTHING."
YES, I DO.
WE ALL OWE HER. ME ESPECIALLY.
"IT'S MORE DIFFICULT TO DISTINGUISH THE GOOD FROM THE BAD EVERY DAY--
"--AND SHE NEEDS PEOPLE THAT SHE CAN TRUST.

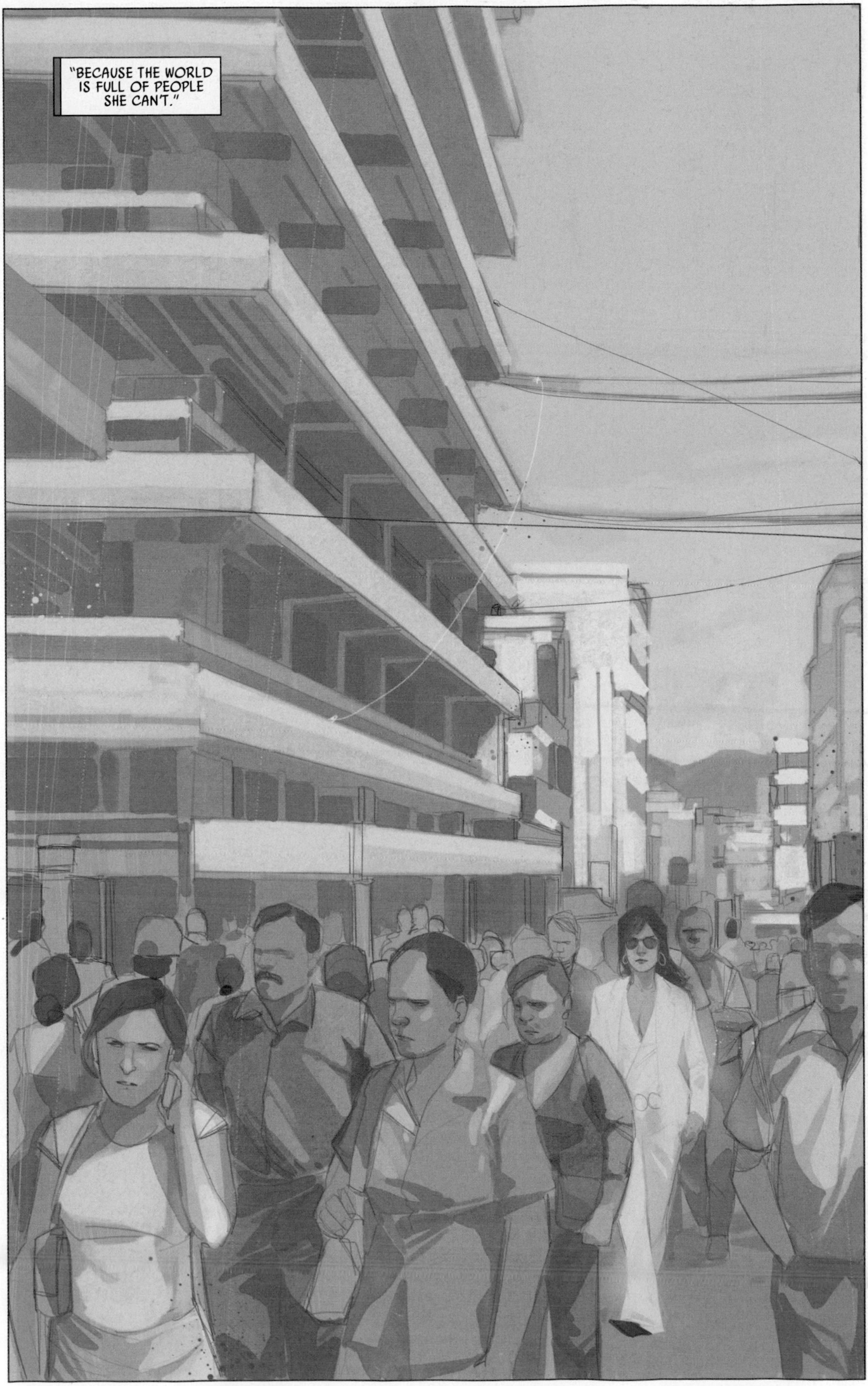
"BECAUSE THE WORLD IS FULL OF PEOPLE SHE CAN'T."

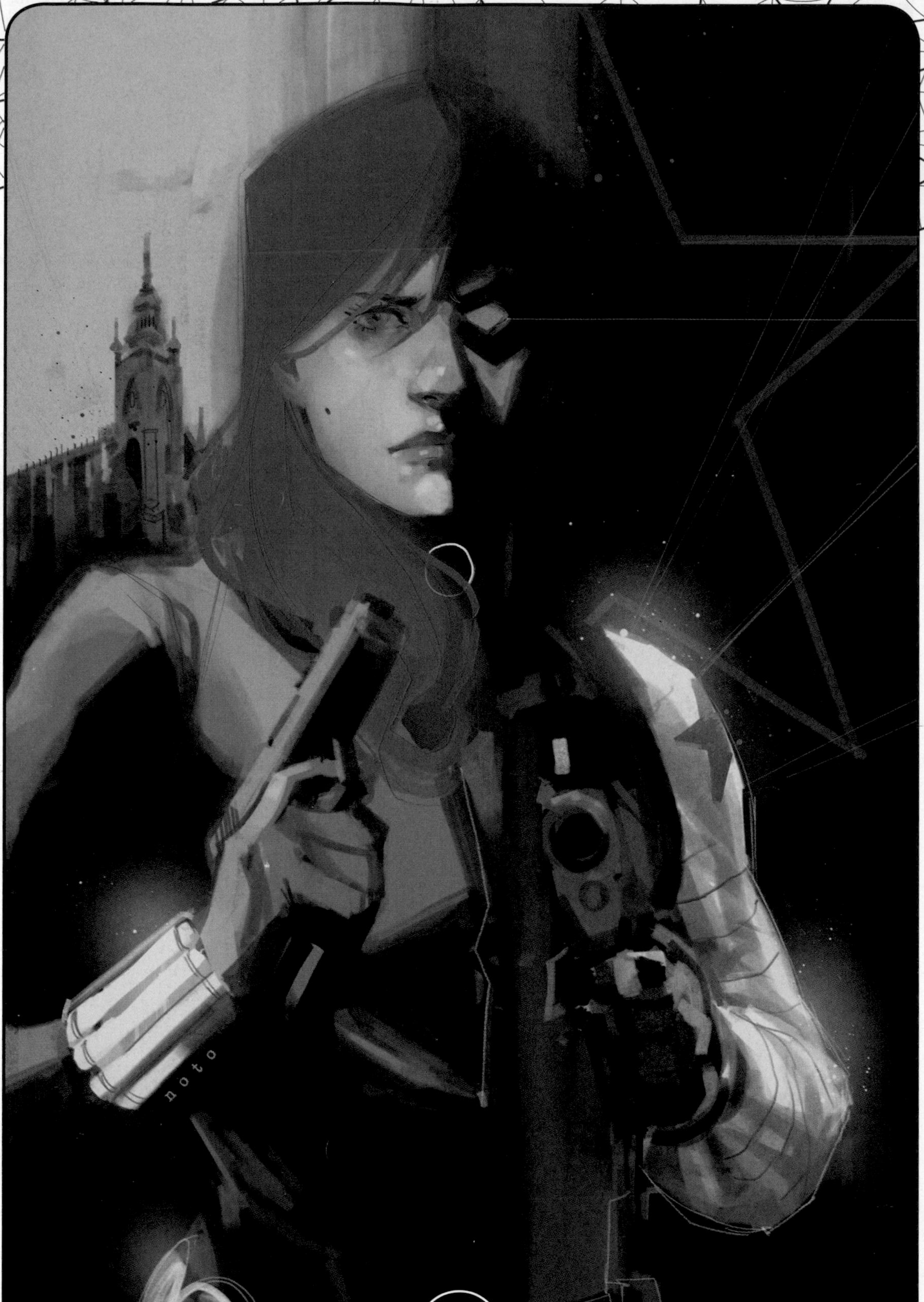
noto
8

BITTER COLD

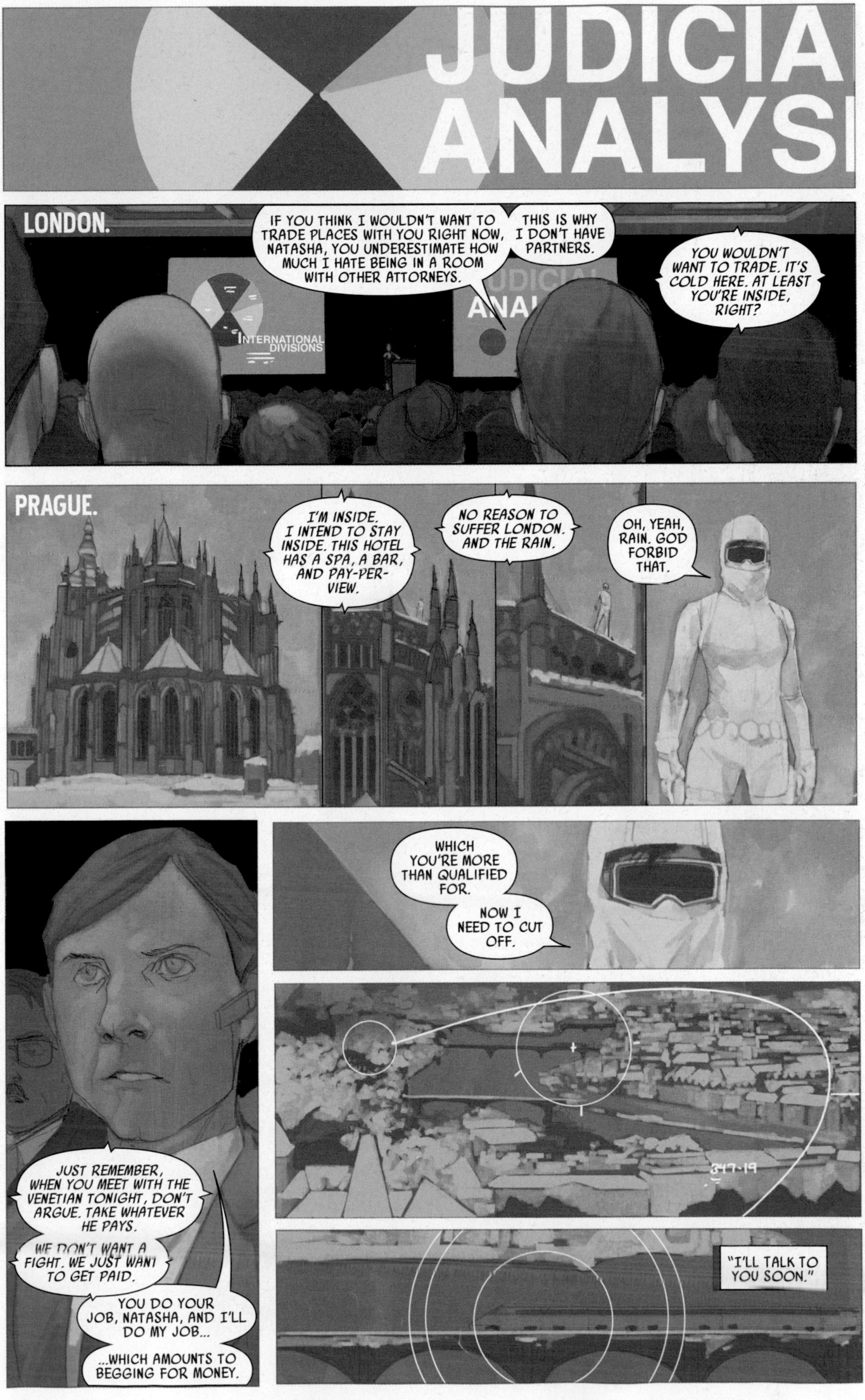
JUDICIA
ANALYSI
LONDON.
INTERNATIONAL DIVISIONS
IF YOU THINK I WOULDN'T WANT TO TRADE PLACES WITH YOU RIGHT NOW, NATASHA, YOU UNDERESTIMATE HOW MUCH I HATE BEING IN A ROOM WITH OTHER ATTORNEYS.
THIS IS WHY I DON'T HAVE PARTNERS.
YOU WOULDN'T WANT TO TRADE. IT'S COLD HERE. AT LEAST YOU'RE INSIDE, RIGHT?
PRAGUE.
I'M INSIDE. I INTEND TO STAY INSIDE. THIS HOTEL HAS A SPA, A BAR, AND PAY-PER-VIEW.
NO REASON TO SUFFER LONDON. AND THE RAIN.
OH, YEAH, RAIN. GOD FORBID THAT.
JUST REMEMBER, WHEN YOU MEET WITH THE VENETIAN TONIGHT, DON'T ARGUE. TAKE WHATEVER HE PAYS.
WE DON'T WANT A FIGHT. WE JUST WANT TO GET PAID.
YOU DO YOUR JOB, NATASHA, AND I'LL DO MY JOB...
...WHICH AMOUNTS TO BEGGING FOR MONEY.
WHICH YOU'RE MORE THAN QUALIFIED FOR.
NOW I NEED TO CUT OFF.
347-19
"I'LL TALK TO YOU SOON."

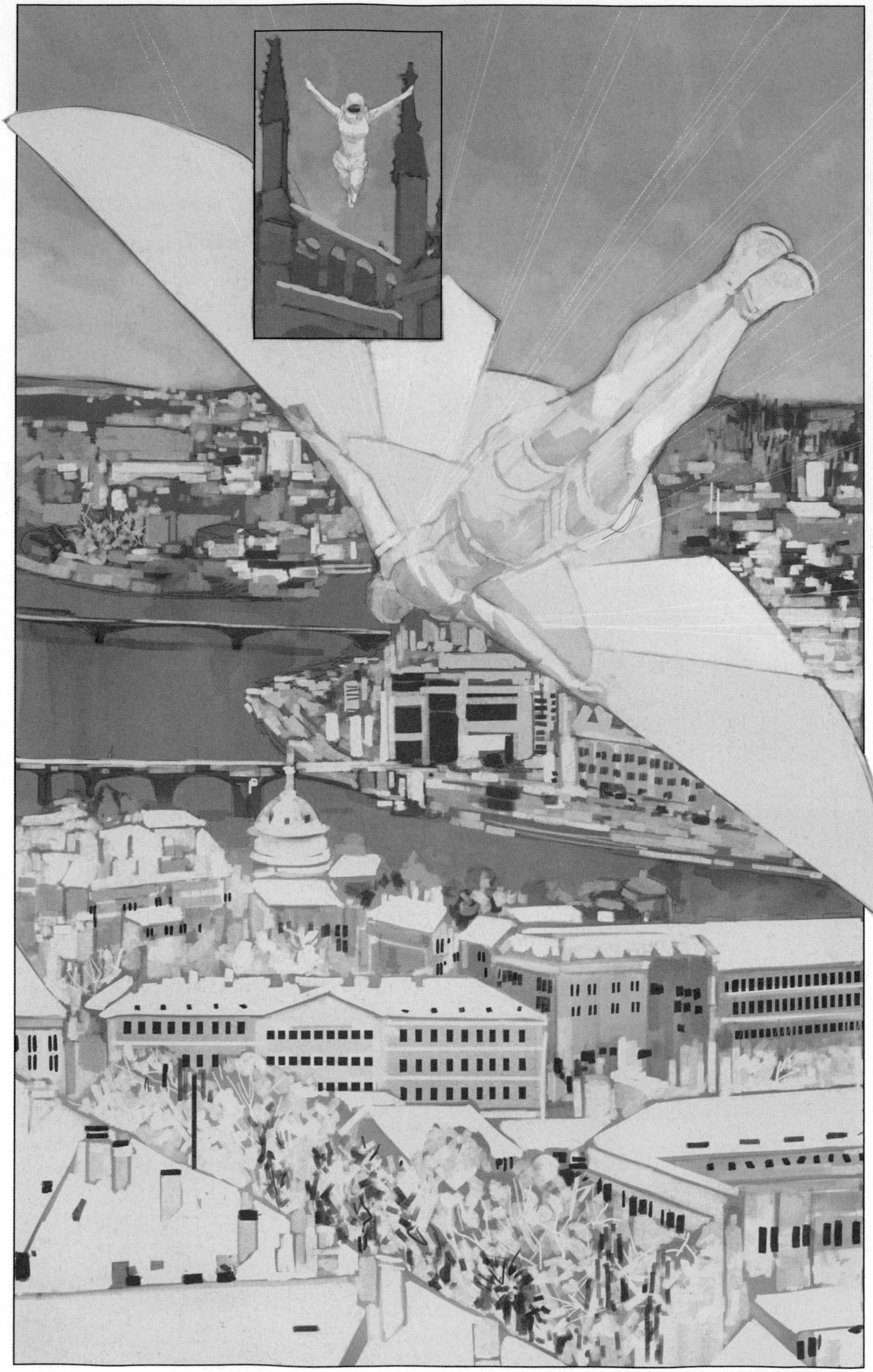

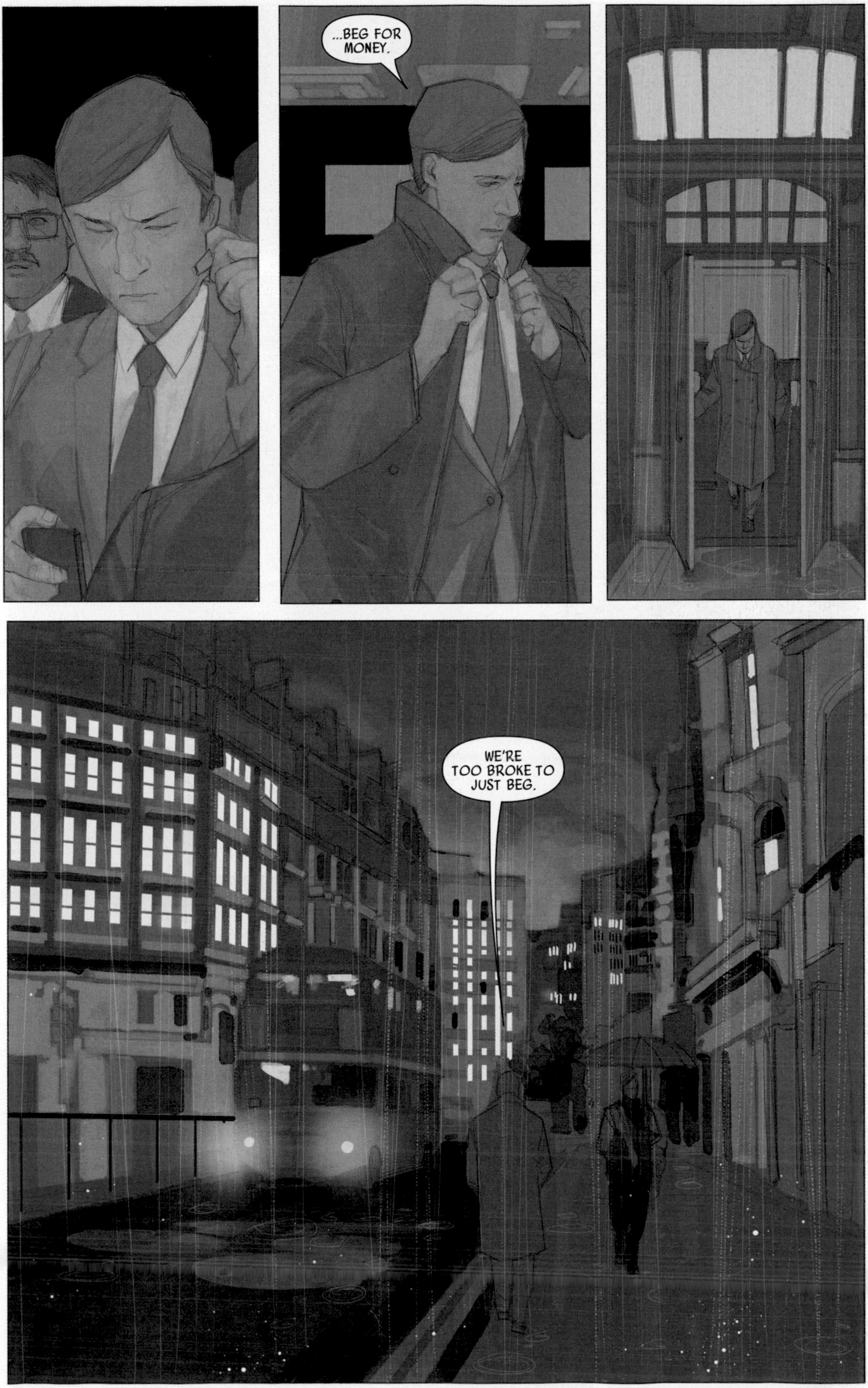
...BEG FOR MONEY.
WE'RE TOO BROKE TO JUST BEG.

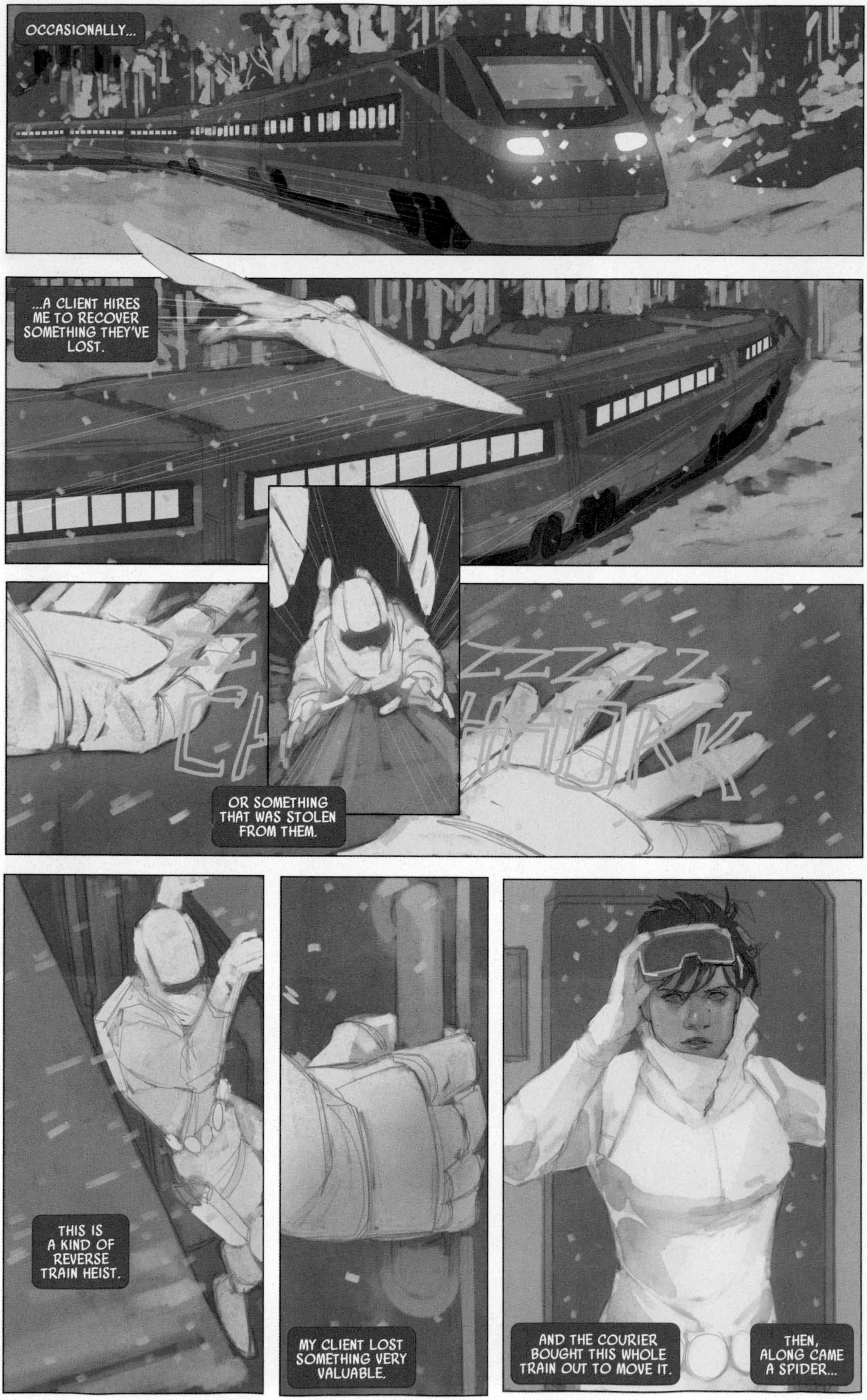
OCCASIONALLY...
...A CLIENT HIRES ME TO RECOVER SOMETHING THEY'VE LOST.
ZZ ZZZZZZ
CHHHHDRK
OR SOMETHING THAT WAS STOLEN FROM THEM.
THIS IS A KIND OF REVERSE TRAIN HEIST.
MY CLIENT LOST SOMETHING VERY VALUABLE.
AND THE COURIER BOUGHT THIS WHOLE TRAIN OUT TO MOVE IT.
THEN, ALONG CAME A SPIDER...

IT'S A QUICK JOB...

...AN EASY PAYCHECK.

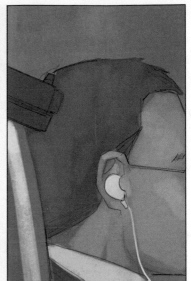

HAND IT OVER.

THANKS FOR YOUR COOPERATION.

WHAT IS THA--

THUMP

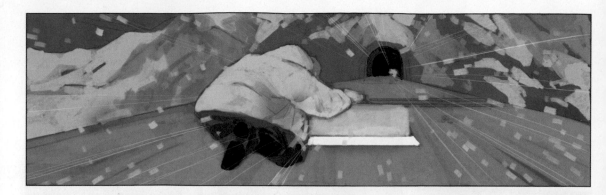

...WINTER SOLDIER?

NAT-- BLACK WIDOW?

WE HAVE TO GET OFF THIS TRAIN. FAST.

KENSINGTON.

MAY I HELP YOU?

YES, YOU CAN.

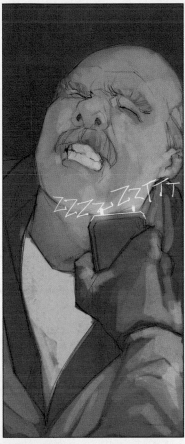

ZZZZ ZZFTT

I'M HERE TO COLLECT ON AN UNPAID BILL.

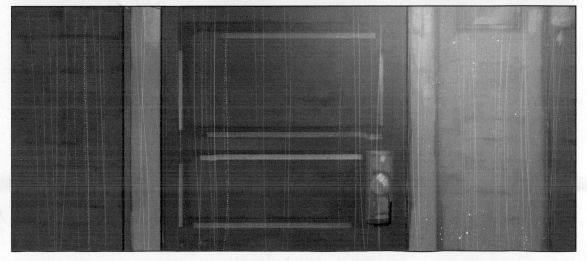

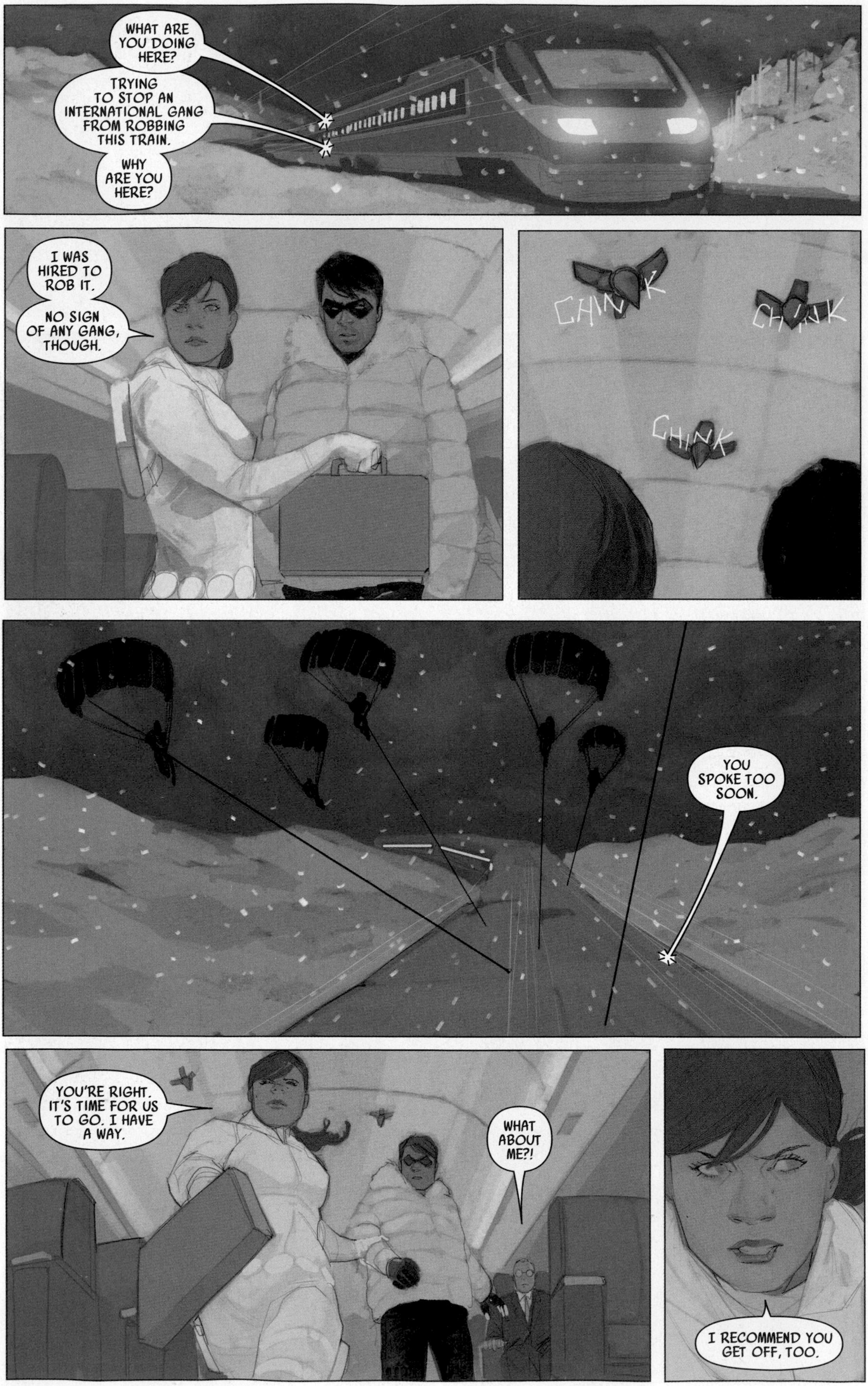
WHAT ARE YOU DOING HERE?
TRYING TO STOP AN INTERNATIONAL GANG FROM ROBBING THIS TRAIN.
WHY ARE YOU HERE?
I WAS HIRED TO ROB IT.
NO SIGN OF ANY GANG, THOUGH.
CHINK
CHINK
CHINK
YOU SPOKE TOO SOON.
YOU'RE RIGHT. IT'S TIME FOR US TO GO. I HAVE A WAY.
WHAT ABOUT ME?!
I RECOMMEND YOU GET OFF, TOO.

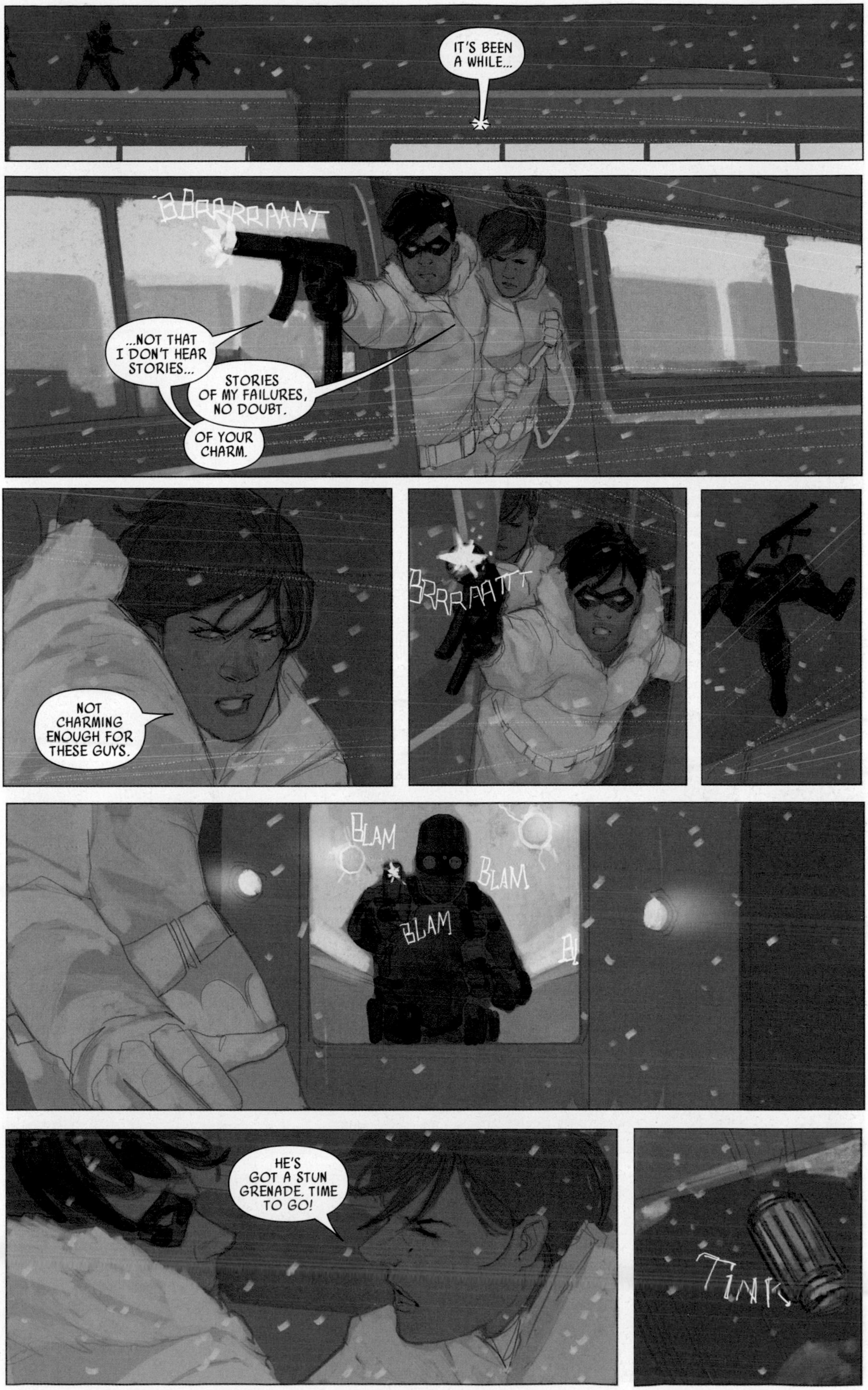
IT'S BEEN A WHILE...
BBRRRRAAAT
...NOT THAT I DON'T HEAR STORIES...
STORIES OF MY FAILURES, NO DOUBT.
OF YOUR CHARM.
NOT CHARMING ENOUGH FOR THESE GUYS.
BRRRAATTT
BLAM
BLAM
BLAM
HE'S GOT A STUN GRENADE. TIME TO GO!
TINK

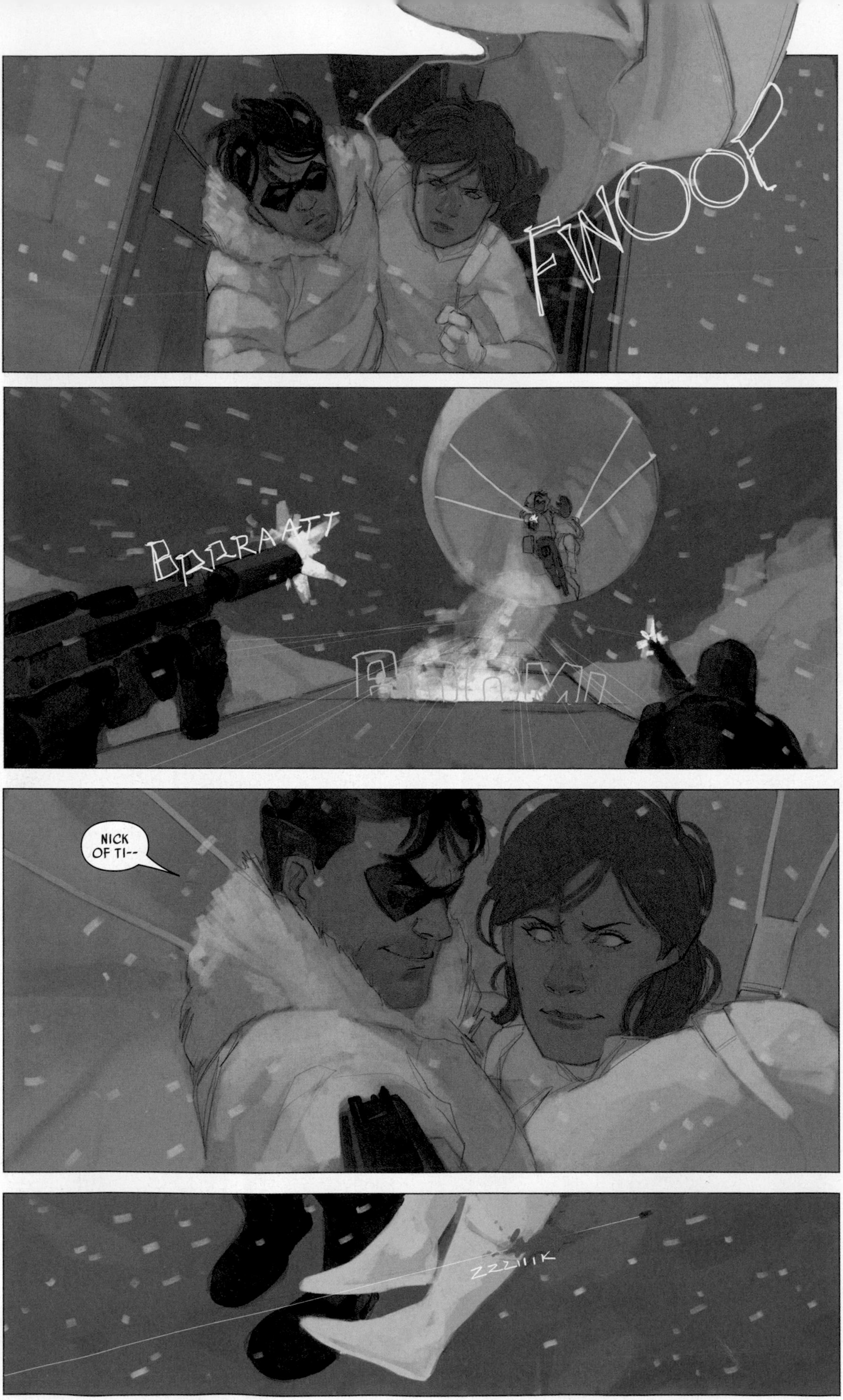
FWOOP
BRRRAATT
NICK OF TI--
ZZZIIIK

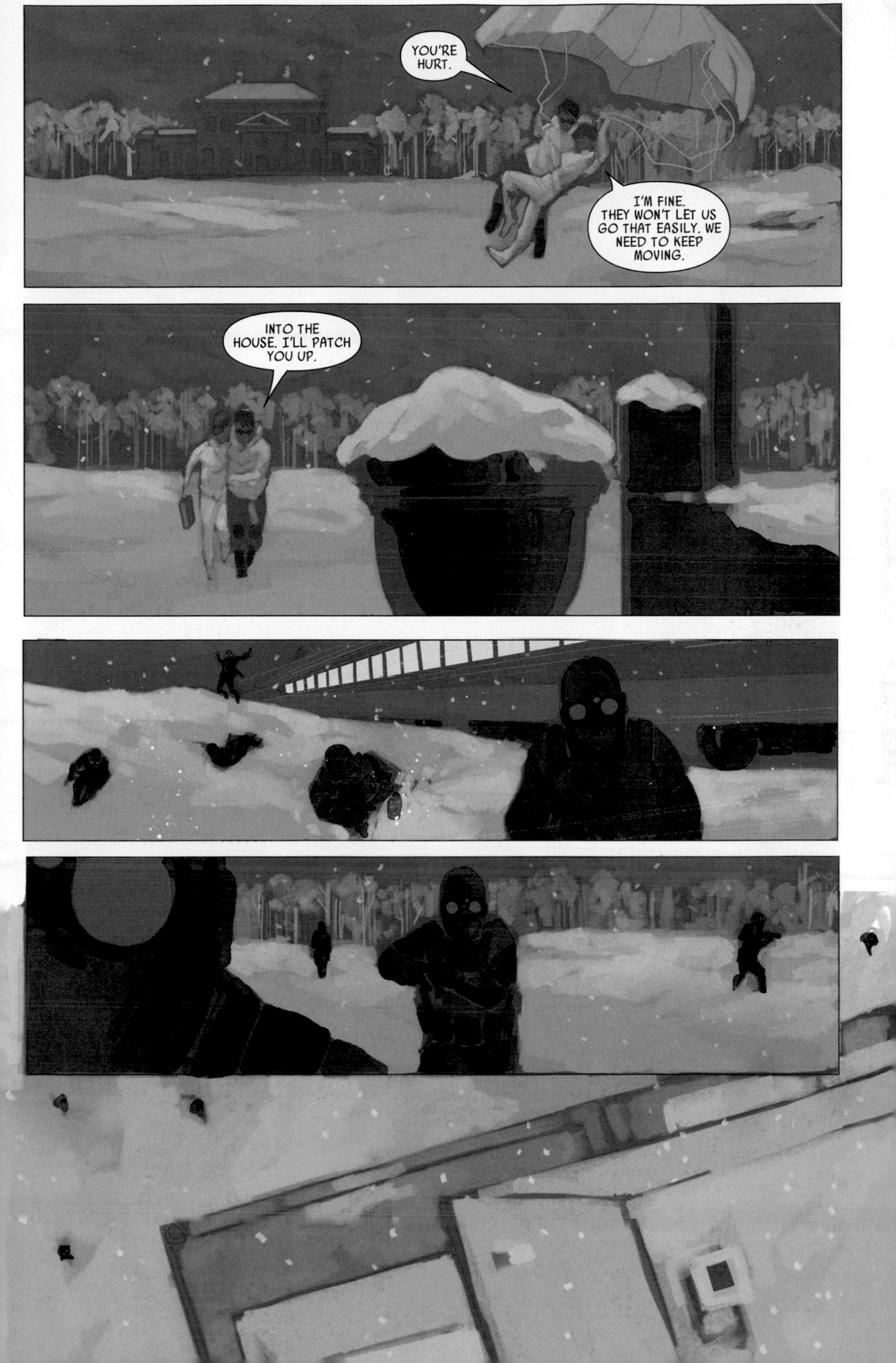
YOU'RE HURT.
I'M FINE. THEY WON'T LET US GO THAT EASILY. WE NEED TO KEEP MOVING.
INTO THE HOUSE. I'LL PATCH YOU UP.

KRASH!

I'M GUESSING THE RESIDENTS ARE SOMEWHERE WARM FOR THE SUMMER.

I'VE NEVER UNDERSTOOD THAT COMPULSION.

NEITHER HAVE I. CLEAR NIGHT SKIES, COLD MORNINGS...

IT MUST MAKE NEW YORK FEEL SO FAR FROM HOME FOR YOU.

IT GETS COLD ENOUGH THERE.

RRRRIP

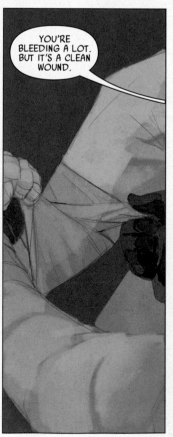

YOU'RE BLEEDING A LOT. BUT IT'S A CLEAN WOUND.

I'LL BE FINE. BUT THEY'RE RIGHT ON OUR ASSES.

THWAK THWAK

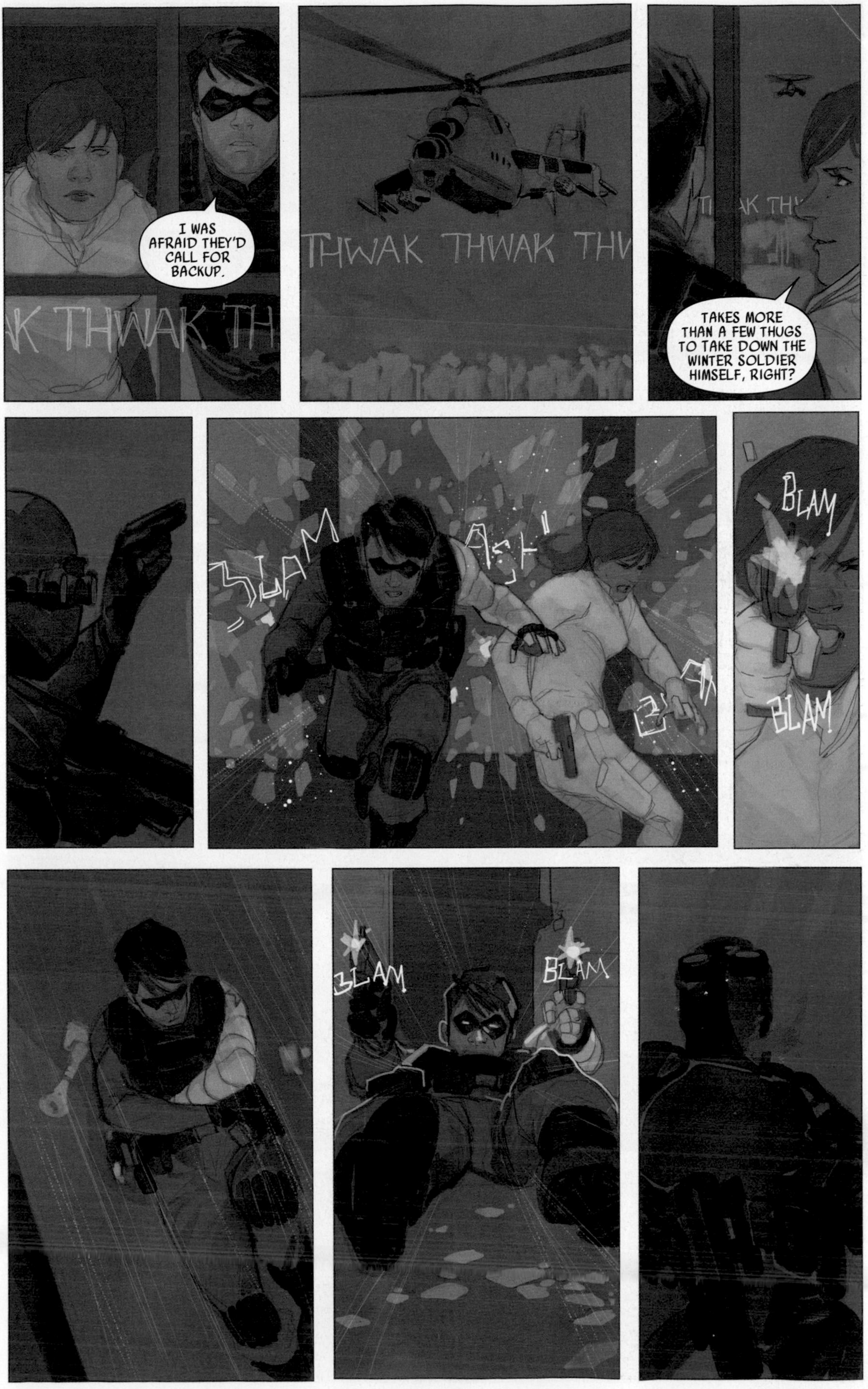
I WAS AFRAID THEY'D CALL FOR BACKUP.
THWAK THWAK
THWAK THWAK
THWAK
TAKES MORE THAN A FEW THUGS TO TAKE DOWN THE WINTER SOLDIER HIMSELF, RIGHT?
BLAM
BLAM
BLAM
BLAM!
BLAM
BLAM

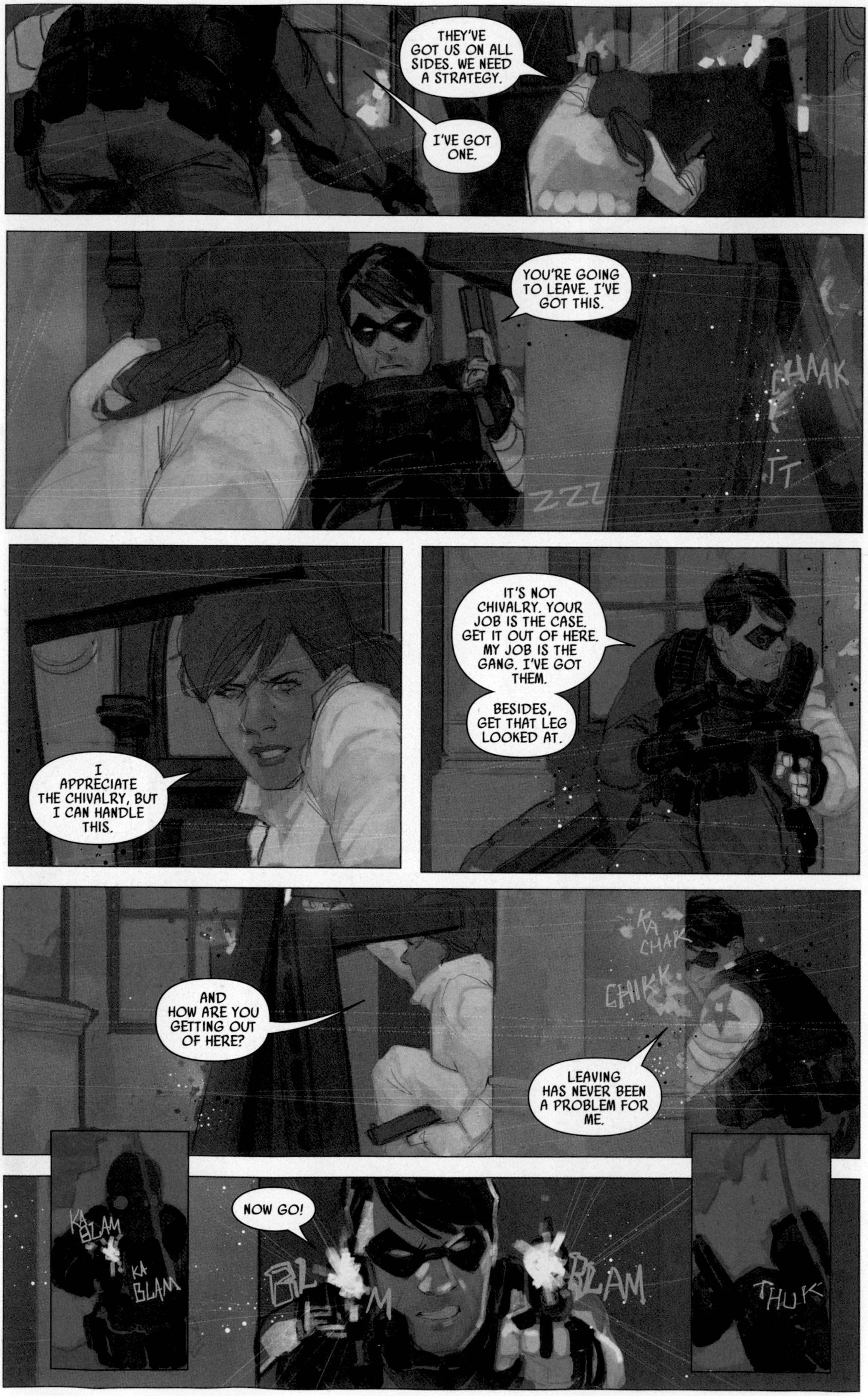
THEY'VE GOT US ON ALL SIDES. WE NEED A STRATEGY.
I'VE GOT ONE.
YOU'RE GOING TO LEAVE. I'VE GOT THIS.
CHAAK
TT
ZZZ
I APPRECIATE THE CHIVALRY, BUT I CAN HANDLE THIS.
IT'S NOT CHIVALRY. YOUR JOB IS THE CASE. GET IT OUT OF HERE. MY JOB IS THE GANG. I'VE GOT THEM.
BESIDES, GET THAT LEG LOOKED AT.
AND HOW ARE YOU GETTING OUT OF HERE?
KA CHAK
CHIKK
LEAVING HAS NEVER BEEN A PROBLEM FOR ME.
KA BLAM
KA BLAM
NOW GO!
BLAM
BLAM
THUK

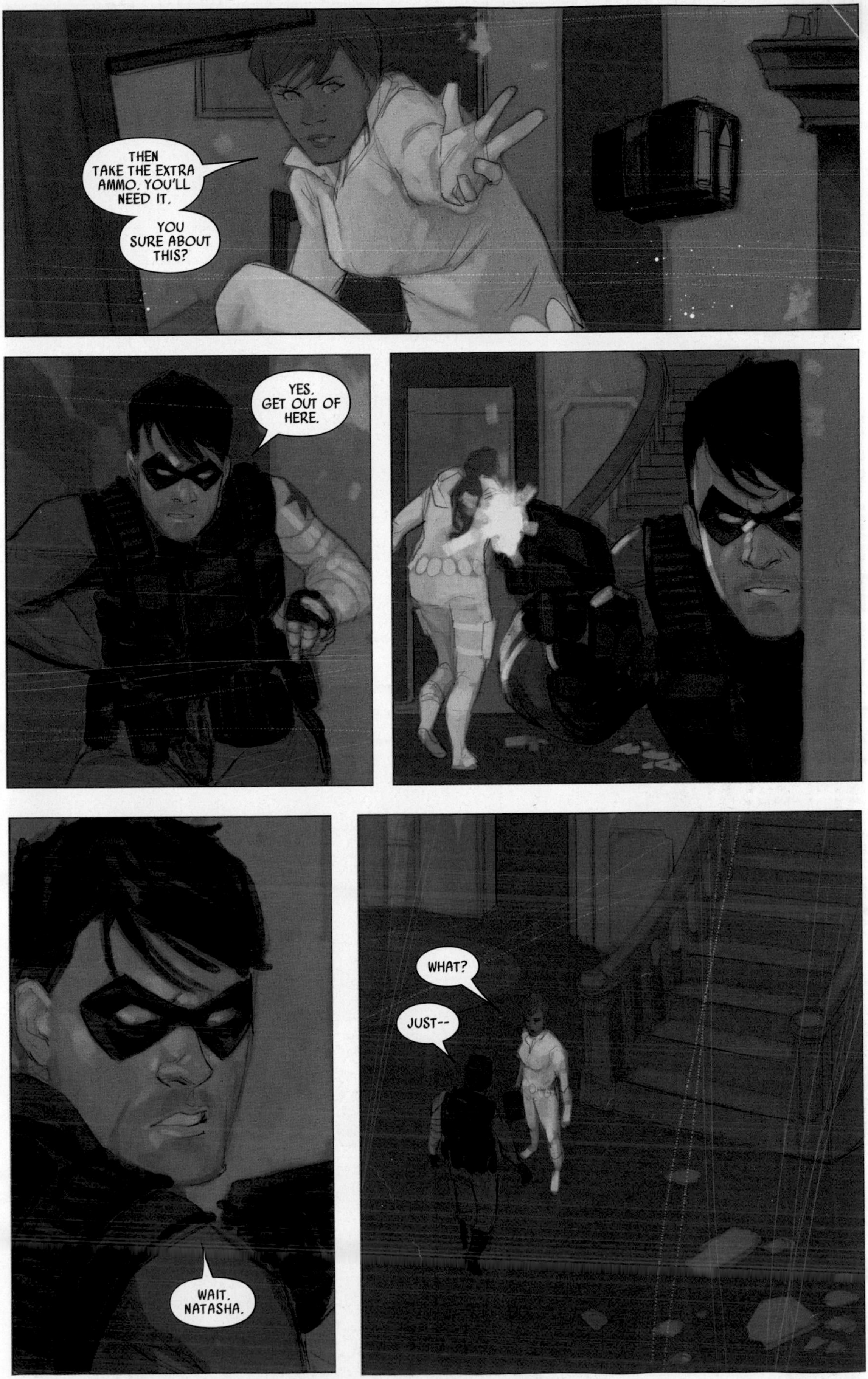
THEN TAKE THE EXTRA AMMO. YOU'LL NEED IT.
YOU SURE ABOUT THIS?
YES. GET OUT OF HERE.
WAIT. NATASHA.
WHAT?
JUST--

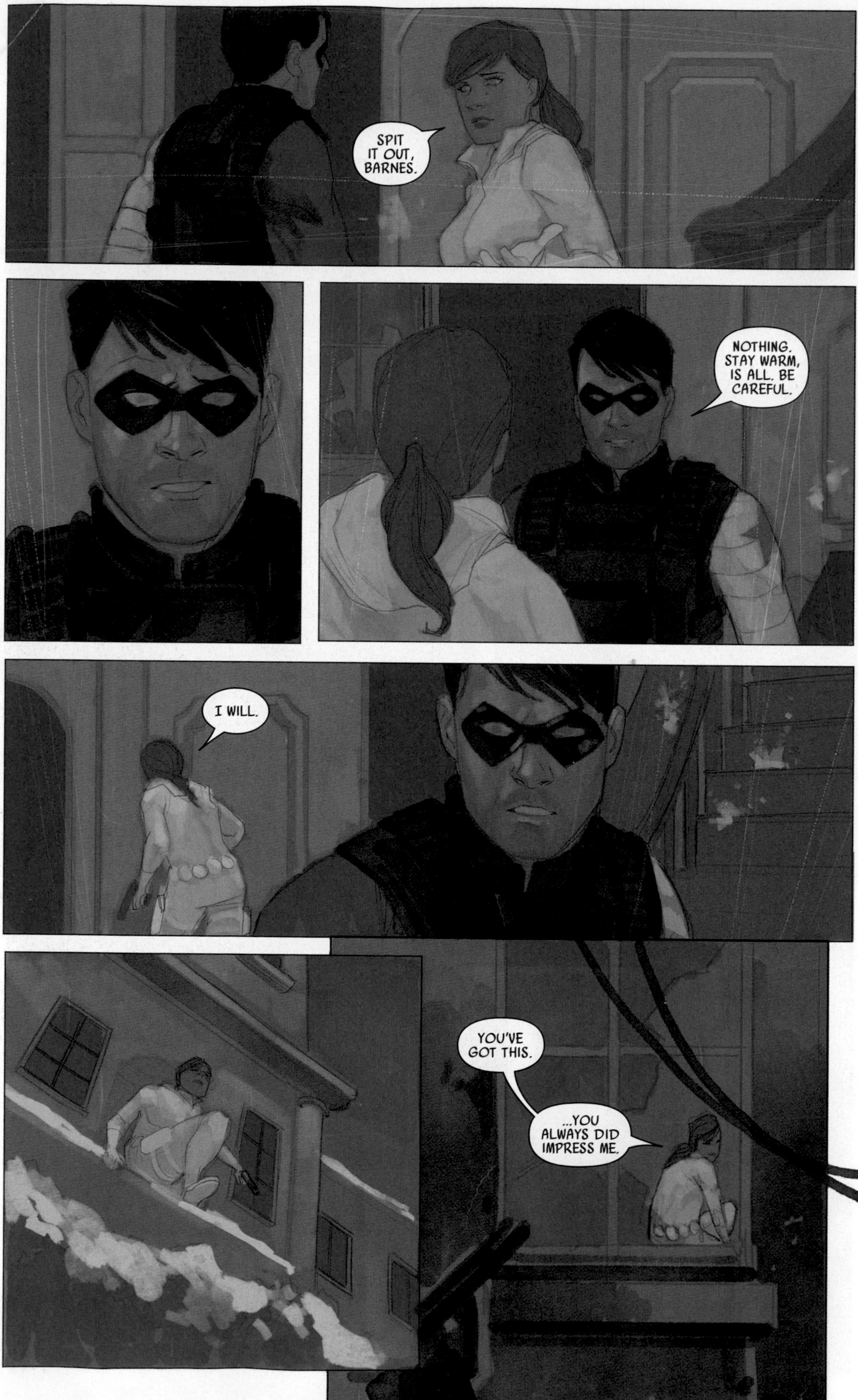
SPIT IT OUT, BARNES.
NOTHING. STAY WARM, IS ALL. BE CAREFUL.
I WILL.
YOU'VE GOT THIS.
...YOU ALWAYS DID IMPRESS ME.

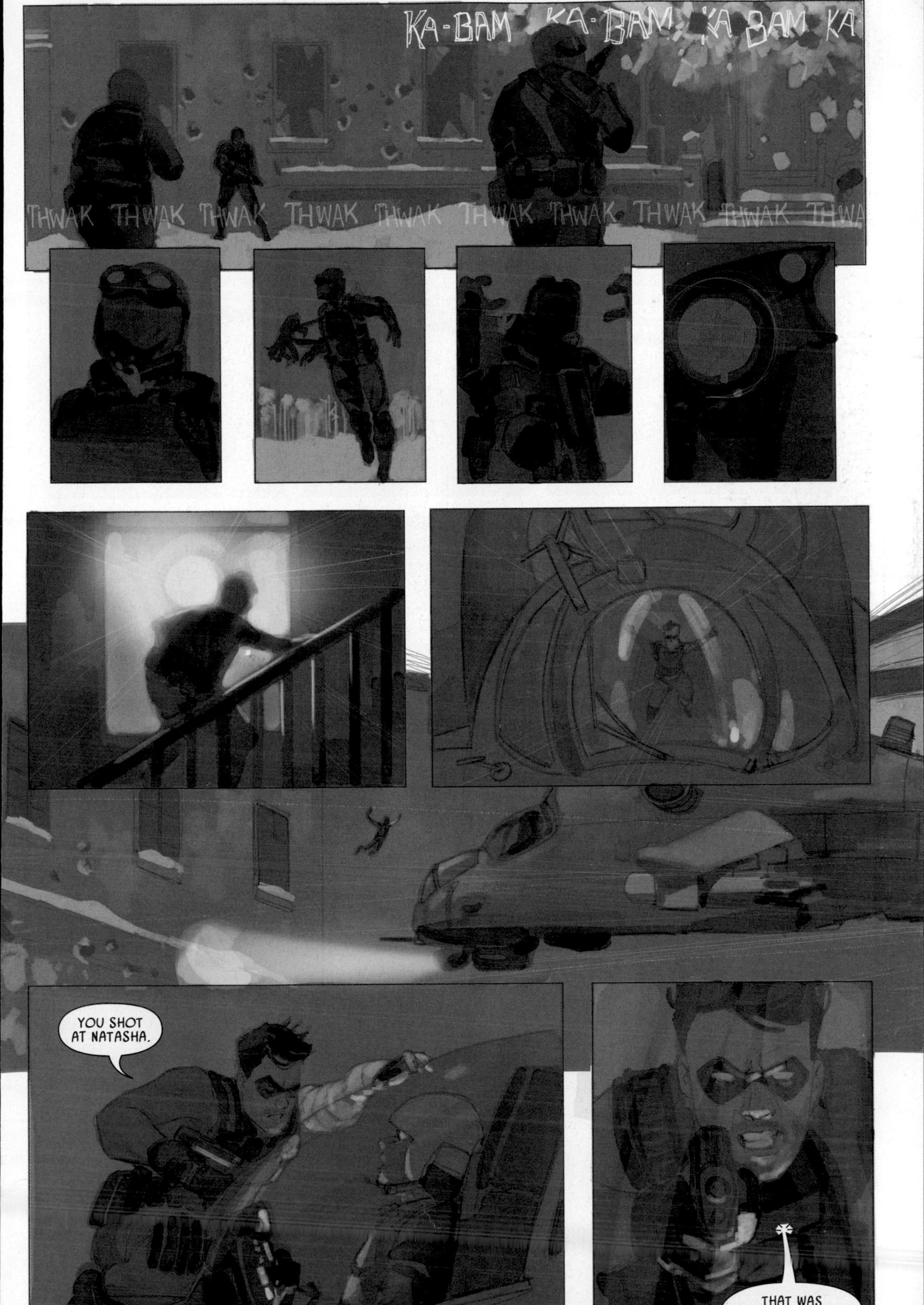
KA-BAM KA-BAM KA-BAM KA-
THWAK THWAK THWAK THWAK THWAK THWAK THWAK THWAK THWAK THWA
YOU SHOT AT NATASHA.
THAT WAS YOUR LAST ACT ON EARTH, PAL.

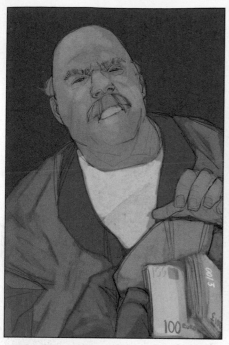

IT WILL DO. THANK YOU KINDLY.

A PLEASURE DOING BUSINESS WITH YOU.

SCREW YOU.

WELL THAT'S ONE SMALL MIRACLE.

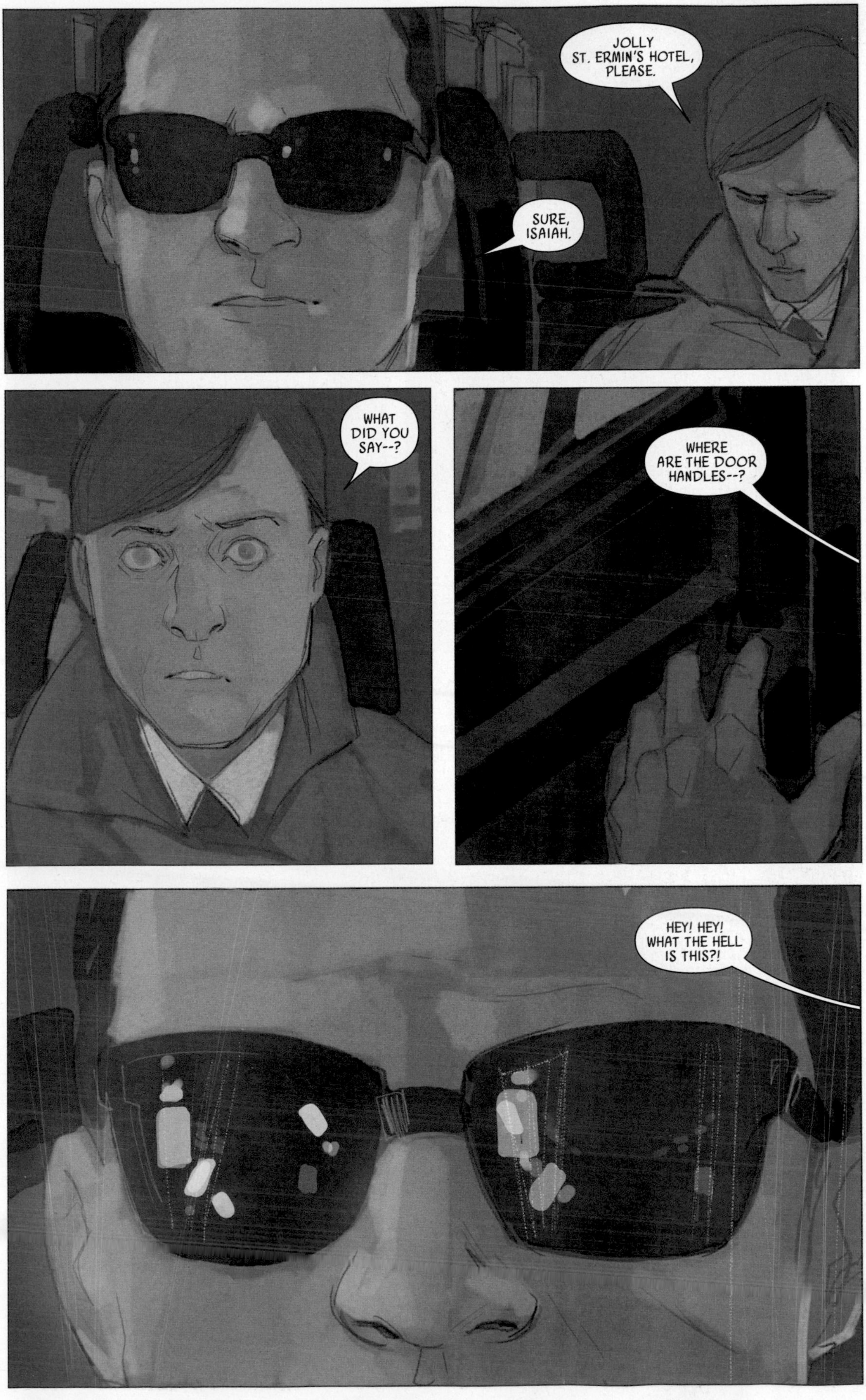
JOLLY
ST. ERMIN'S HOTEL,
PLEASE.
SURE,
ISAIAH.
WHAT
DID YOU
SAY--?
WHERE
ARE THE DOOR
HANDLES--?
HEY! HEY!
WHAT THE HELL
IS THIS?!

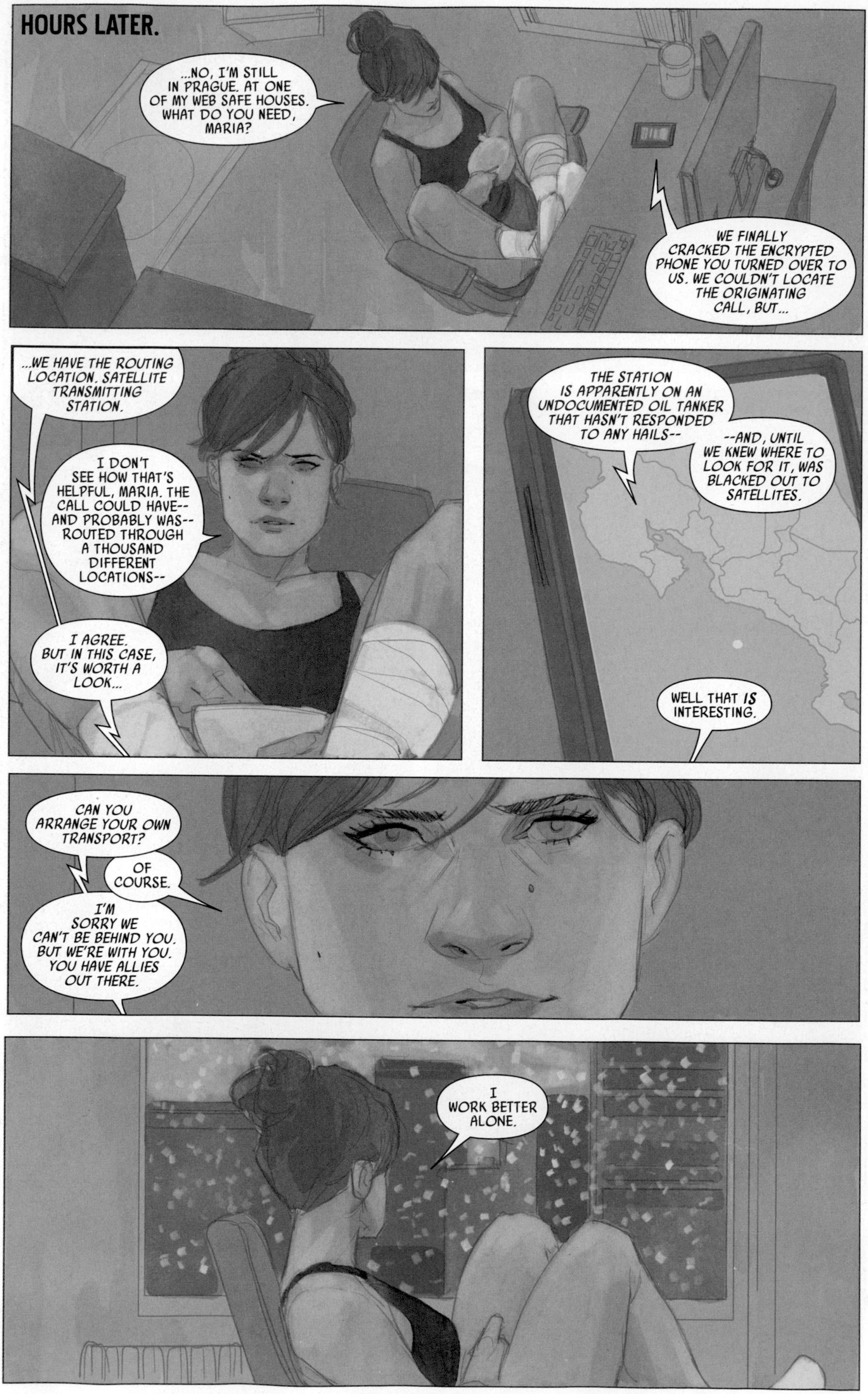
HOURS LATER.
...NO, I'M STILL IN PRAGUE. AT ONE OF MY WEB SAFE HOUSES. WHAT DO YOU NEED, MARIA?
WE FINALLY CRACKED THE ENCRYPTED PHONE YOU TURNED OVER TO US. WE COULDN'T LOCATE THE ORIGINATING CALL, BUT...
...WE HAVE THE ROUTING LOCATION. SATELLITE TRANSMITTING STATION.
I DON'T SEE HOW THAT'S HELPFUL, MARIA. THE CALL COULD HAVE-- AND PROBABLY WAS-- ROUTED THROUGH A THOUSAND DIFFERENT LOCATIONS--
I AGREE. BUT IN THIS CASE, IT'S WORTH A LOOK...
THE STATION IS APPARENTLY ON AN UNDOCUMENTED OIL TANKER THAT HASN'T RESPONDED TO ANY HAILS--
--AND, UNTIL WE KNEW WHERE TO LOOK FOR IT, WAS BLACKED OUT TO SATELLITES.
WELL THAT **IS** INTERESTING.
CAN YOU ARRANGE YOUR OWN TRANSPORT?
OF COURSE.
I'M SORRY WE CAN'T BE BEHIND YOU. BUT WE'RE WITH YOU. YOU HAVE ALLIES OUT THERE.
I WORK BETTER ALONE.

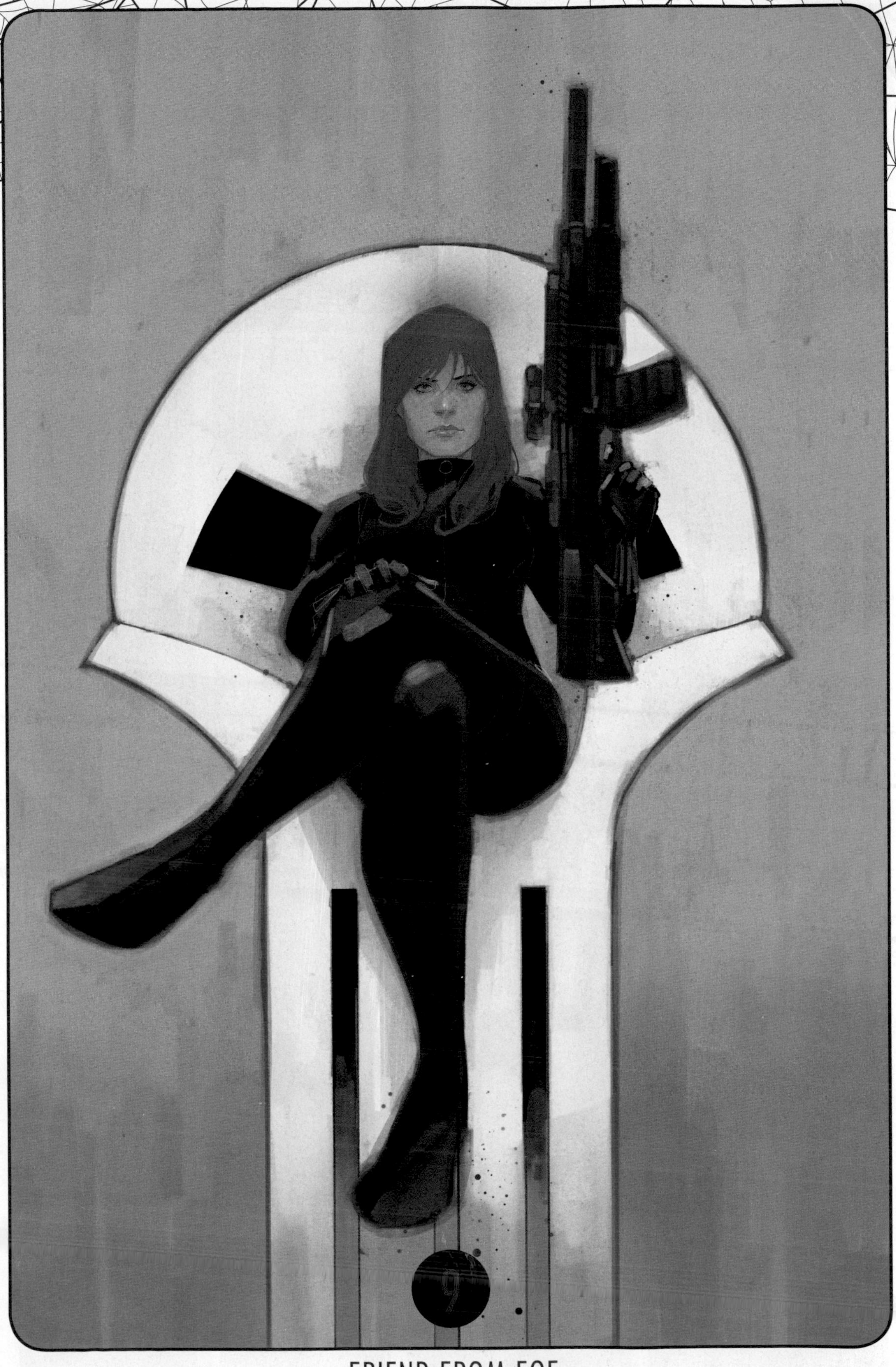
9

FRIEND FROM FOE

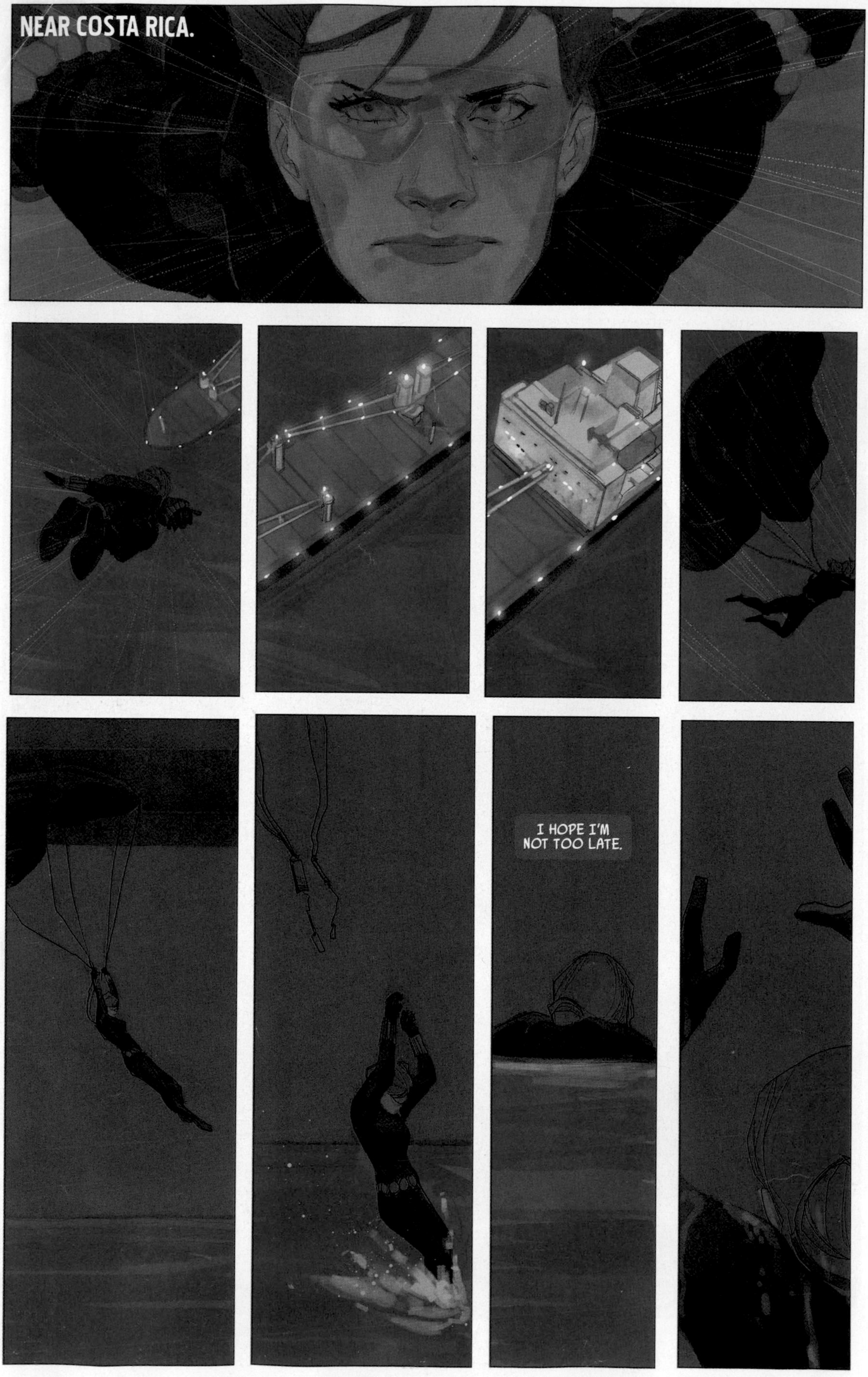
NEAR COSTA RICA.
I HOPE I'M NOT TOO LATE.

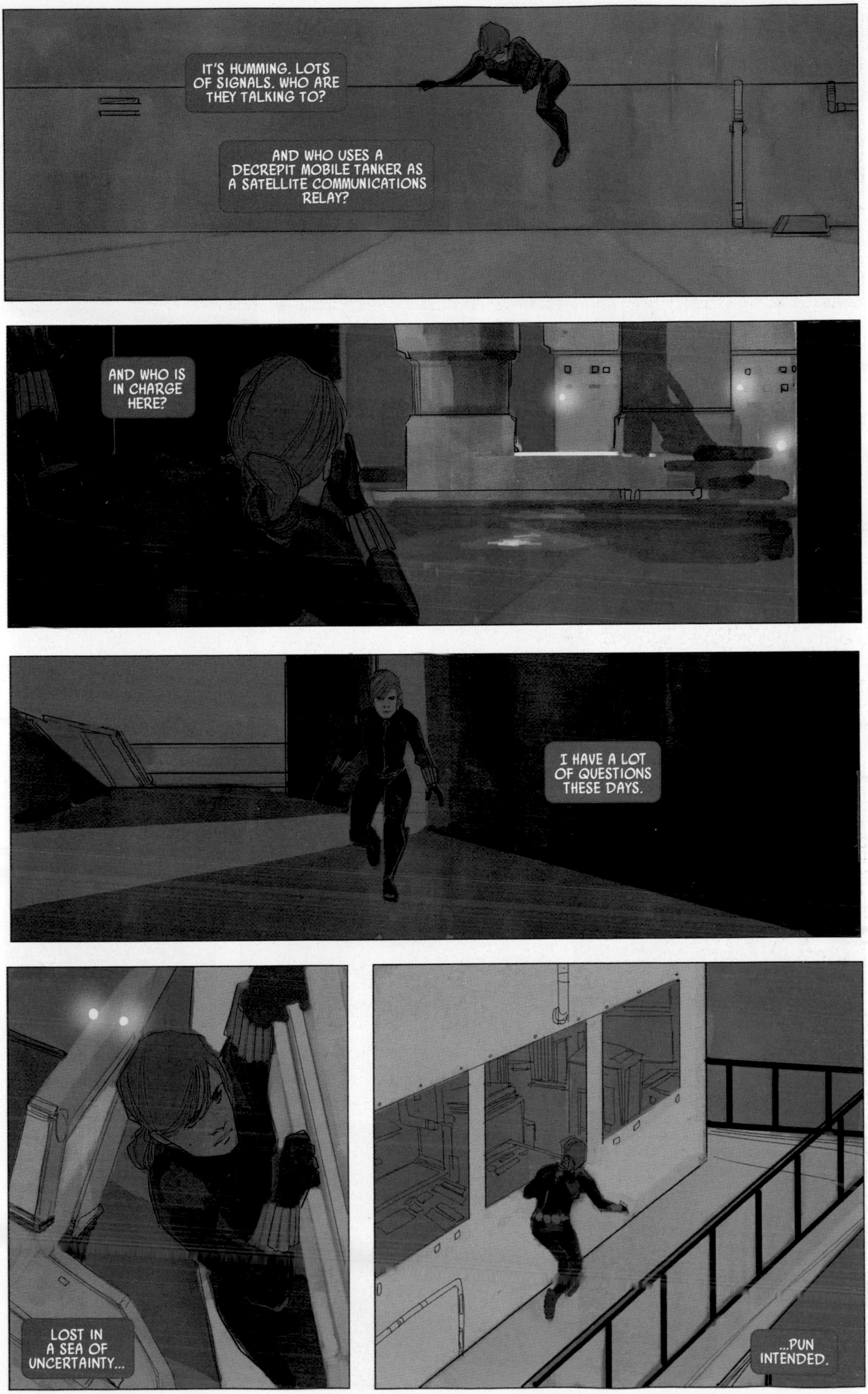
IT'S HUMMING. LOTS OF SIGNALS. WHO ARE THEY TALKING TO?
AND WHO USES A DECREPIT MOBILE TANKER AS A SATELLITE COMMUNICATIONS RELAY?
AND WHO IS IN CHARGE HERE?
I HAVE A LOT OF QUESTIONS THESE DAYS.
LOST IN A SEA OF UNCERTAINTY...
...PUN INTENDED.

NO ONE ON THE BRIDGE...

THAT PHRASE "EERILY QUIET" COMES TO MIND...

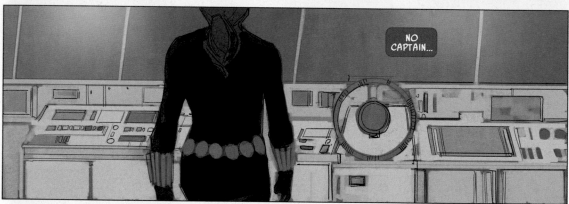

NO CAPTAIN...

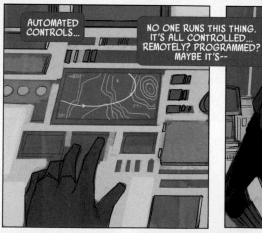

AUTOMATED CONTROLS...

NO ONE RUNS THIS THING. IT'S ALL CONTROLLED... REMOTELY? PROGRAMMED? MAYBE IT'S--

BZZZZZ

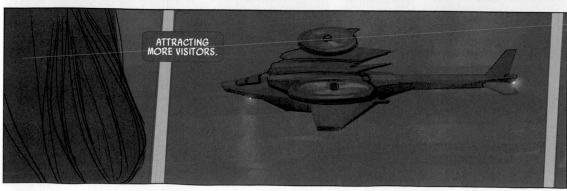

ATTRACTING MORE VISITORS.

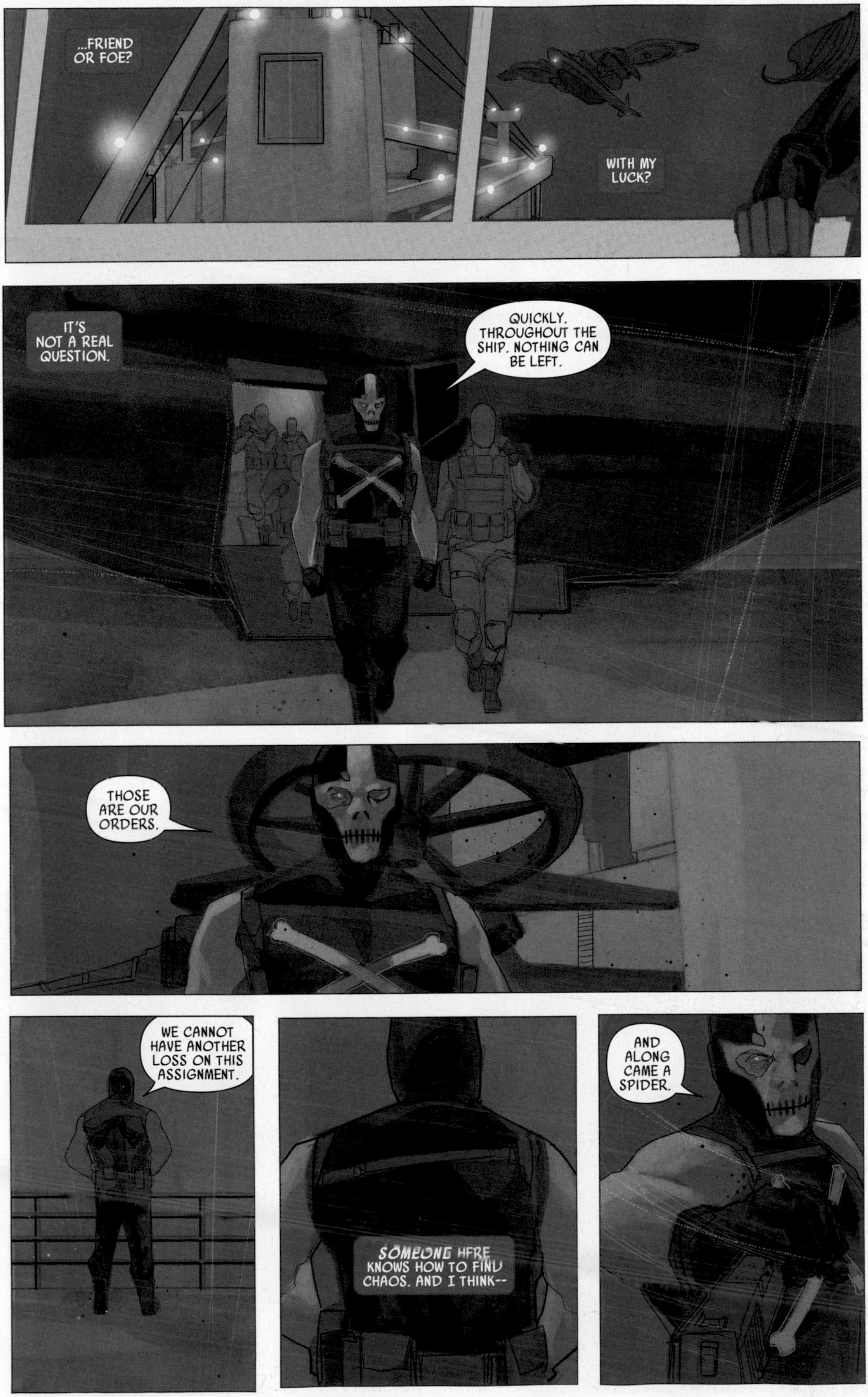
...FRIEND OR FOE?
WITH MY LUCK?
IT'S NOT A REAL QUESTION.
QUICKLY. THROUGHOUT THE SHIP. NOTHING CAN BE LEFT.
THOSE ARE OUR ORDERS.
WE CANNOT HAVE ANOTHER LOSS ON THIS ASSIGNMENT.
SOMEONE HERE KNOWS HOW TO FIND CHAOS. AND I THINK--
AND ALONG CAME A SPIDER.

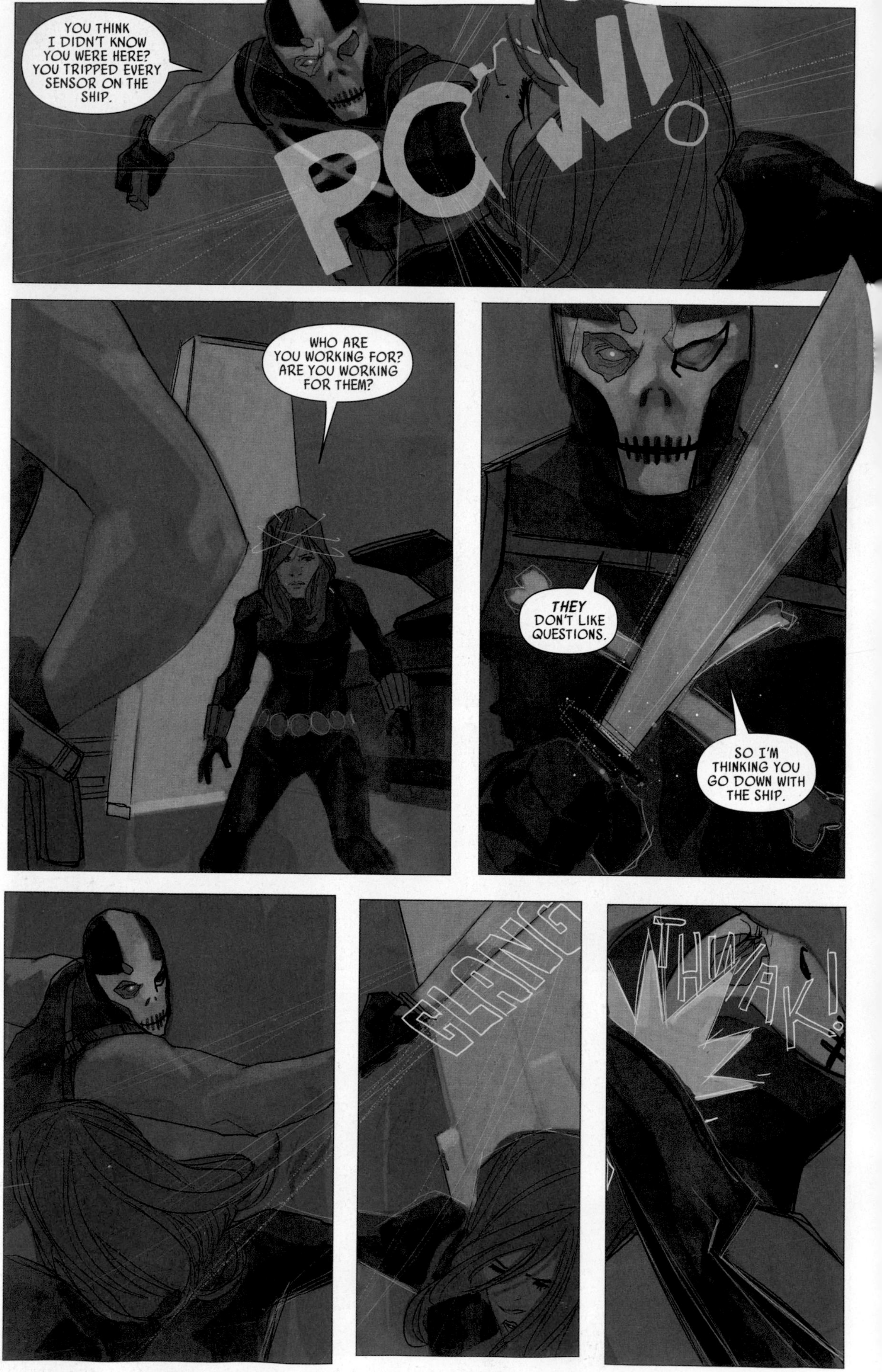
YOU THINK I DIDN'T KNOW YOU WERE HERE? YOU TRIPPED EVERY SENSOR ON THE SHIP.
POW!
WHO ARE YOU WORKING FOR? ARE YOU WORKING FOR THEM?
THEY DON'T LIKE QUESTIONS.
SO I'M THINKING YOU GO DOWN WITH THE SHIP.
CLANG
THWAK!

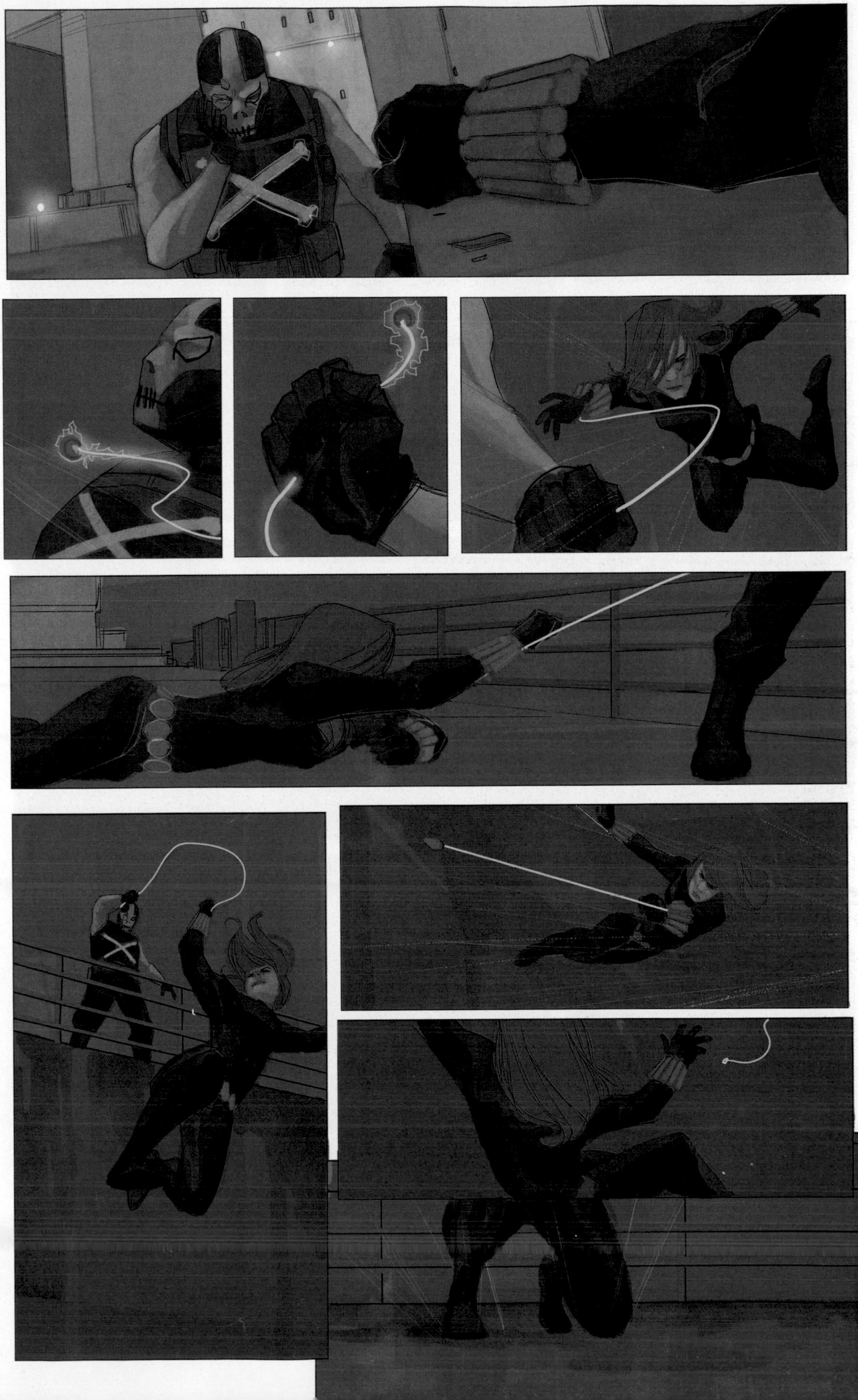

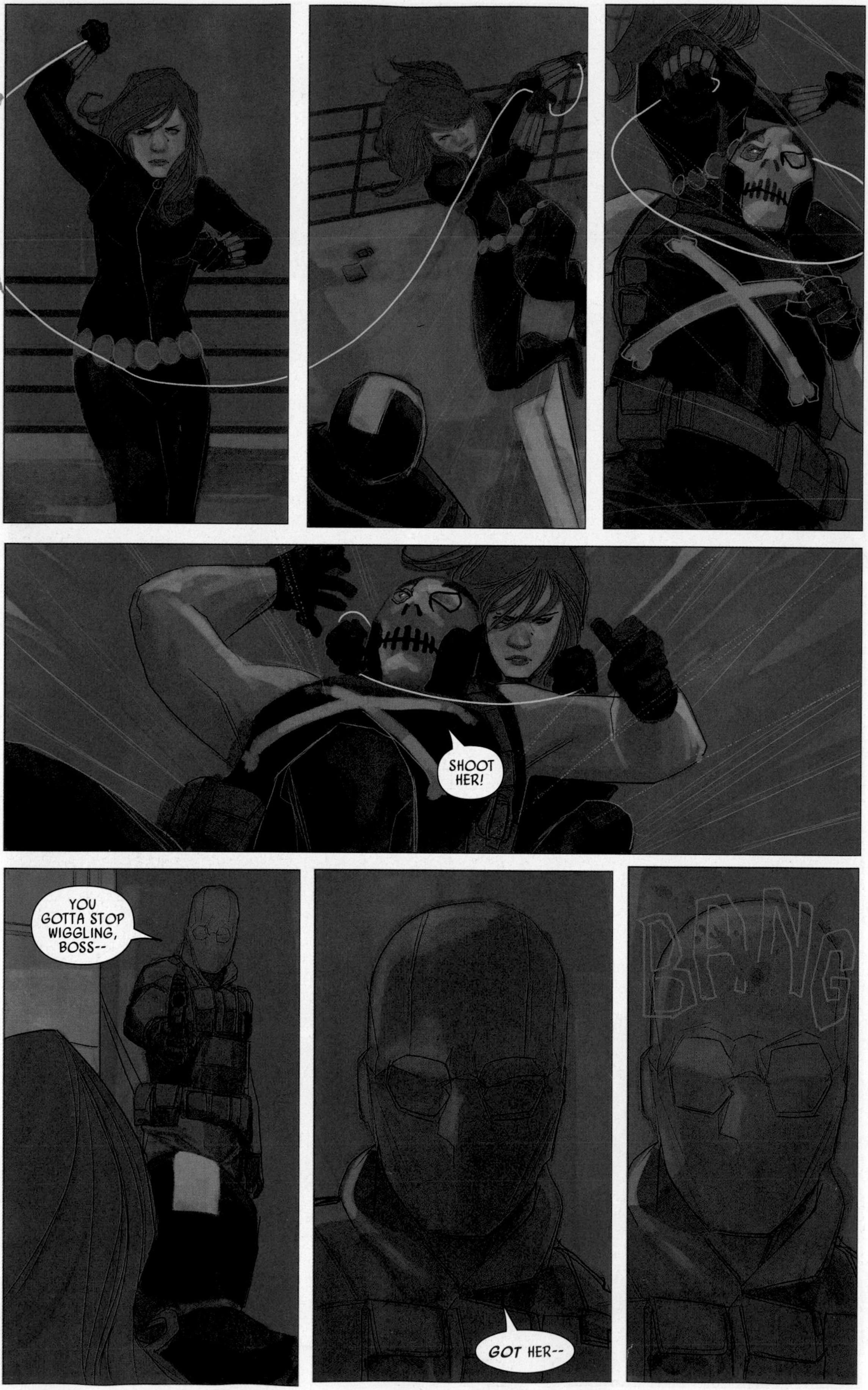
SHOOT HER!
YOU GOTTA STOP WIGGLING, BOSS--
GOT HER--
BANG

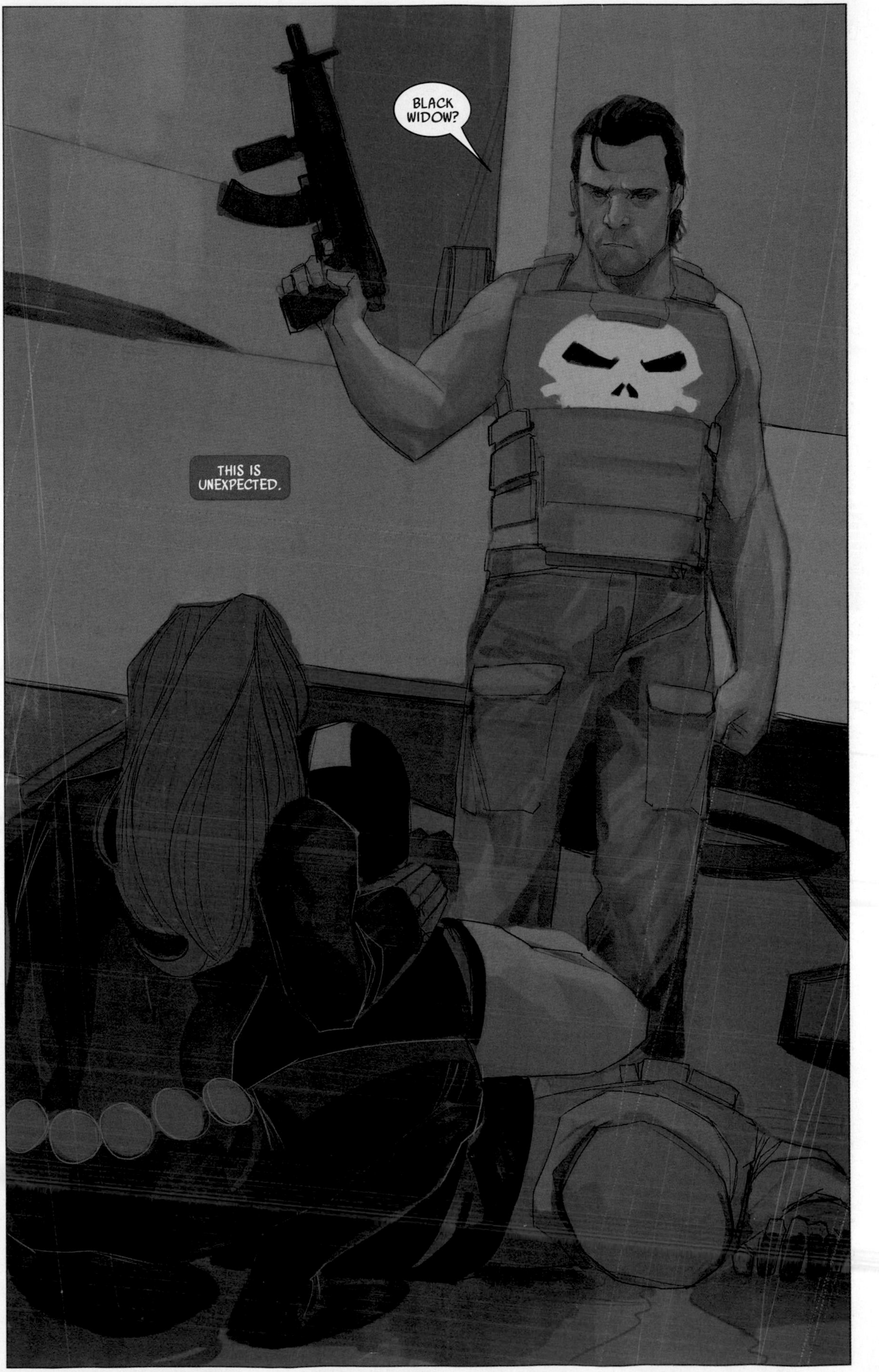
BLACK WIDOW?
THIS IS UNEXPECTED.

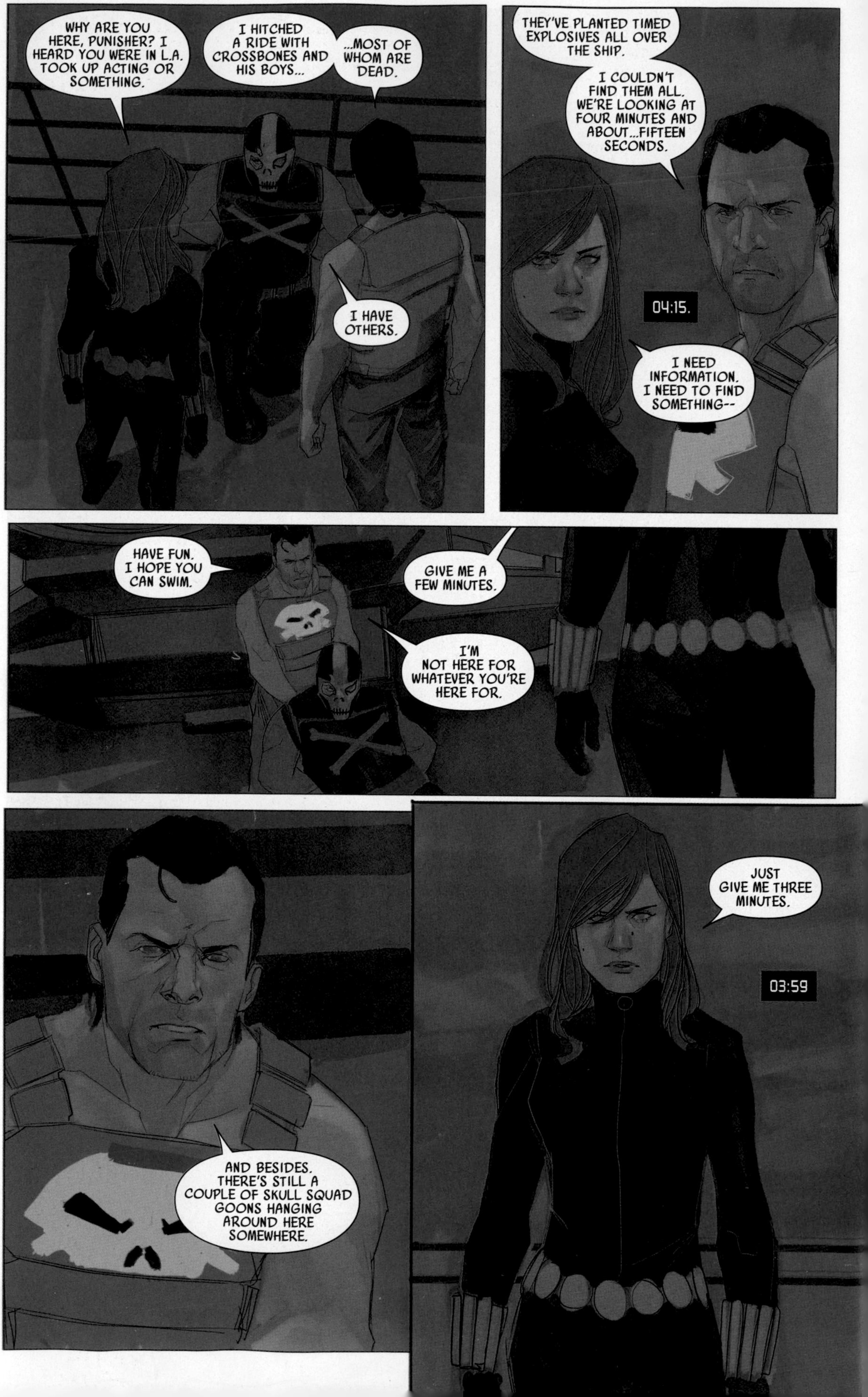
WHY ARE YOU HERE, PUNISHER? I HEARD YOU WERE IN L.A. TOOK UP ACTING OR SOMETHING.
I HITCHED A RIDE WITH CROSSBONES AND HIS BOYS...
...MOST OF WHOM ARE DEAD.
I HAVE OTHERS.
THEY'VE PLANTED TIMED EXPLOSIVES ALL OVER THE SHIP.
I COULDN'T FIND THEM ALL. WE'RE LOOKING AT FOUR MINUTES AND ABOUT...FIFTEEN SECONDS.
04:15.
I NEED INFORMATION. I NEED TO FIND SOMETHING--
HAVE FUN. I HOPE YOU CAN SWIM.
GIVE ME A FEW MINUTES.
I'M NOT HERE FOR WHATEVER YOU'RE HERE FOR.
AND BESIDES. THERE'S STILL A COUPLE OF SKULL SQUAD GOONS HANGING AROUND HERE SOMEWHERE.
JUST GIVE ME THREE MINUTES.
03:59

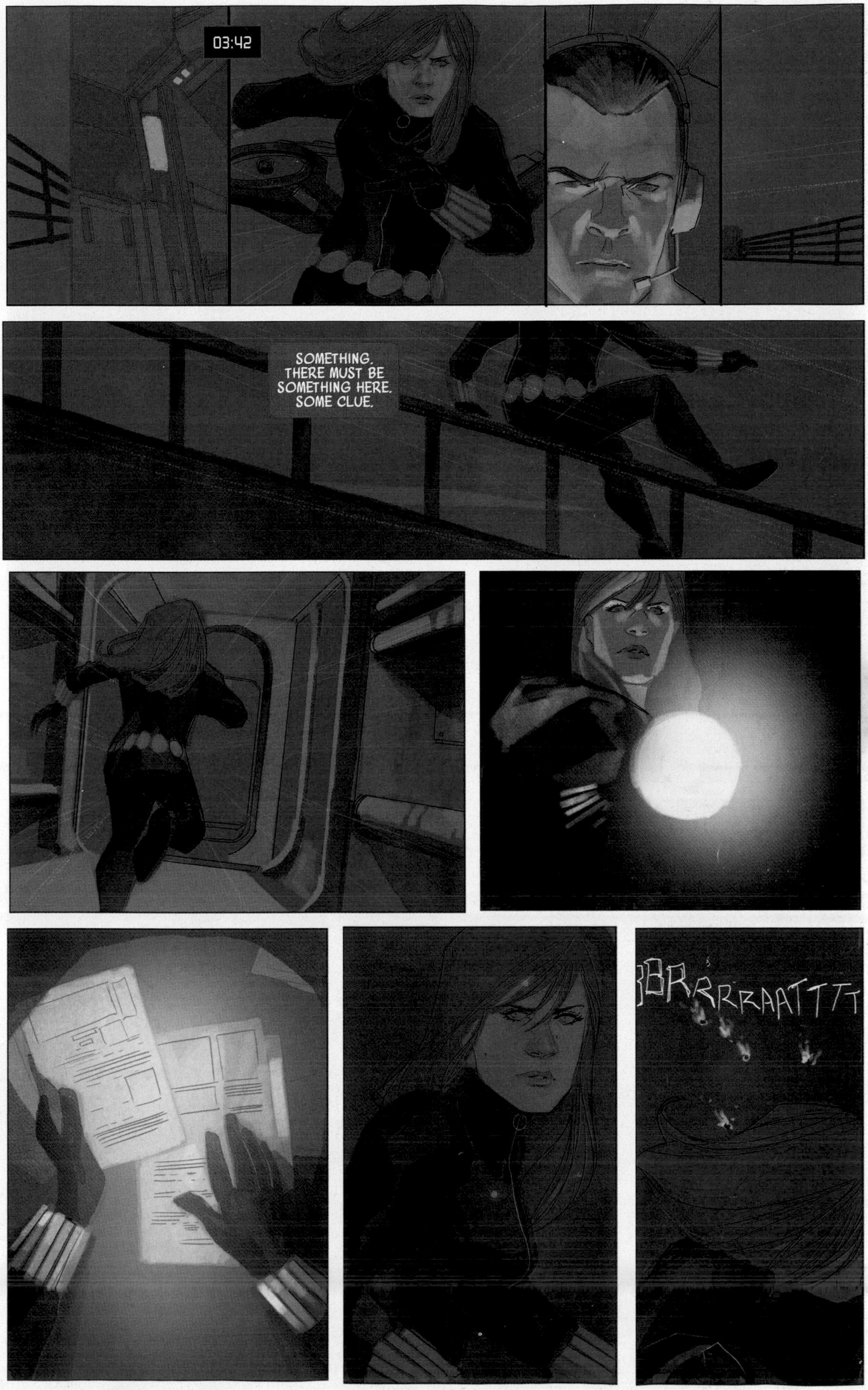
03:42
SOMETHING. THERE MUST BE SOMETHING HERE. SOME CLUE.
BRRRRAATTTT

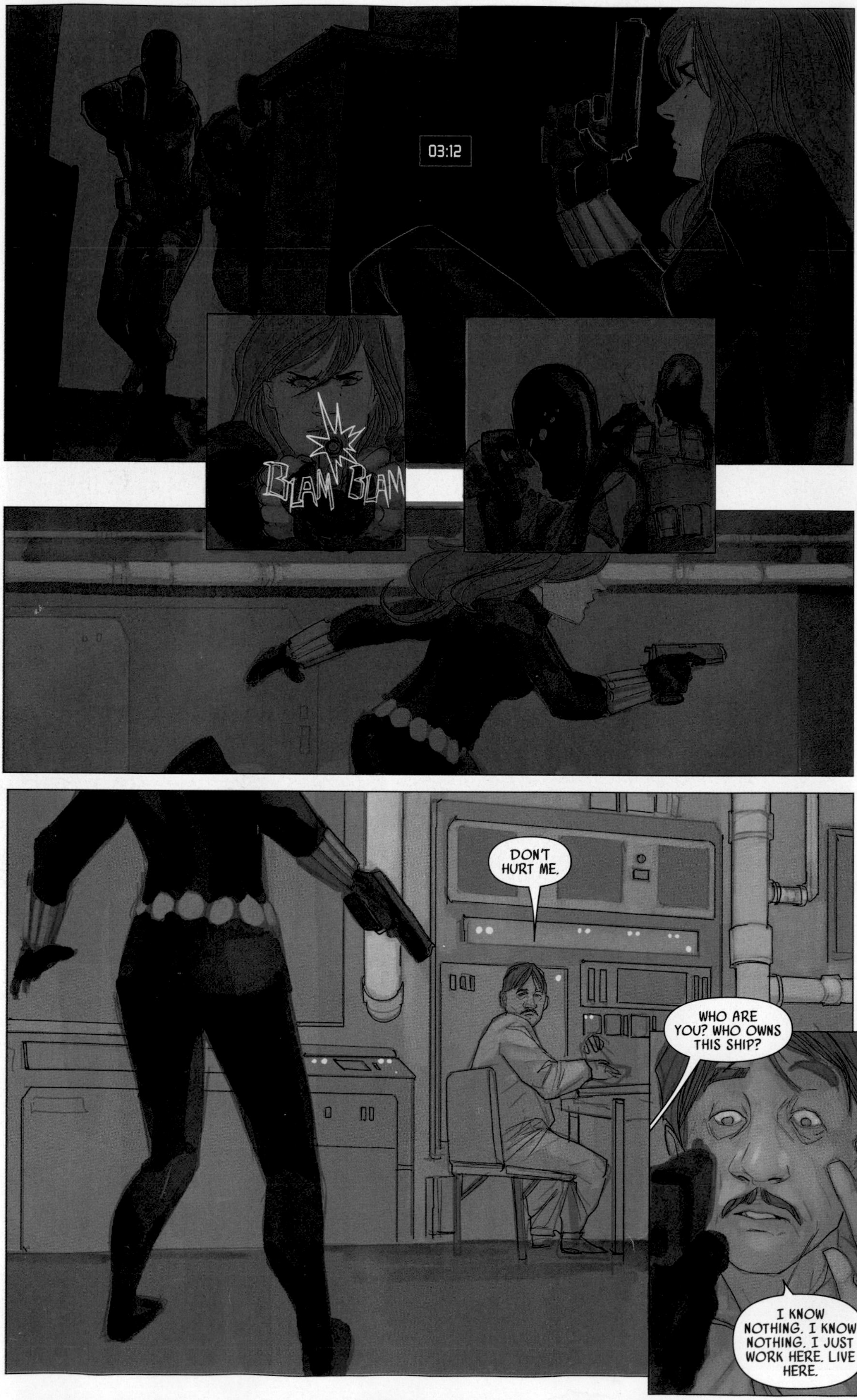
03:12
BLAM BLAM
DON'T HURT ME.
WHO ARE YOU? WHO OWNS THIS SHIP?
I KNOW NOTHING. I KNOW NOTHING. I JUST WORK HERE. LIVE HERE.

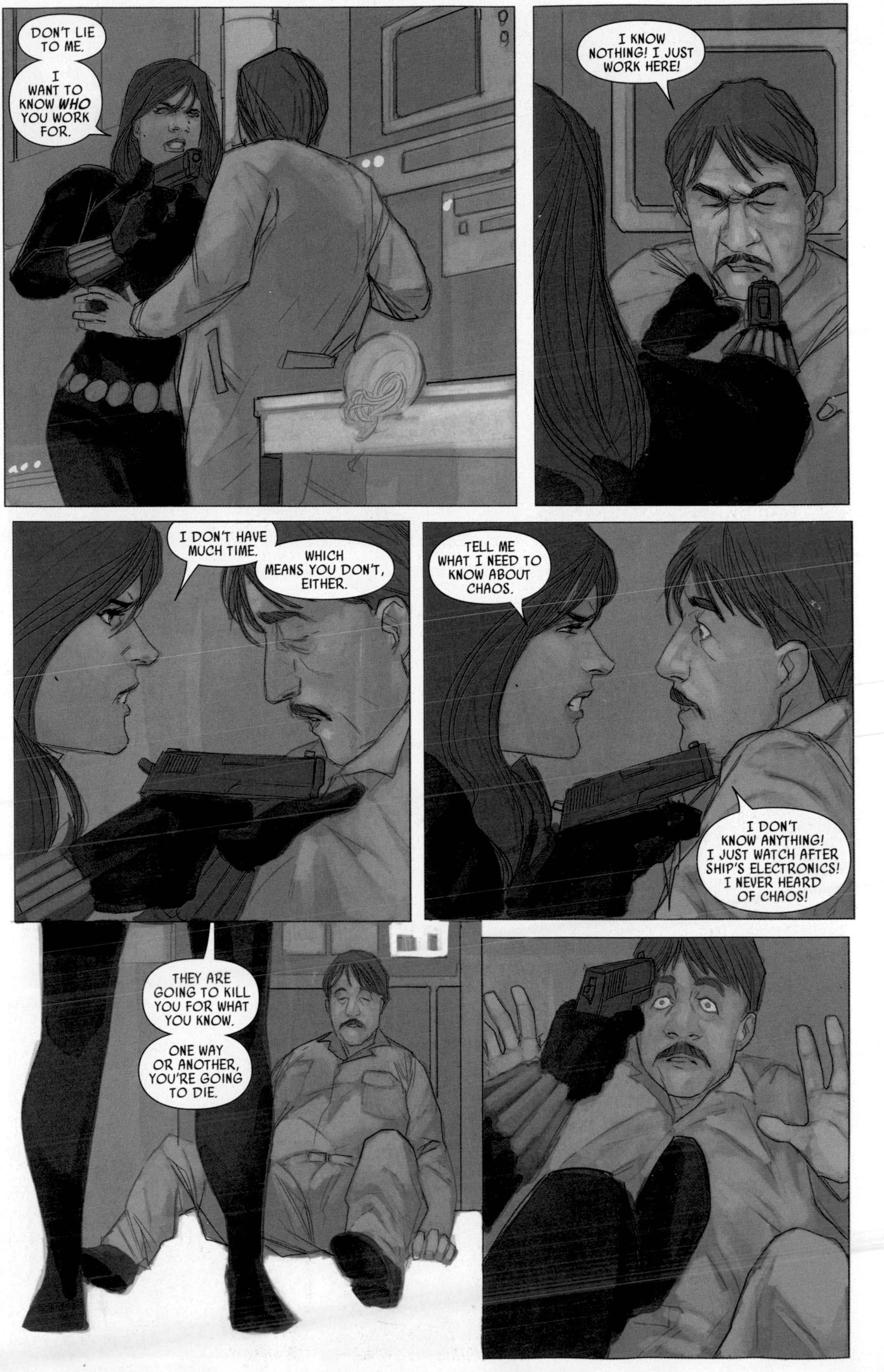
DON'T LIE TO ME.
I WANT TO KNOW WHO YOU WORK FOR.
I KNOW NOTHING! I JUST WORK HERE!
I DON'T HAVE MUCH TIME.
WHICH MEANS YOU DON'T, EITHER.
TELL ME WHAT I NEED TO KNOW ABOUT CHAOS.
I DON'T KNOW ANYTHING! I JUST WATCH AFTER SHIP'S ELECTRONICS! I NEVER HEARD OF CHAOS!
THEY ARE GOING TO KILL YOU FOR WHAT YOU KNOW.
ONE WAY OR ANOTHER, YOU'RE GOING TO DIE.

I'M GOING TO GIVE YOU THIRTY SECONDS.

01:31

I TOLD YOU WHAT I KNOW. I TOLD YOU I ONLY FIX THINGS. I JUST TAKE CARE OF SHIP.

YOU'RE EITHER LYING, OR YOU'RE OF NO USE TO ME.

01:11

A BULLET TO THE KNEECAP I THINK WILL MAKE CLEAR WHICH--

01:05

HEY!

NO.

00:59

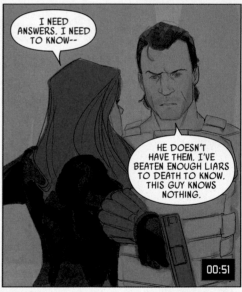

I NEED ANSWERS. I NEED TO KNOW--

HE DOESN'T HAVE THEM. I'VE BEATEN ENOUGH LIARS TO DEATH TO KNOW. THIS GUY KNOWS NOTHING.

00:51

I DON'T KNOW WHAT YOU'RE UP AGAINST, BUT TAKE IT FROM ME--

--DON'T LET YOUR EMOTIONS LEAD THE WAY.

NOW LET'S SPLIT.

00:48

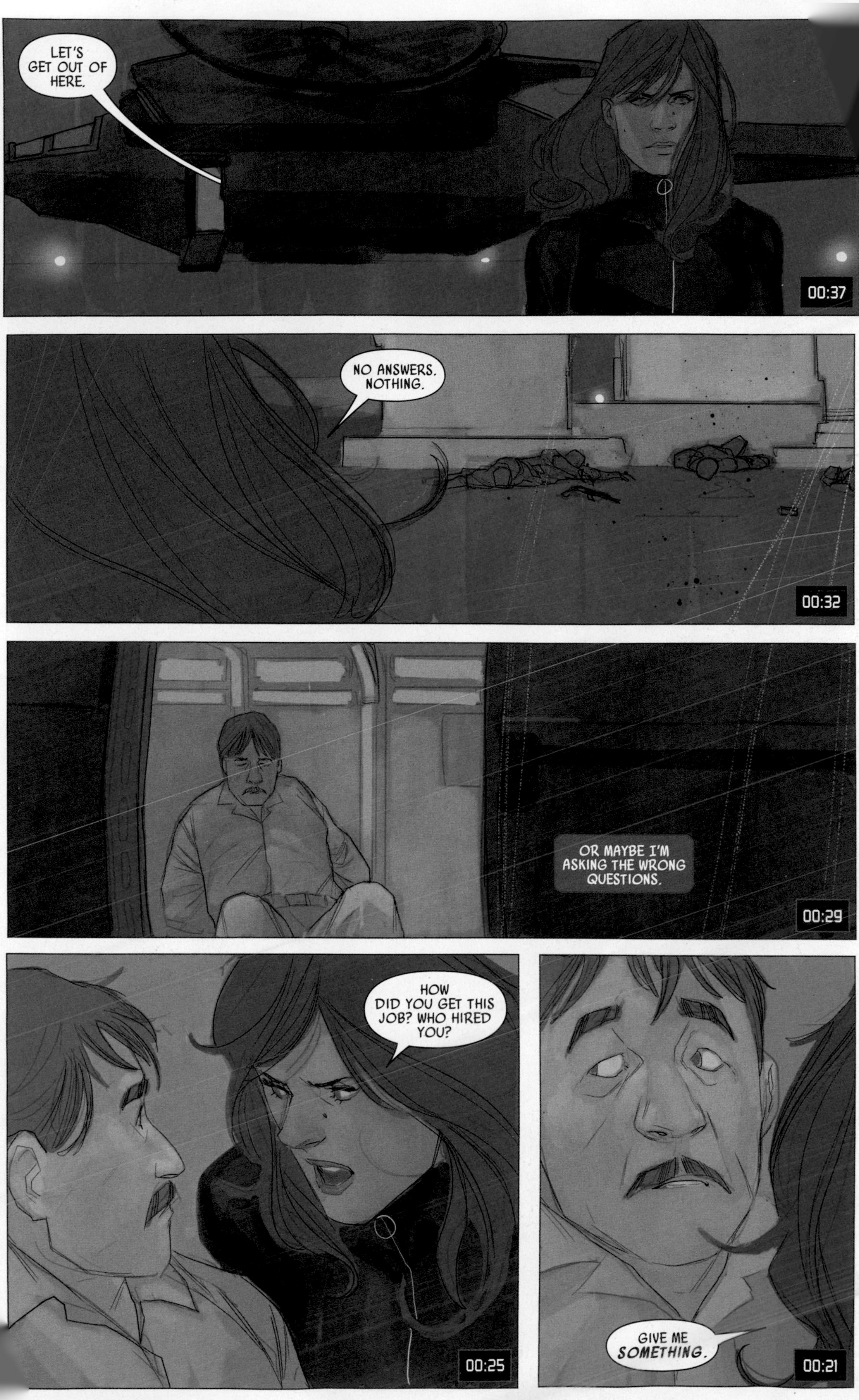
LET'S GET OUT OF HERE.
00:37
NO ANSWERS. NOTHING.
00:32
OR MAYBE I'M ASKING THE WRONG QUESTIONS.
00:29
HOW DID YOU GET THIS JOB? WHO HIRED YOU?
00:25
GIVE ME SOMETHING.
00:21

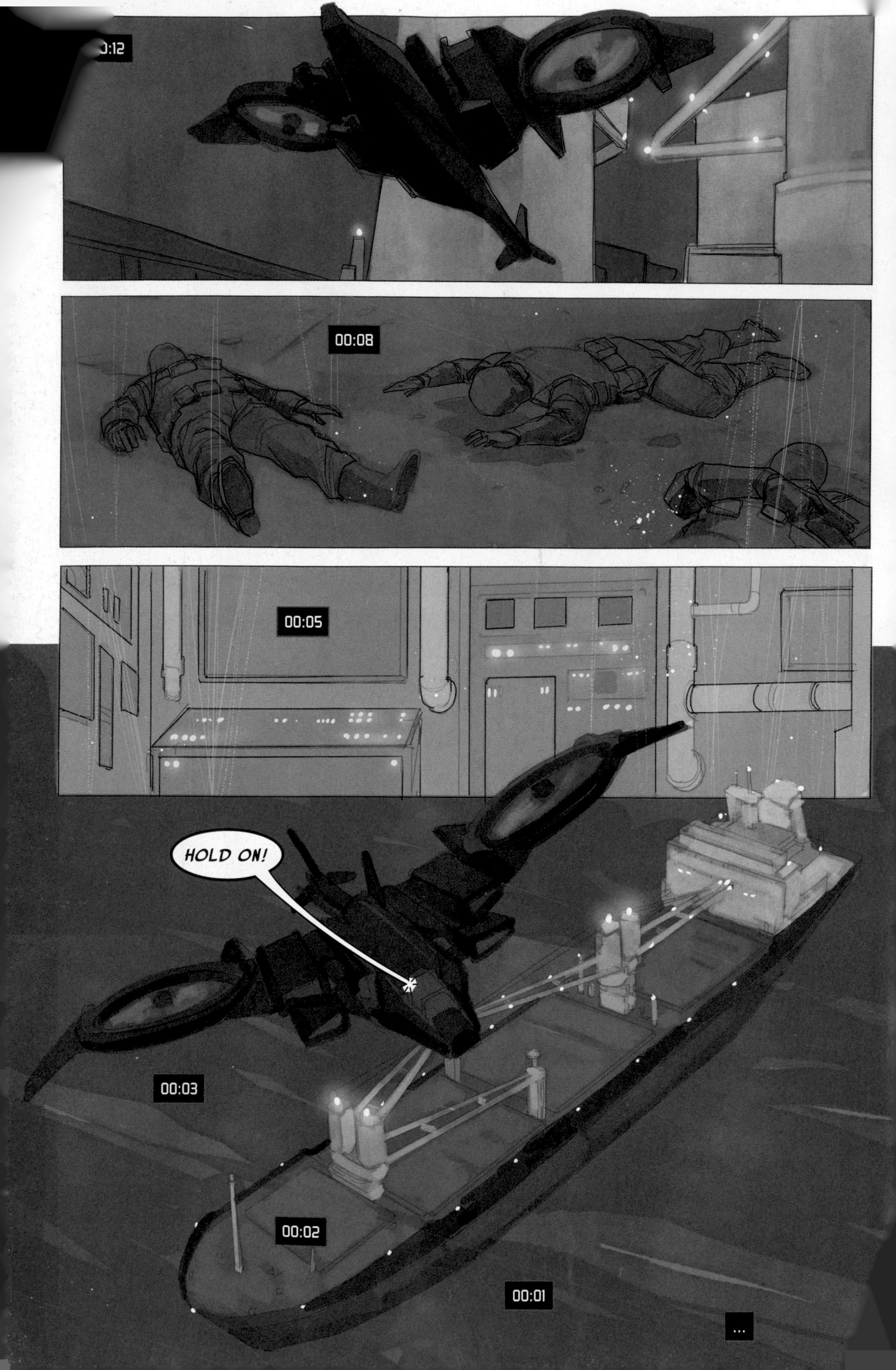

0:12
00:08
00:05
HOLD ON!
00:03
00:02
00:01
...

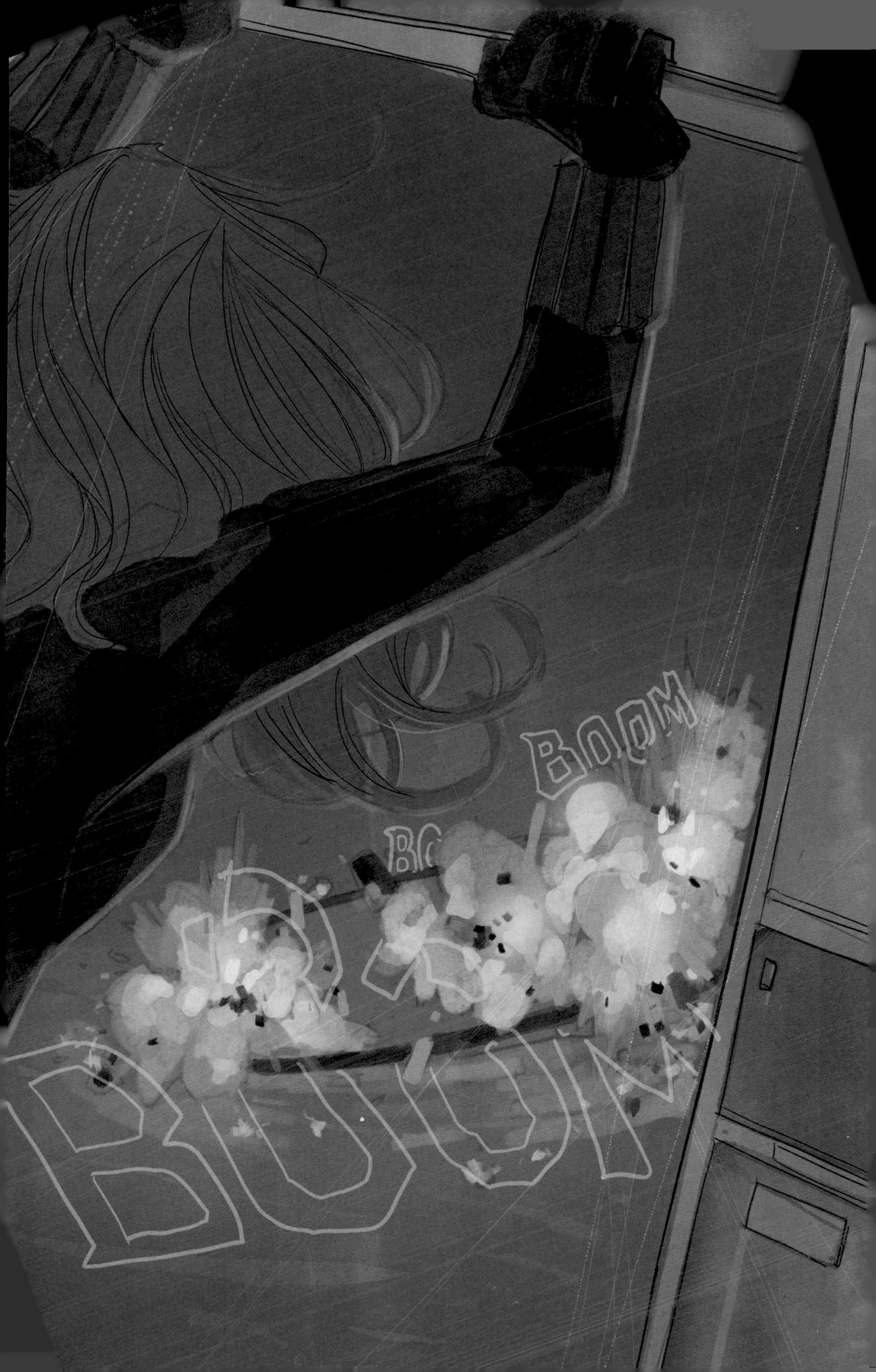
BOOM
BO
BOOM

THEY WOULD DESTROY THE BOAT, FOR YOU?

NOT ME. EVERYTHING. THEY ERASE EVERY TRACK.

THEY MUST HAVE MISSED *SOMETHING*. WHO HIRED YOU?

SOME GUY BOUGHT THE BOAT HIRED ME. THAT WAS IT.

HIS *NAME*. GIVE ME HIS *NAME*.

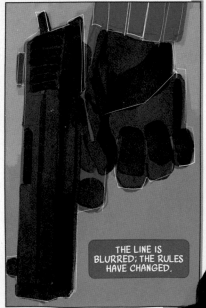

THE LINE IS BLURRED; THE RULES HAVE CHANGED.

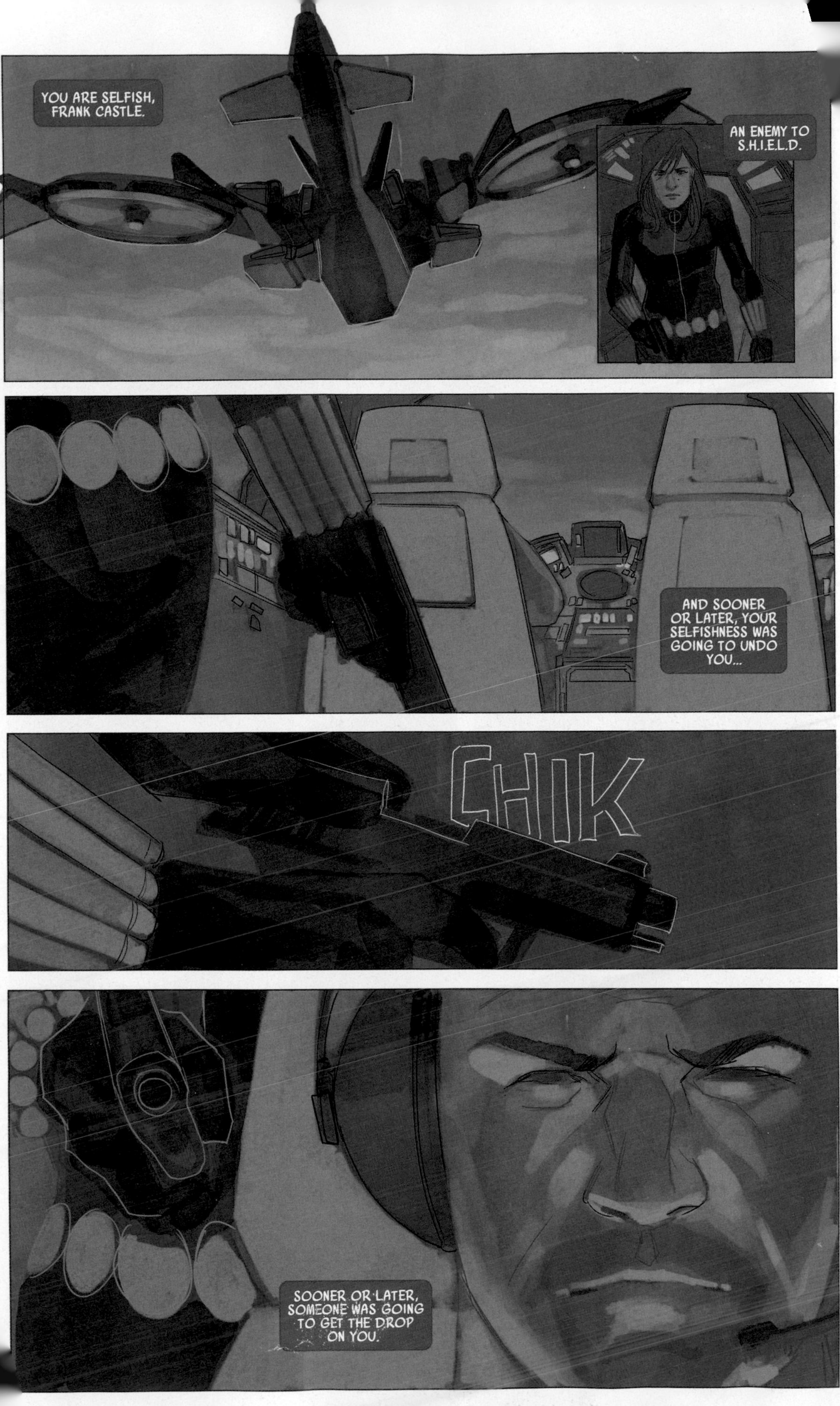
YOU ARE SELFISH, FRANK CASTLE.
AN ENEMY TO S.H.I.E.L.D.
AND SOONER OR LATER, YOUR SELFISHNESS WAS GOING TO UNDO YOU...
CHIK
SOONER OR LATER, SOMEONE WAS GOING TO GET THE DROP ON YOU.

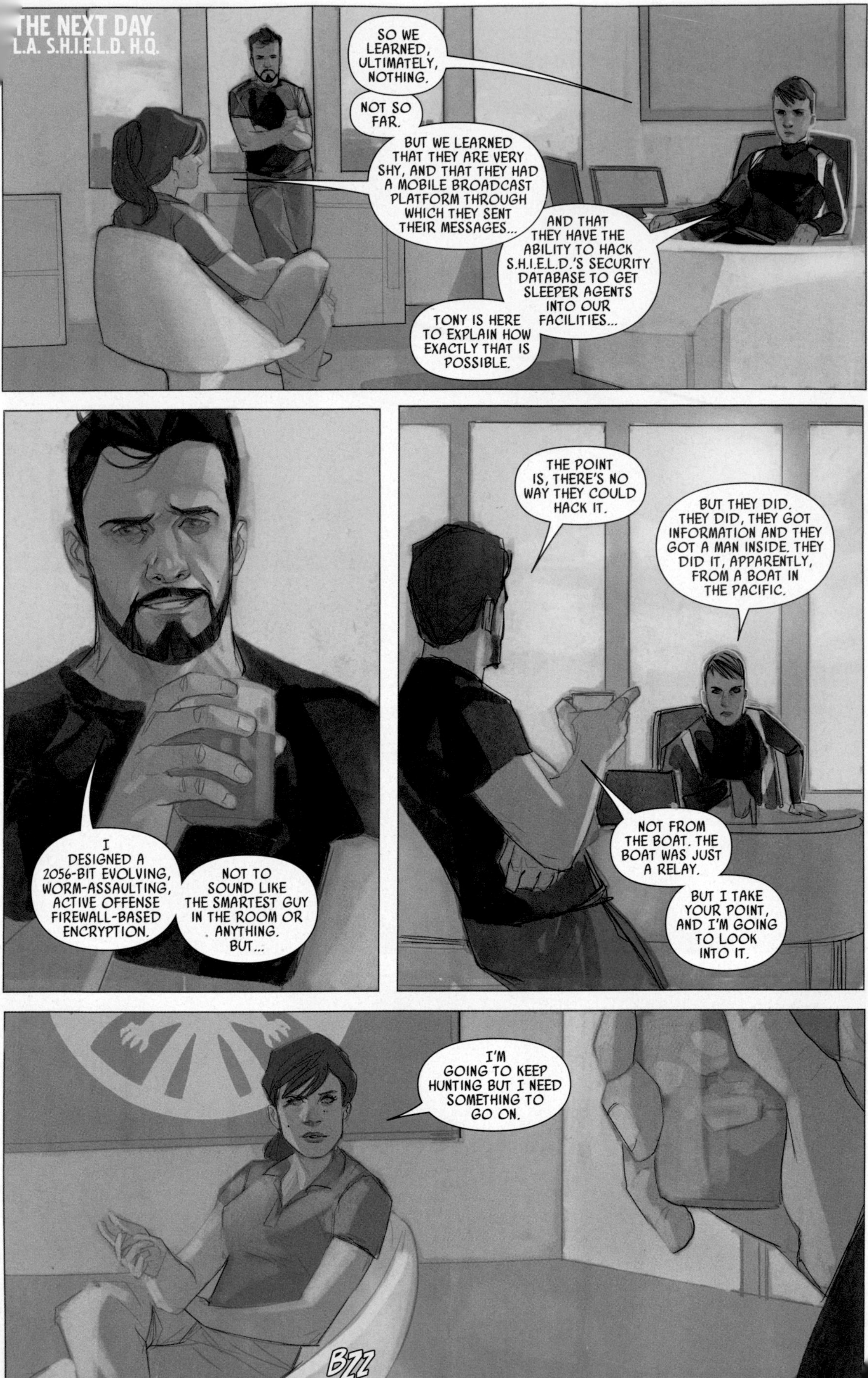
THE NEXT DAY. L.A. S.H.I.E.L.D. H.Q.
SO WE LEARNED, ULTIMATELY, NOTHING.
NOT SO FAR.
BUT WE LEARNED THAT THEY ARE VERY SHY, AND THAT THEY HAD A MOBILE BROADCAST PLATFORM THROUGH WHICH THEY SENT THEIR MESSAGES...
AND THAT THEY HAVE THE ABILITY TO HACK S.H.I.E.L.D.'S SECURITY DATABASE TO GET SLEEPER AGENTS INTO OUR FACILITIES...
TONY IS HERE TO EXPLAIN HOW EXACTLY THAT IS POSSIBLE.
I DESIGNED A 2056-BIT EVOLVING, WORM-ASSAULTING, ACTIVE OFFENSE FIREWALL-BASED ENCRYPTION.
NOT TO SOUND LIKE THE SMARTEST GUY IN THE ROOM OR ANYTHING. BUT...
THE POINT IS, THERE'S NO WAY THEY COULD HACK IT.
BUT THEY DID. THEY DID, THEY GOT INFORMATION AND THEY GOT A MAN INSIDE. THEY DID IT, APPARENTLY, FROM A BOAT IN THE PACIFIC.
NOT FROM THE BOAT. THE BOAT WAS JUST A RELAY.
BUT I TAKE YOUR POINT, AND I'M GOING TO LOOK INTO IT.
I'M GOING TO KEEP HUNTING BUT I NEED SOMETHING TO GO ON.
BZZ

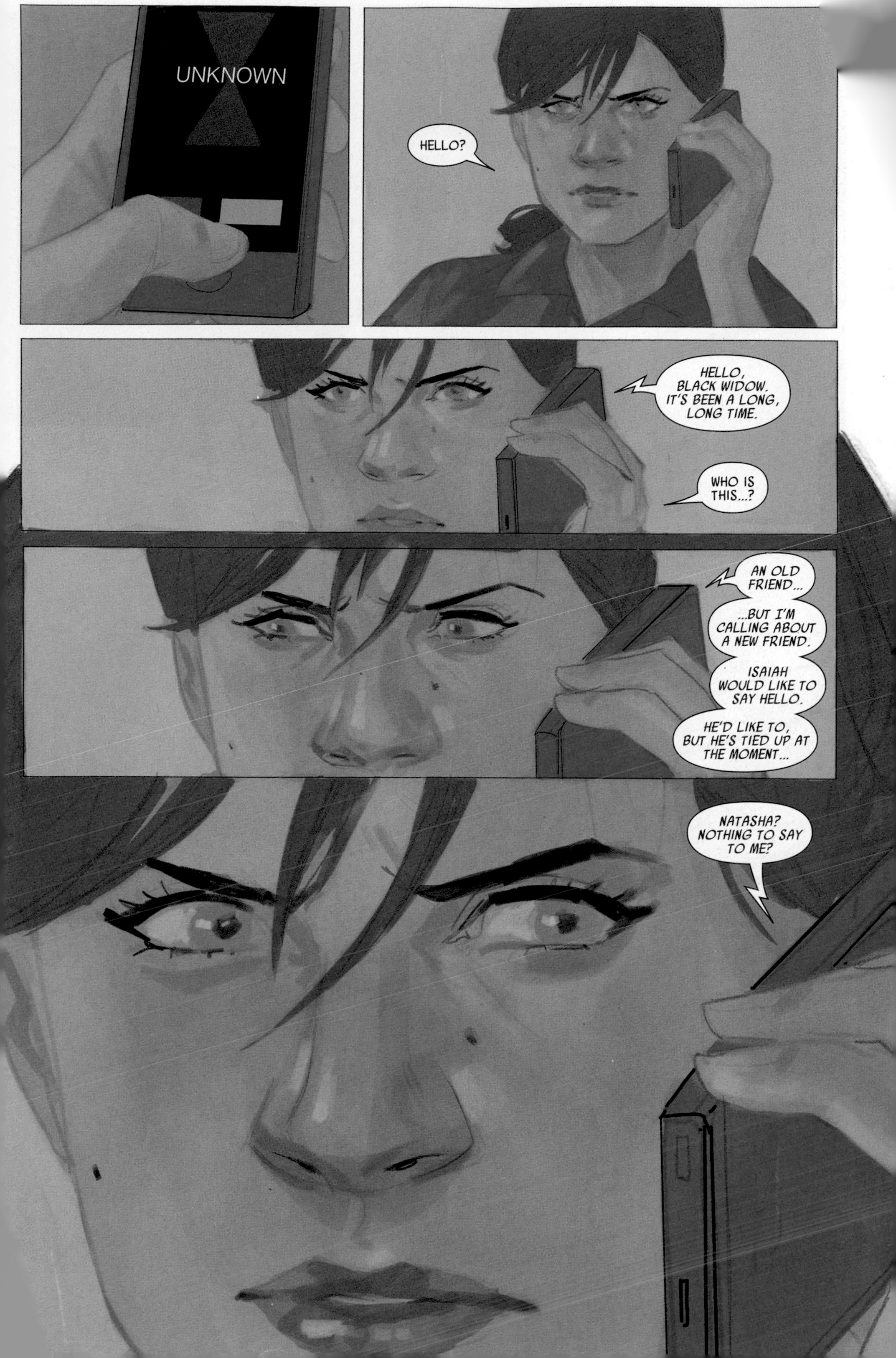
UNKNOWN
HELLO?
HELLO, BLACK WIDOW. IT'S BEEN A LONG, LONG TIME.
WHO IS THIS...?
AN OLD FRIEND...
...BUT I'M CALLING ABOUT A NEW FRIEND.
ISAIAH WOULD LIKE TO SAY HELLO.
HE'D LIKE TO, BUT HE'S TIED UP AT THE MOMENT...
NATASHA? NOTHING TO SAY TO ME?

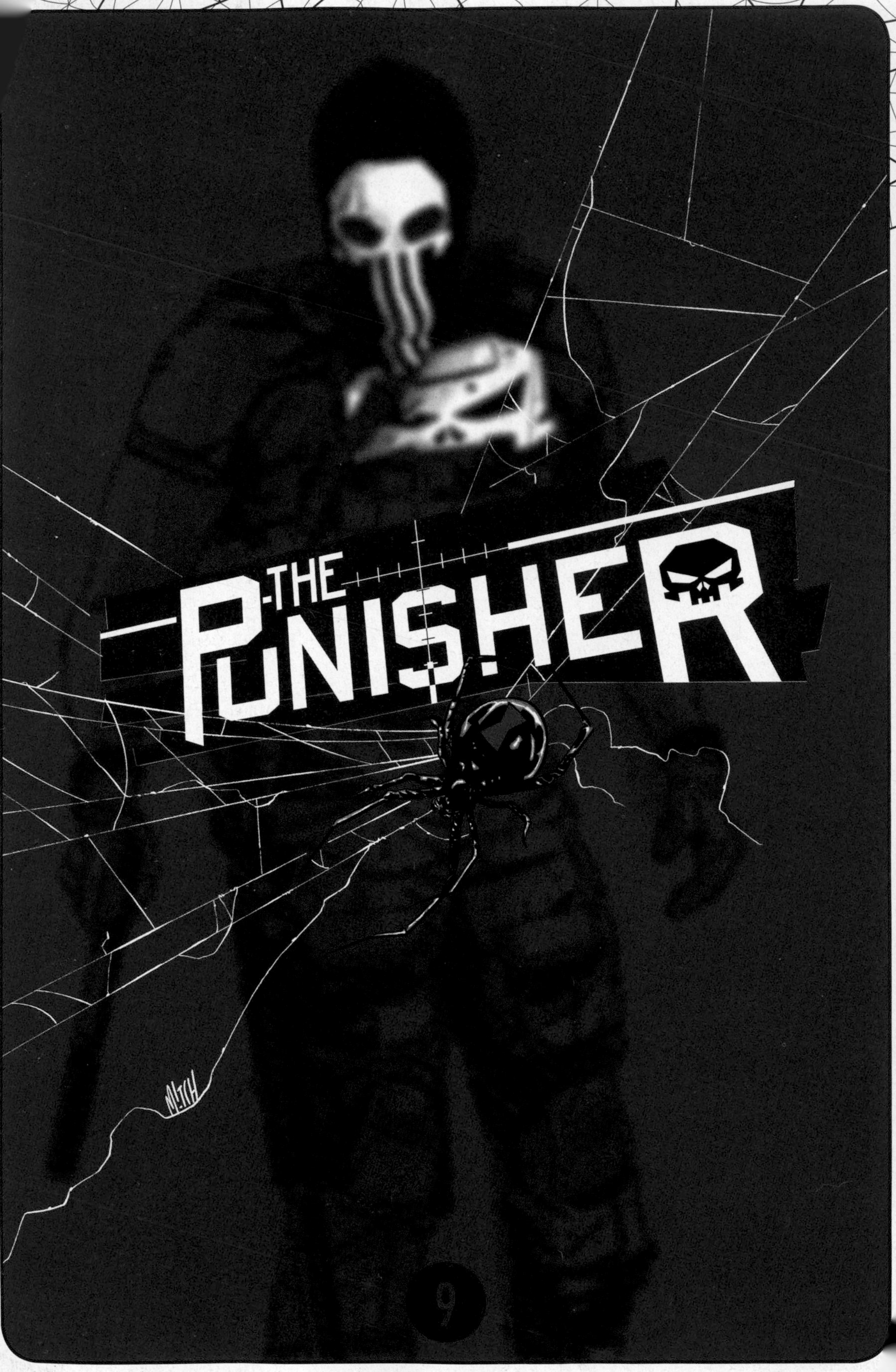
THE PUNISHER
9

FRIEND FROM FOE

FRANK CASTLE was once a decorated Marine officer, an upstanding citizen and family man. Then his family was violently taken from him when they were accidentally killed in a mob hit. From that day on, Frank Castle shed his old identity and became a force of cold, calculated retribution and vigilantism known as

THE PUNISHER

PREVIOUSLY

At the end of the Punisher's war against the Dos Soles, Frank was shot in the chest by the new Howling Commandos. While attempting to discreetly seek medical attention south of the border, he was captured by "El Diablito" Ortiz, a South American crime lord who decided to sell him to the highest bidder--a buyer who sent the mercenary Crossbones to collect the Punisher.

With the help of a Special Forces soldier also captured by El Diablito's men, Frank nearly escaped. But when they became boxed in by the bad guys, Frank sacrificed himself so the soldier could escape by allowing Crossbones to take him captive.

FRIEND FROM FOE

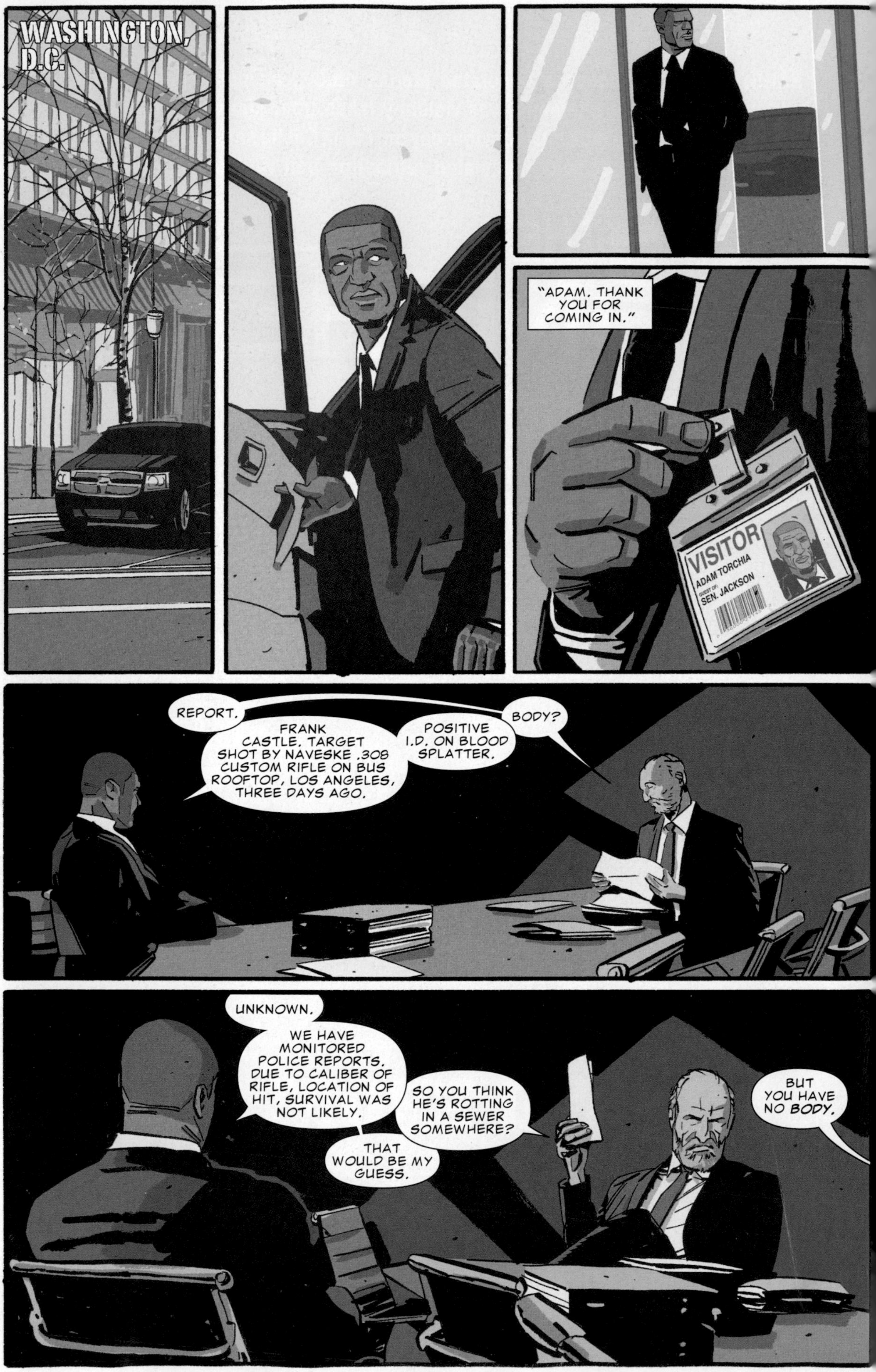
WASHINGTON, D.C.
"ADAM. THANK YOU FOR COMING IN."
VISITOR
ADAM TORCHIA
GUEST OF:
SEN. JACKSON
REPORT.
FRANK CASTLE. TARGET SHOT BY NAVESKE .308 CUSTOM RIFLE ON BUS ROOFTOP, LOS ANGELES, THREE DAYS AGO.
BODY?
POSITIVE I.D. ON BLOOD SPLATTER.
UNKNOWN.
WE HAVE MONITORED POLICE REPORTS. DUE TO CALIBER OF RIFLE, LOCATION OF HIT, SURVIVAL WAS NOT LIKELY.
SO YOU THINK HE'S ROTTING IN A SEWER SOMEWHERE?
THAT WOULD BE MY GUESS.
BUT YOU HAVE NO BODY.

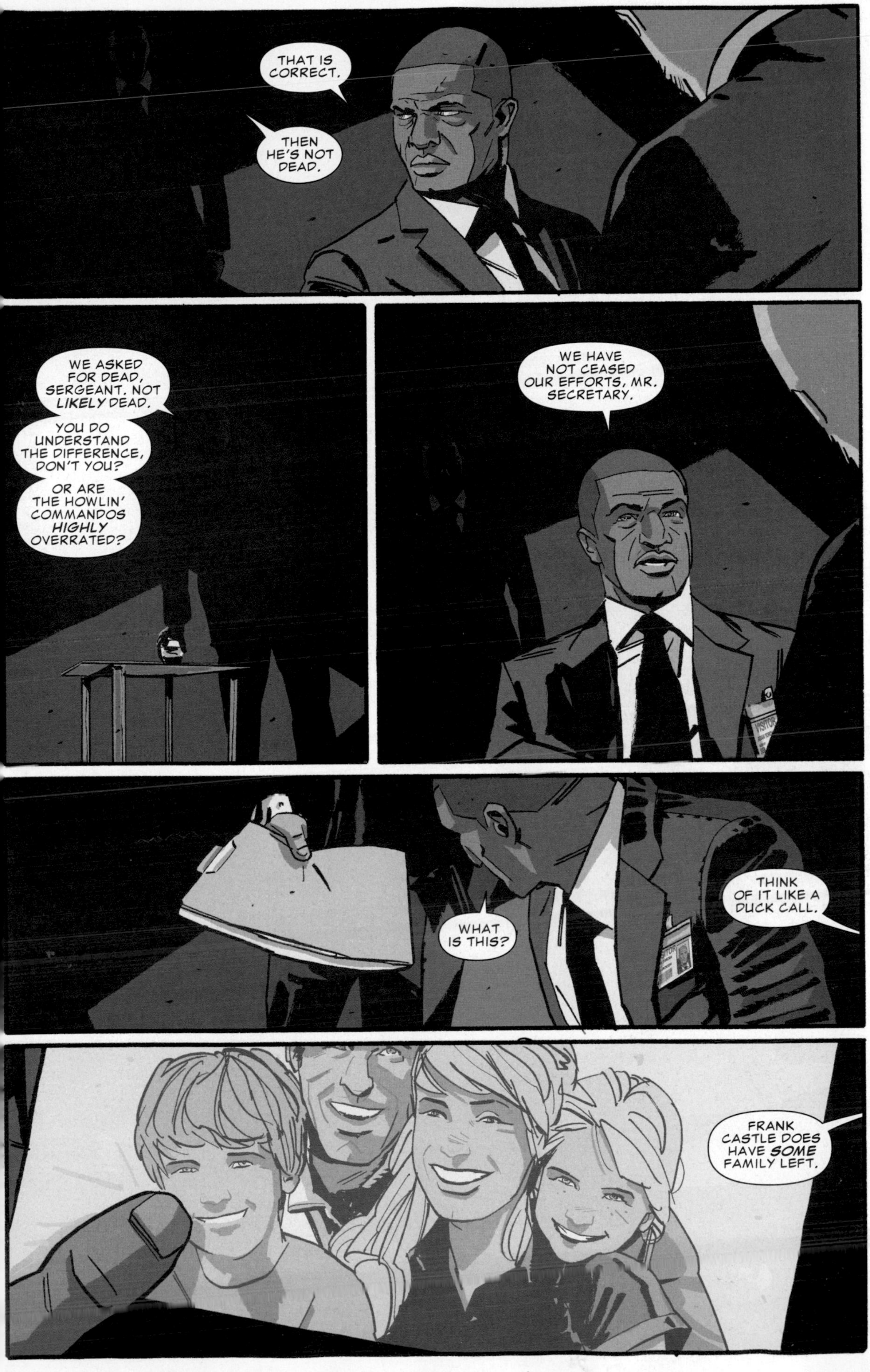
THAT IS CORRECT.
THEN HE'S NOT DEAD.
WE ASKED FOR DEAD, SERGEANT. NOT LIKELY DEAD.
YOU DO UNDERSTAND THE DIFFERENCE, DON'T YOU?
OR ARE THE HOWLIN' COMMANDOS HIGHLY OVERRATED?
WE HAVE NOT CEASED OUR EFFORTS, MR. SECRETARY.
WHAT IS THIS?
THINK OF IT LIKE A DUCK CALL.
FRANK CASTLE DOES HAVE SOME FAMILY LEFT.

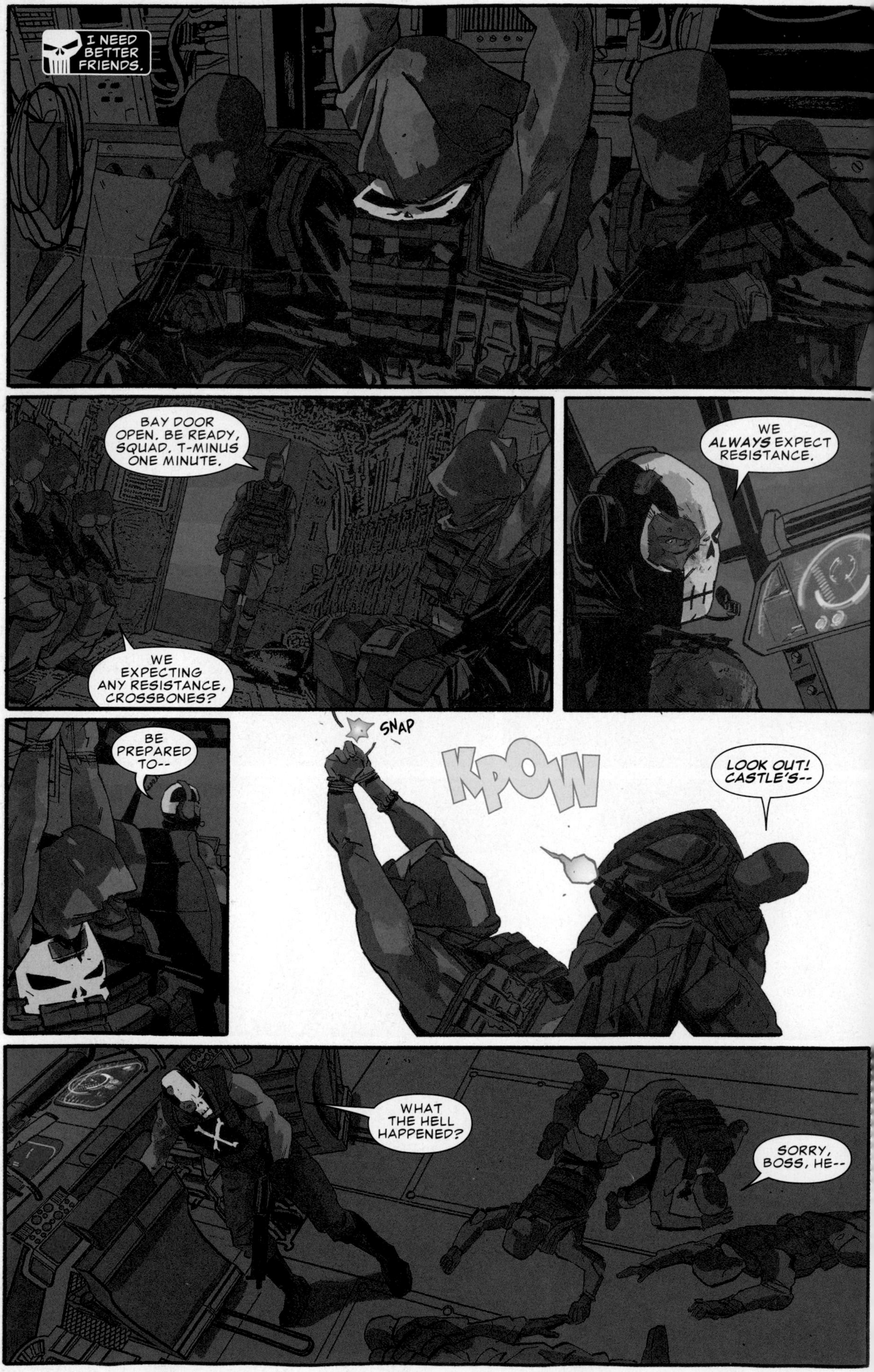
I NEED BETTER FRIENDS.
BAY DOOR OPEN. BE READY, SQUAD. T-MINUS ONE MINUTE.
WE EXPECTING ANY RESISTANCE, CROSSBONES?
WE ALWAYS EXPECT RESISTANCE.
BE PREPARED TO--
SNAP
KPOW
LOOK OUT! CASTLE'S--
WHAT THE HELL HAPPENED?
SORRY, BOSS, HE--

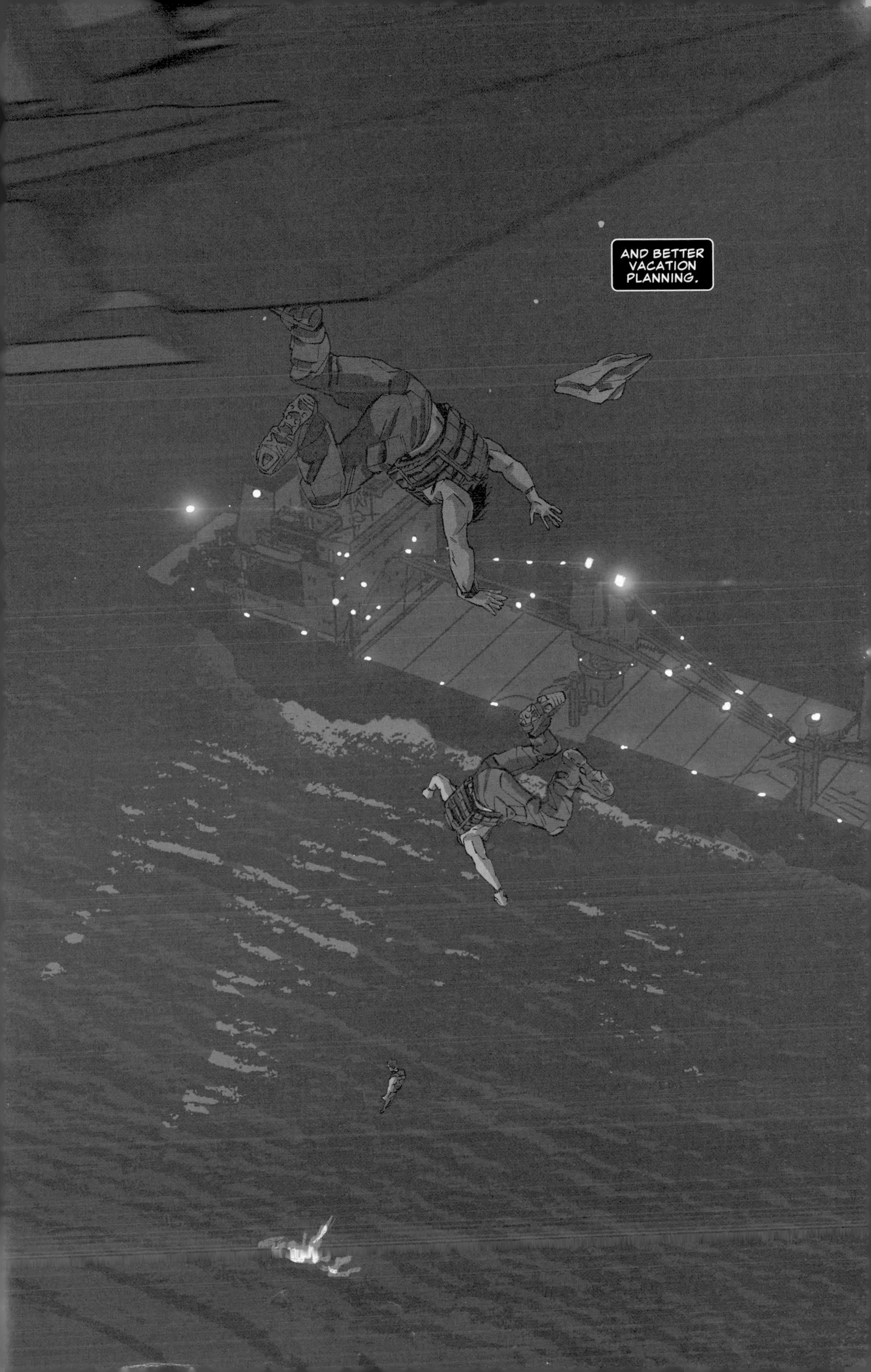
AND BETTER VACATION PLANNING.

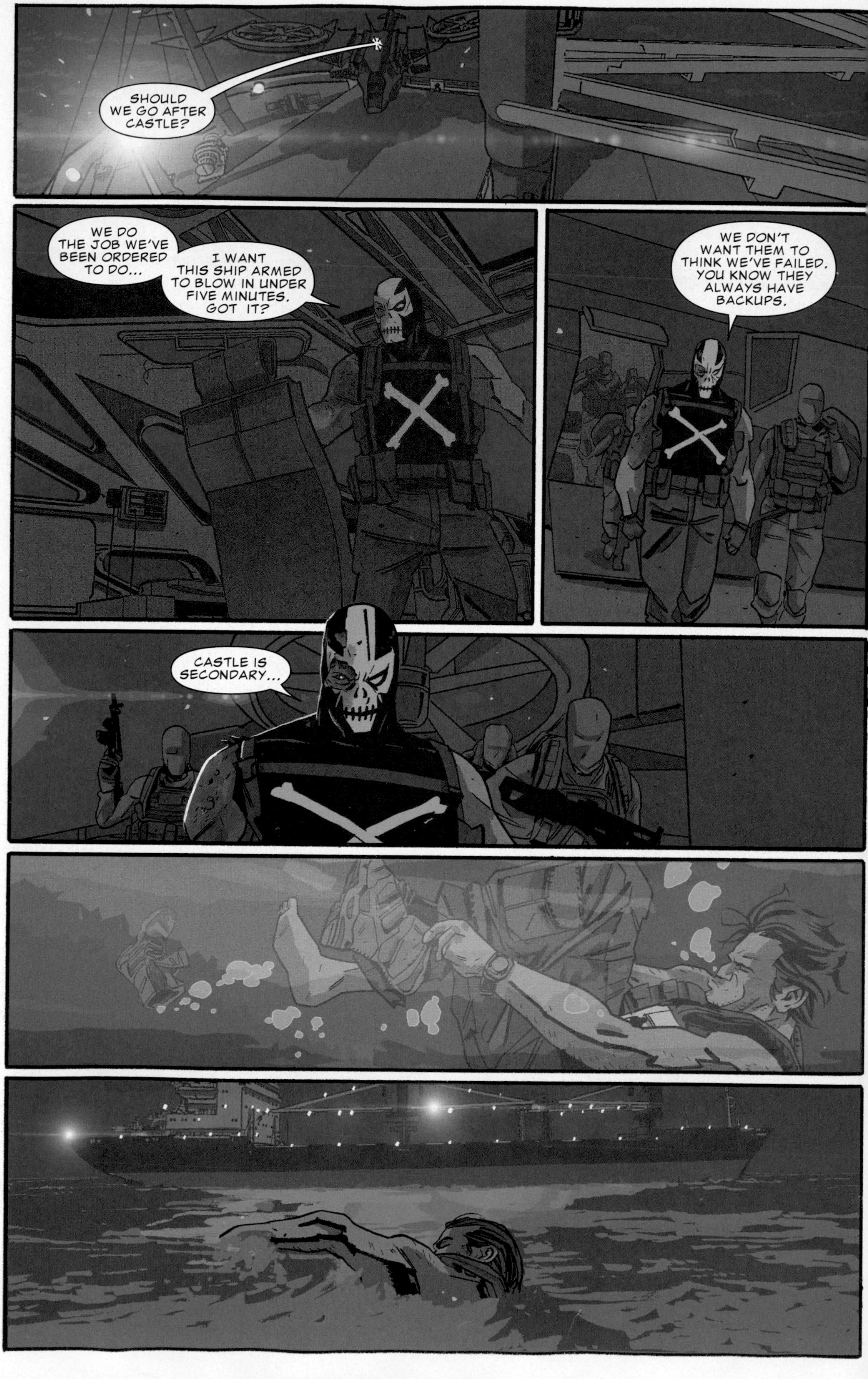
SHOULD WE GO AFTER CASTLE?
WE DO THE JOB WE'VE BEEN ORDERED TO DO...
I WANT THIS SHIP ARMED TO BLOW IN UNDER FIVE MINUTES. GOT IT?
WE DON'T WANT THEM TO THINK WE'VE FAILED. YOU KNOW THEY ALWAYS HAVE BACKUPS.
CASTLE IS SECONDARY...

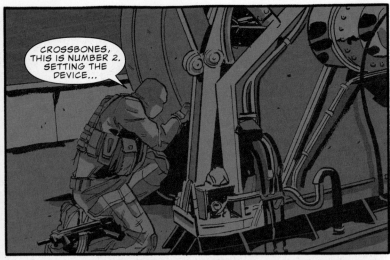

CROSSBONES, THIS IS NUMBER 2. SETTING THE DEVICE...

SYNCING NOW.

I--

WHAM

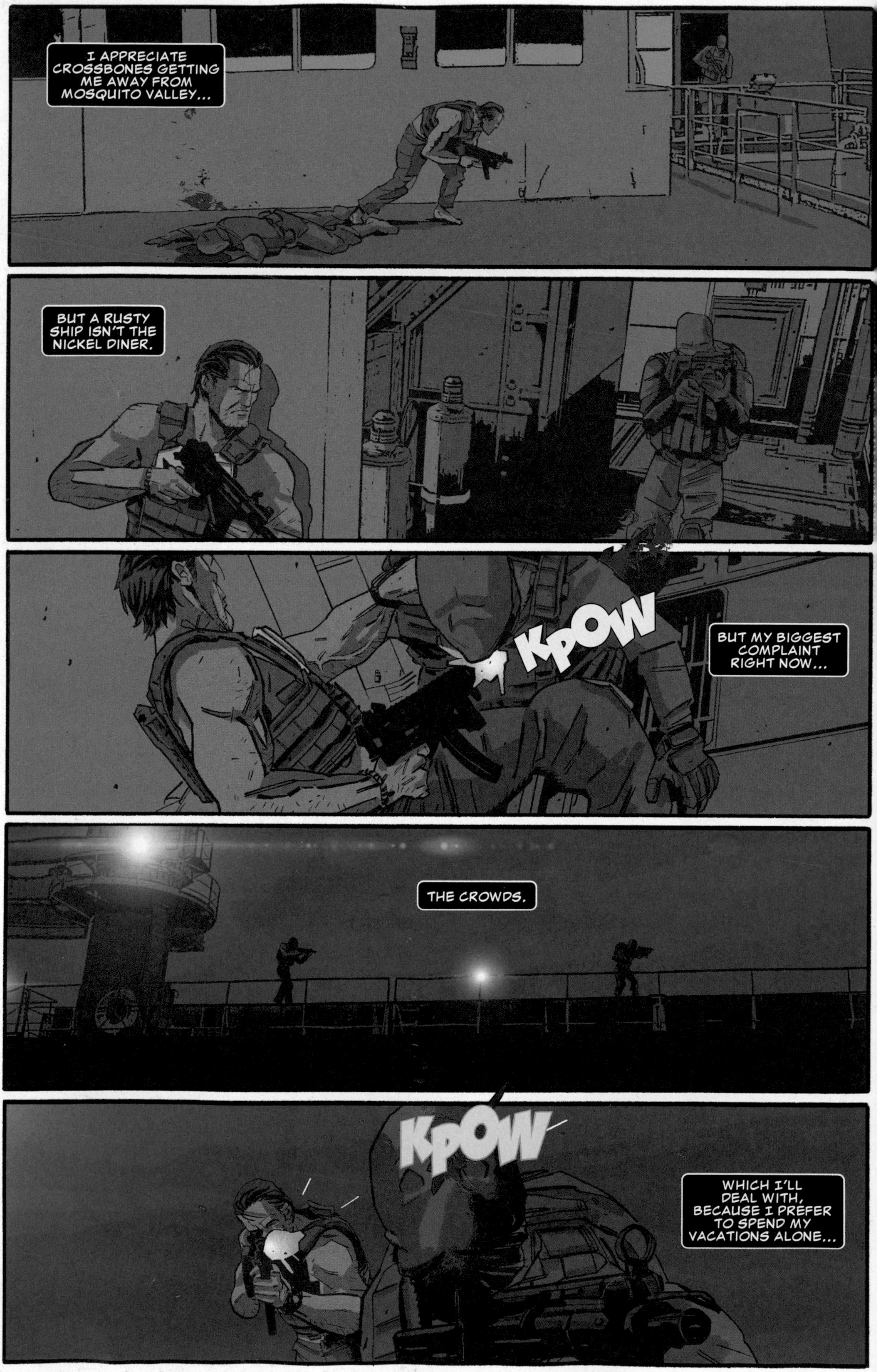
I APPRECIATE CROSSBONES GETTING ME AWAY FROM MOSQUITO VALLEY...
BUT A RUSTY SHIP ISN'T THE NICKEL DINER.
KPOW
BUT MY BIGGEST COMPLAINT RIGHT NOW...
THE CROWDS.
KPOW
WHICH I'LL DEAL WITH, BECAUSE I PREFER TO SPEND MY VACATIONS ALONE...

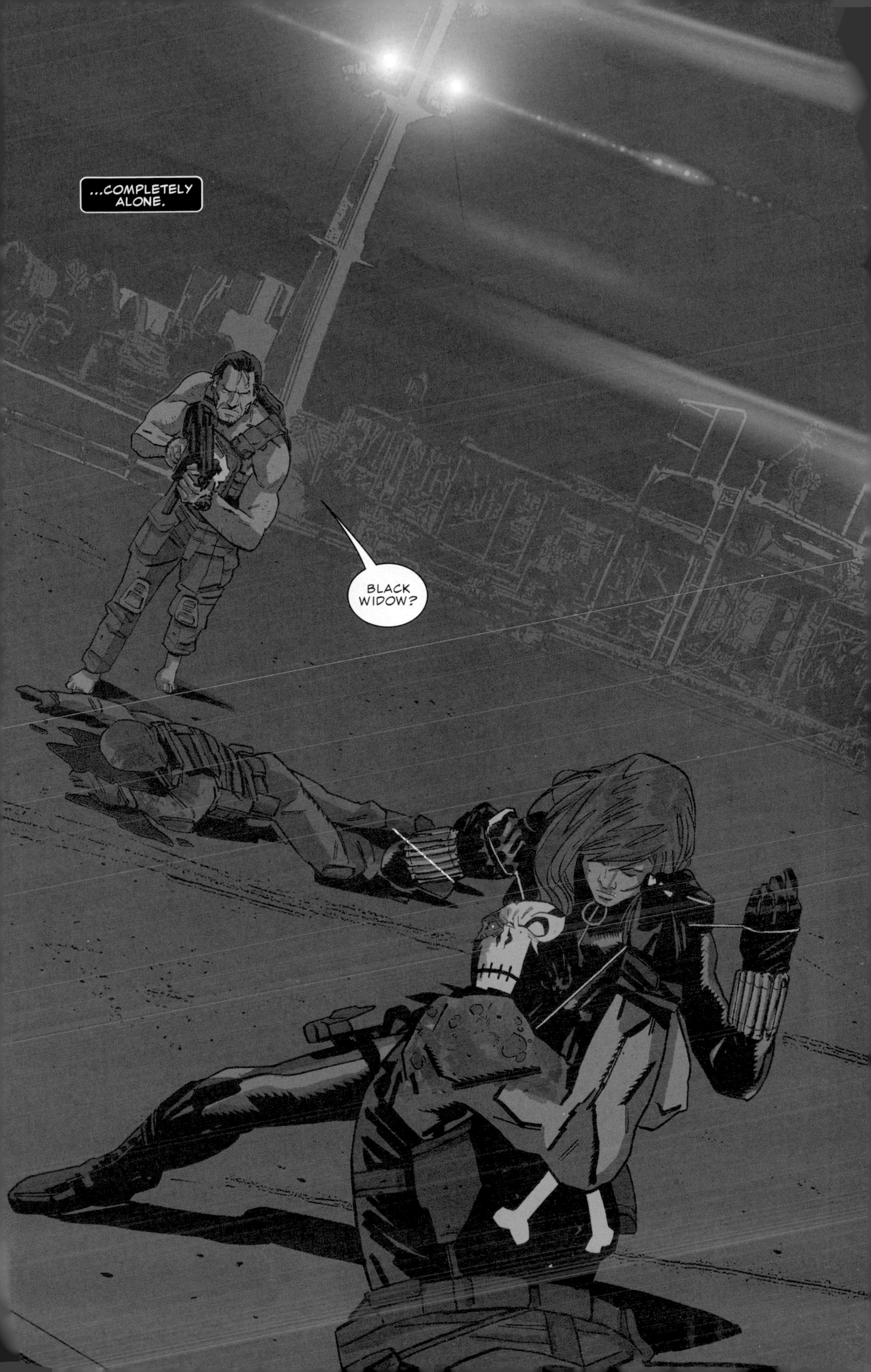
...COMPLETELY ALONE.
BLACK WIDOW?

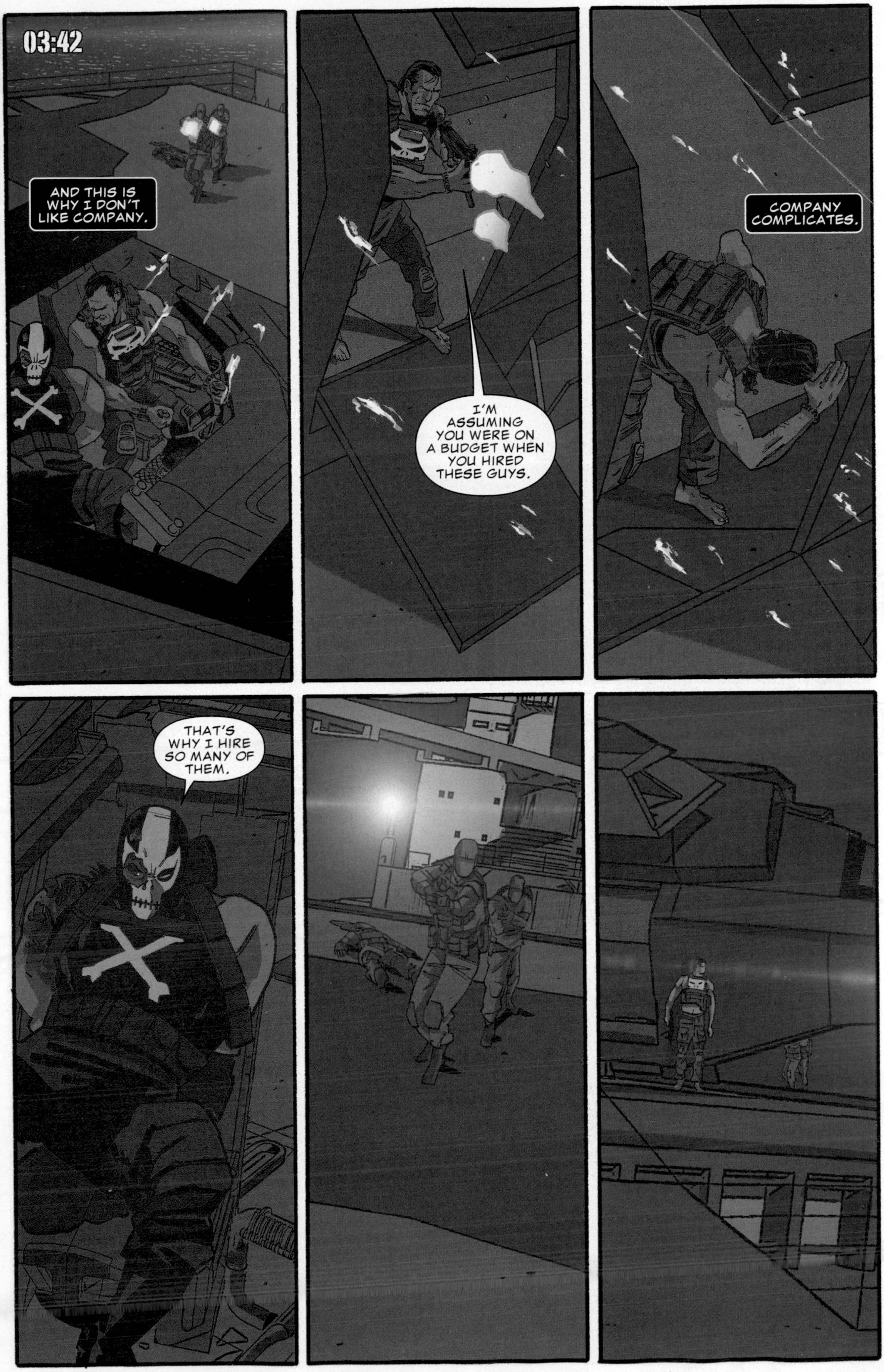
03:42
AND THIS IS WHY I DON'T LIKE COMPANY.
I'M ASSUMING YOU WERE ON A BUDGET WHEN YOU HIRED THESE GUYS.
COMPANY COMPLICATES.
THAT'S WHY I HIRE SO MANY OF THEM.

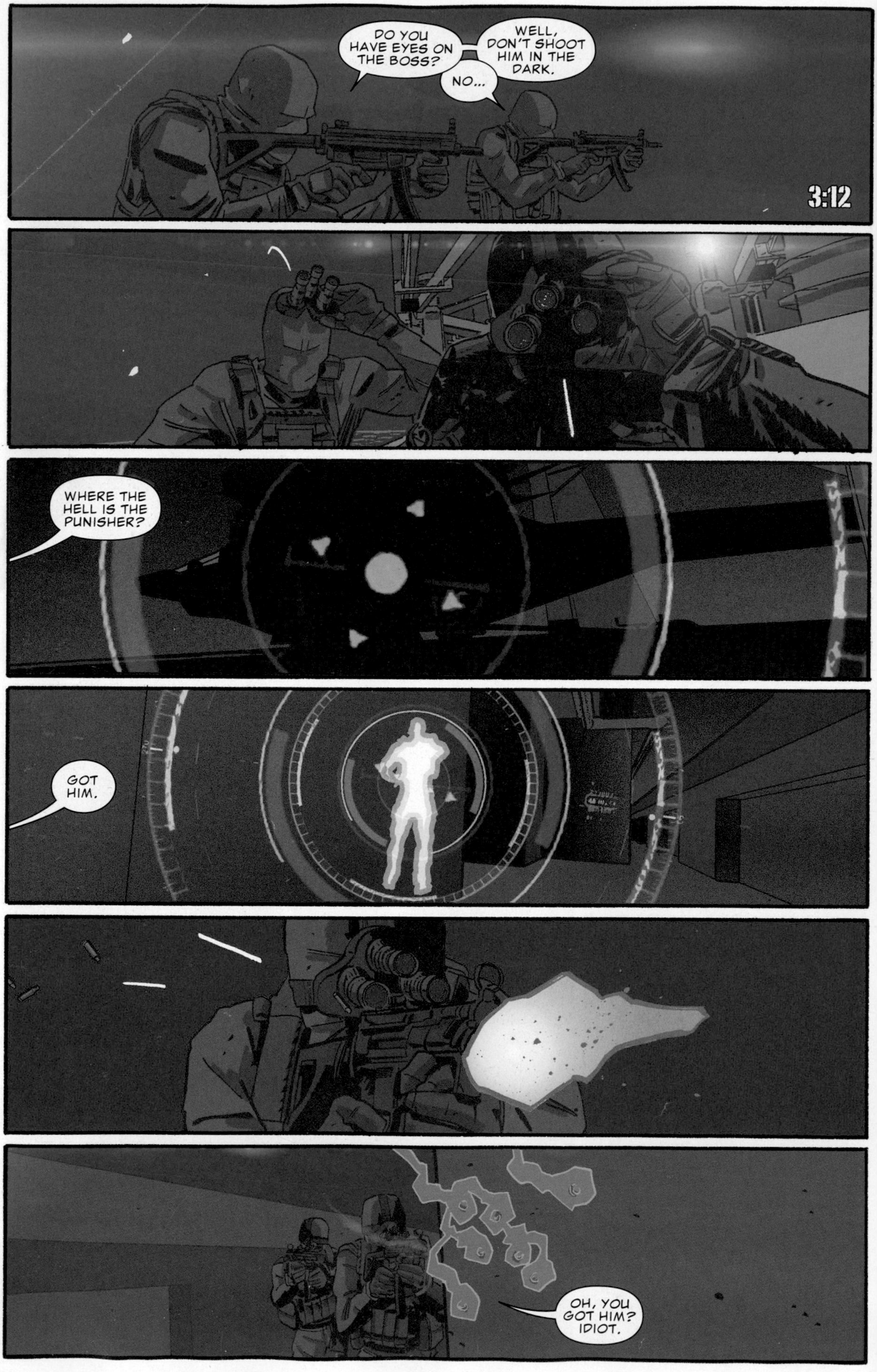
DO YOU HAVE EYES ON THE BOSS?
NO...
WELL, DON'T SHOOT HIM IN THE DARK.
3:12
WHERE THE HELL IS THE PUNISHER?
GOT HIM.
OH, YOU GOT HIM? IDIOT.

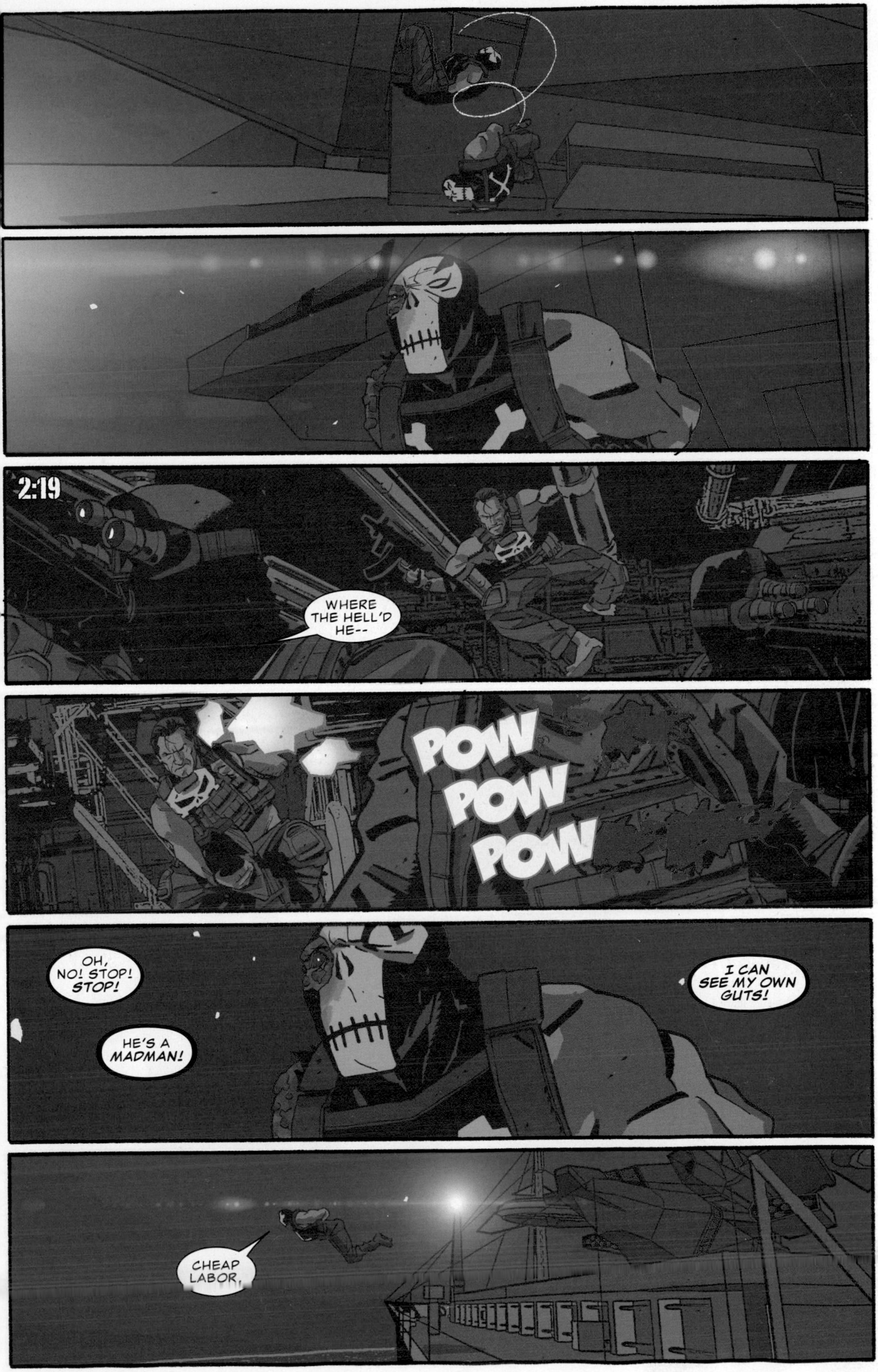
2:19
WHERE THE HELL'D HE--
POW
POW
POW
OH, NO! STOP! STOP!
HE'S A MADMAN!
I CAN SEE MY OWN GUTS!
CHEAP LABOR.

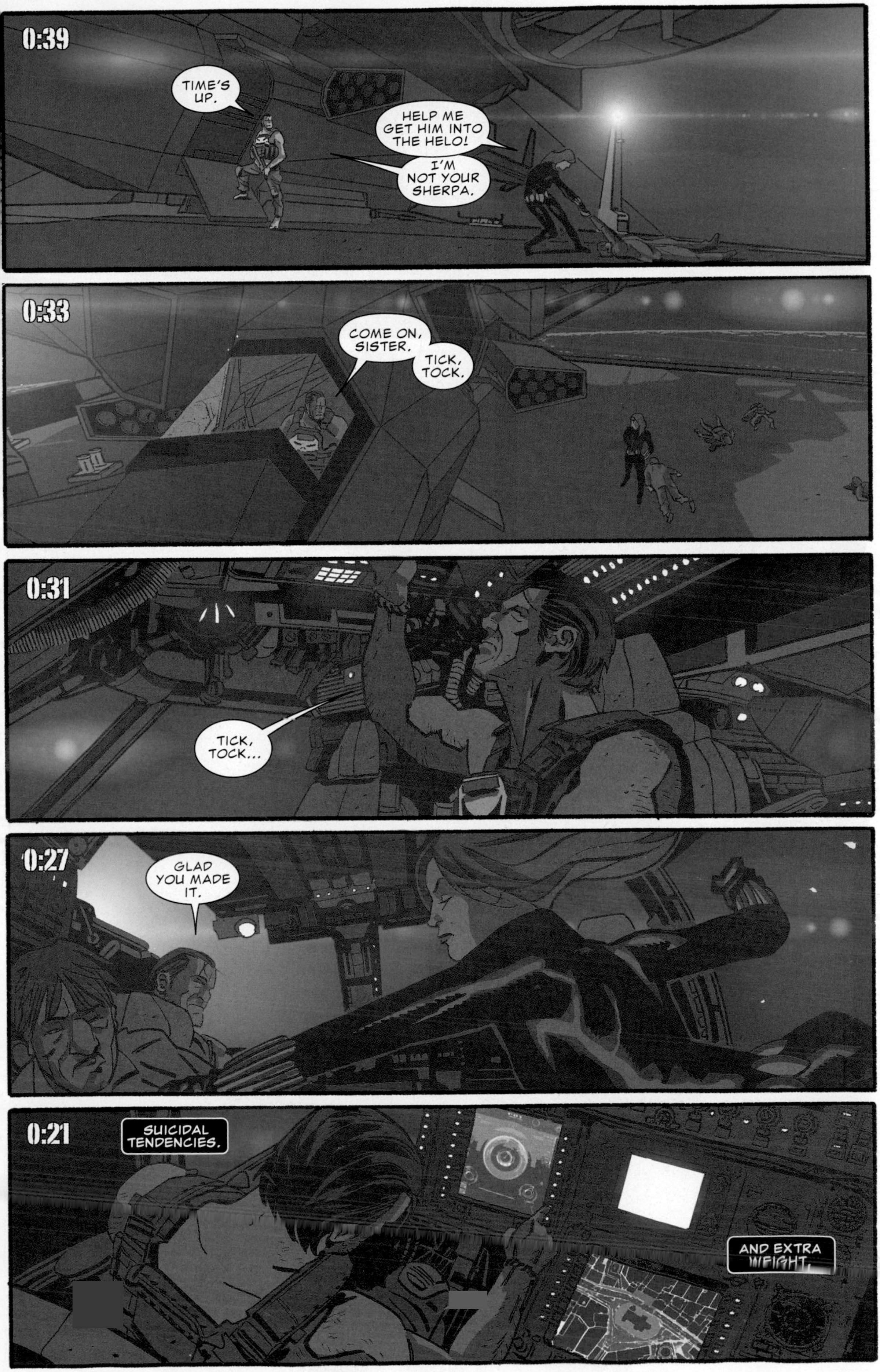

0:39
TIME'S UP.
HELP ME GET HIM INTO THE HELO!
I'M NOT YOUR SHERPA.
0:33
COME ON, SISTER.
TICK, TOCK.
0:31
TICK, TOCK...
0:27
GLAD YOU MADE IT.
0:21
SUICIDAL TENDENCIES.
AND EXTRA WEIGHT.

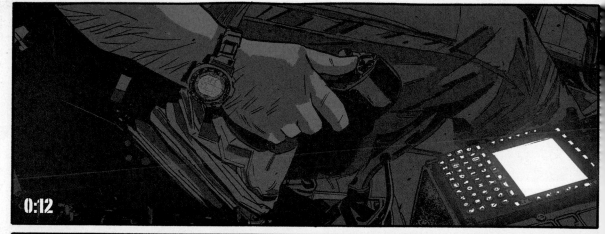

0:12

0:08

AT LEAST I'M GOING HOME...

0:05

0:03...

HOLD ON!

...WHERE I ACTUALLY CAN BE ALONE. IT'S BEEN FAR TOO LONG.

...0:02

...0:01

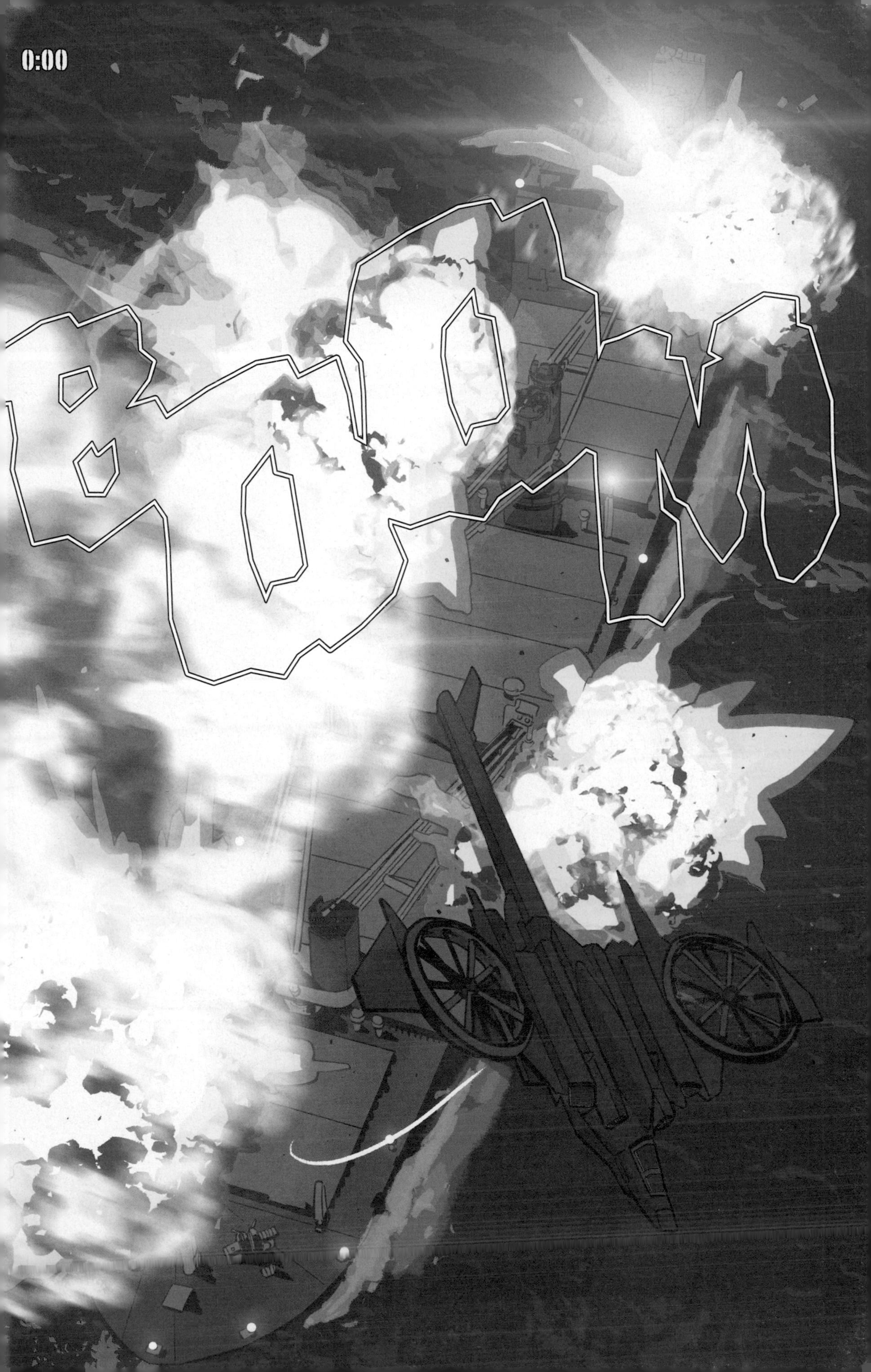
0:00
BOOM

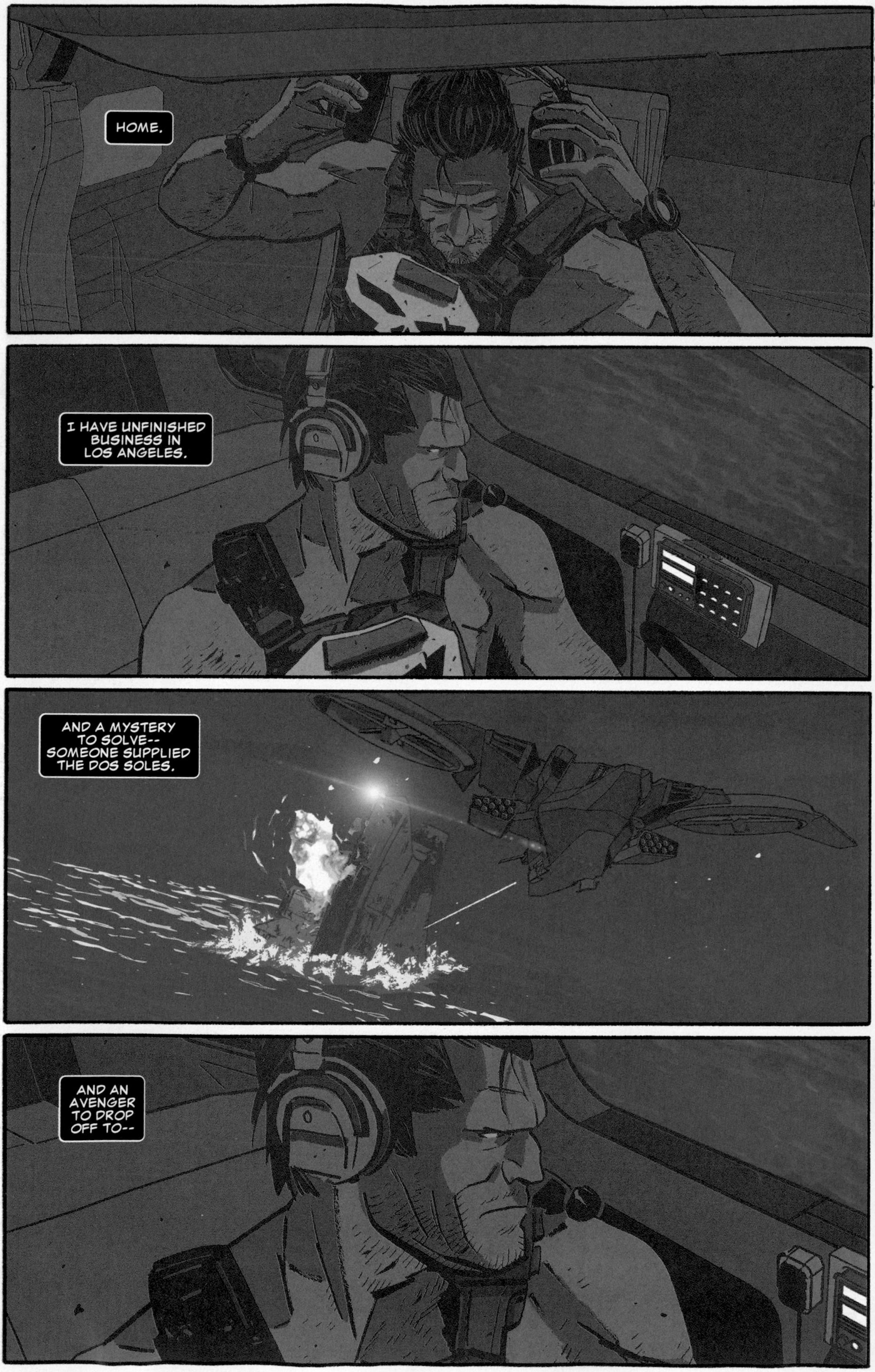
HOME.
I HAVE UNFINISHED BUSINESS IN LOS ANGELES.
AND A MYSTERY TO SOLVE-- SOMEONE SUPPLIED THE DOS SOLES.
AND AN AVENGER TO DROP OFF TO--

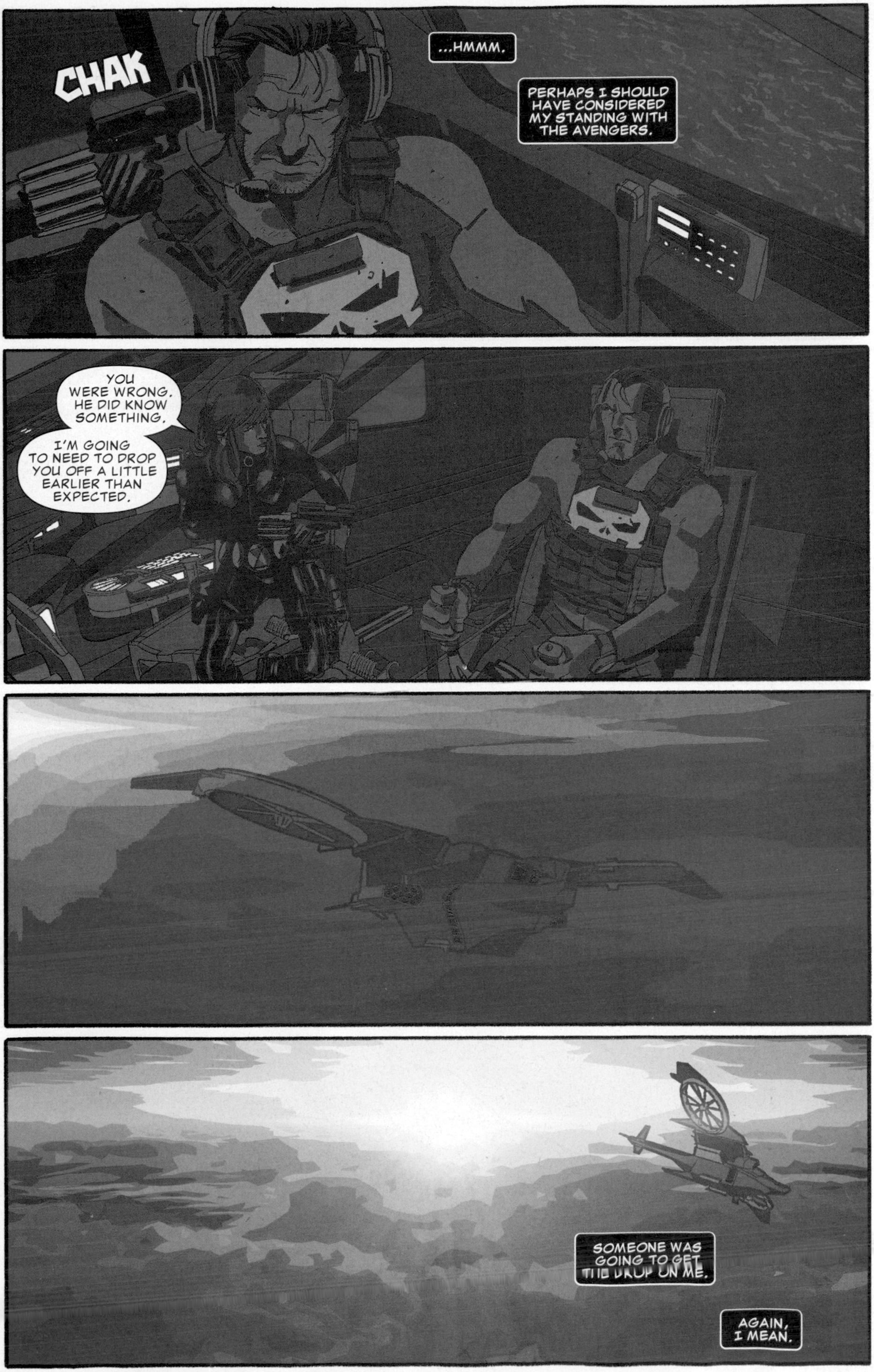
CHAK
...HMMM.
PERHAPS I SHOULD HAVE CONSIDERED MY STANDING WITH THE AVENGERS.
YOU WERE WRONG. HE DID KNOW SOMETHING.
I'M GOING TO NEED TO DROP YOU OFF A LITTLE EARLIER THAN EXPECTED.
SOMEONE WAS GOING TO GET THE DROP ON ME.
AGAIN, I MEAN.

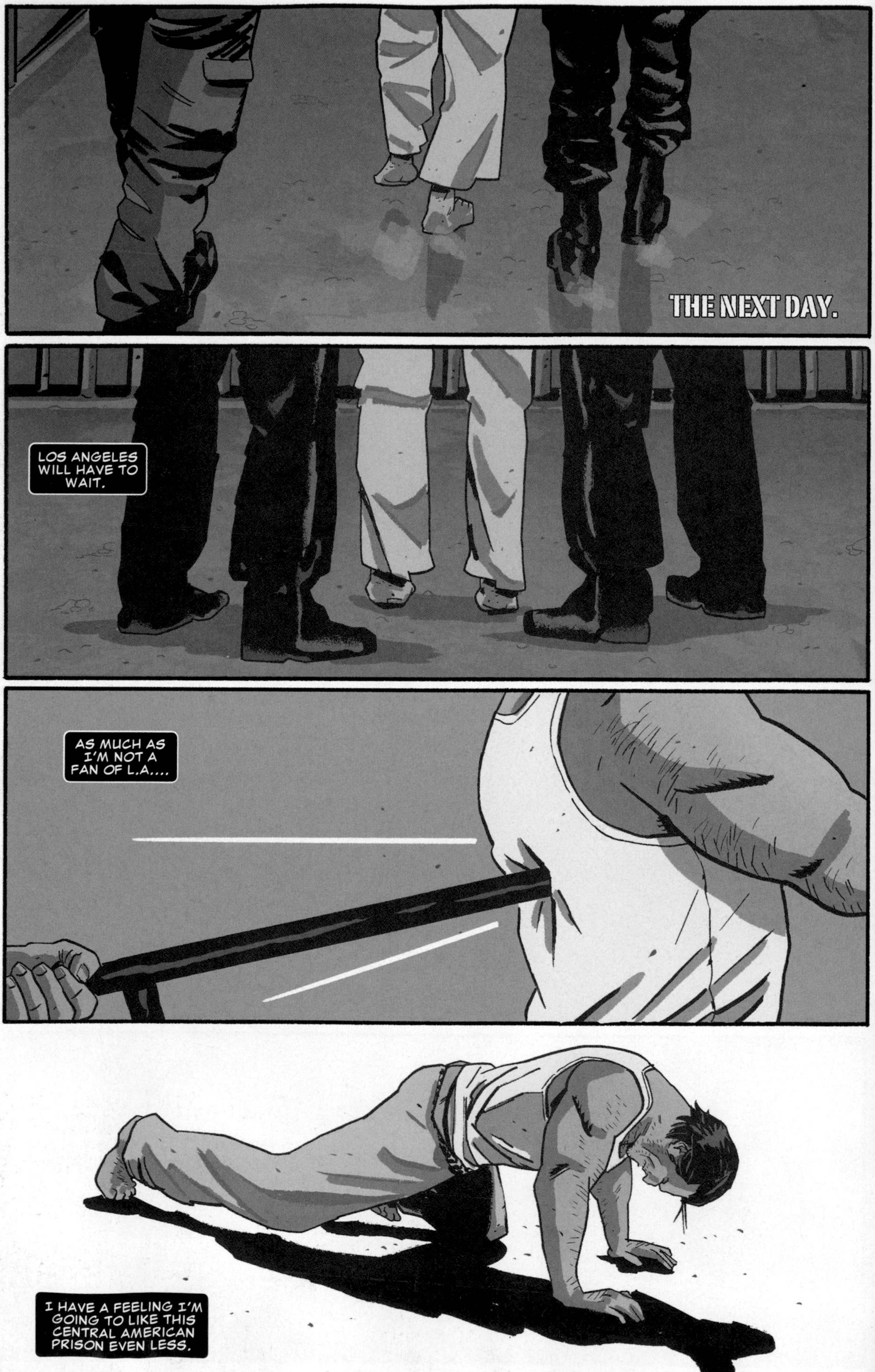
THE NEXT DAY.
LOS ANGELES WILL HAVE TO WAIT.
AS MUCH AS I'M NOT A FAN OF L.A....
I HAVE A FEELING I'M GOING TO LIKE THIS CENTRAL AMERICAN PRISON EVEN LESS.

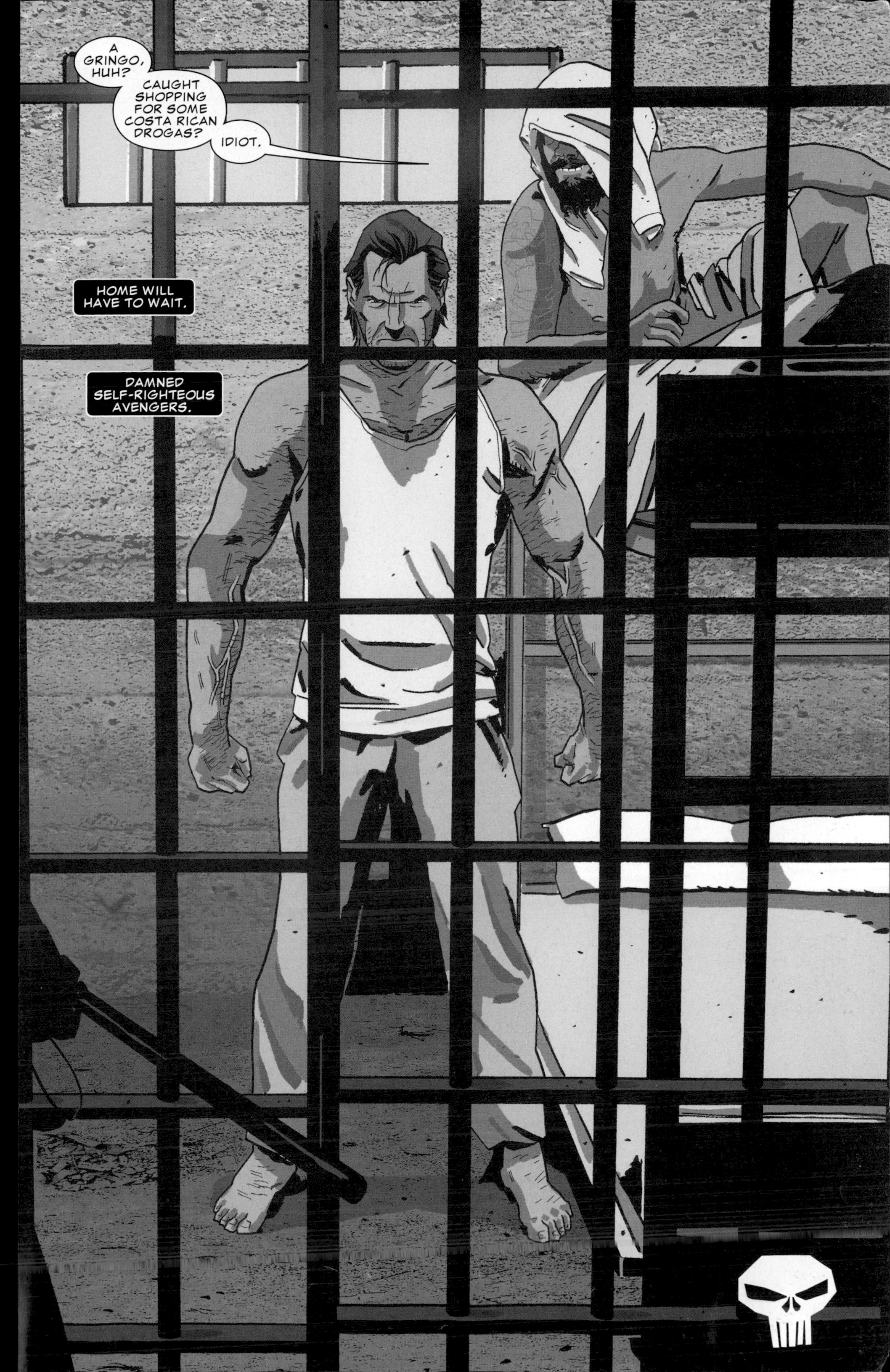
A GRINGO, HUH?
CAUGHT SHOPPING FOR SOME COSTA RICAN DROGAS?
IDIOT.
HOME WILL HAVE TO WAIT.
DAMNED SELF-RIGHTEOUS AVENGERS.

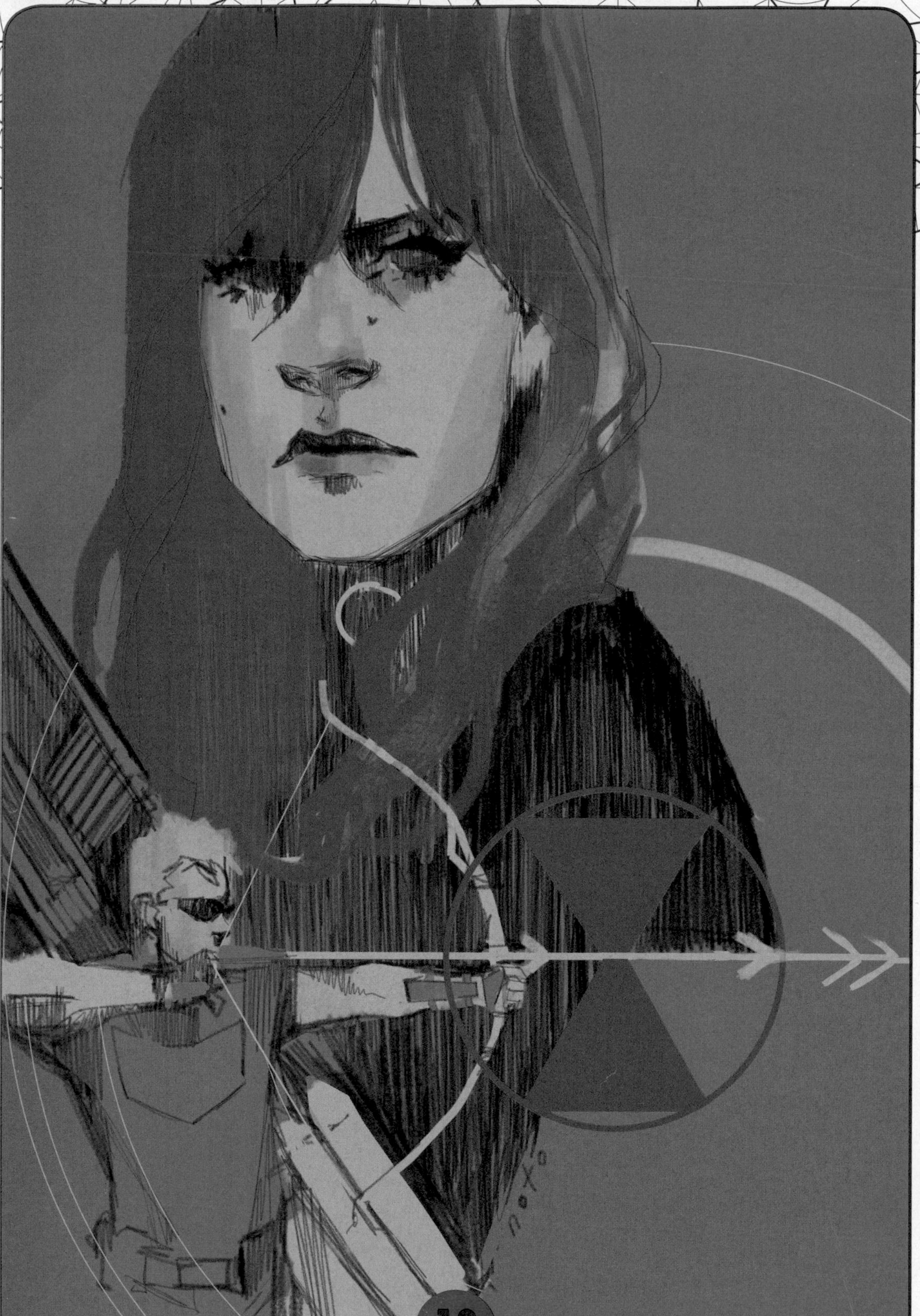
10

TOTAL RECALL

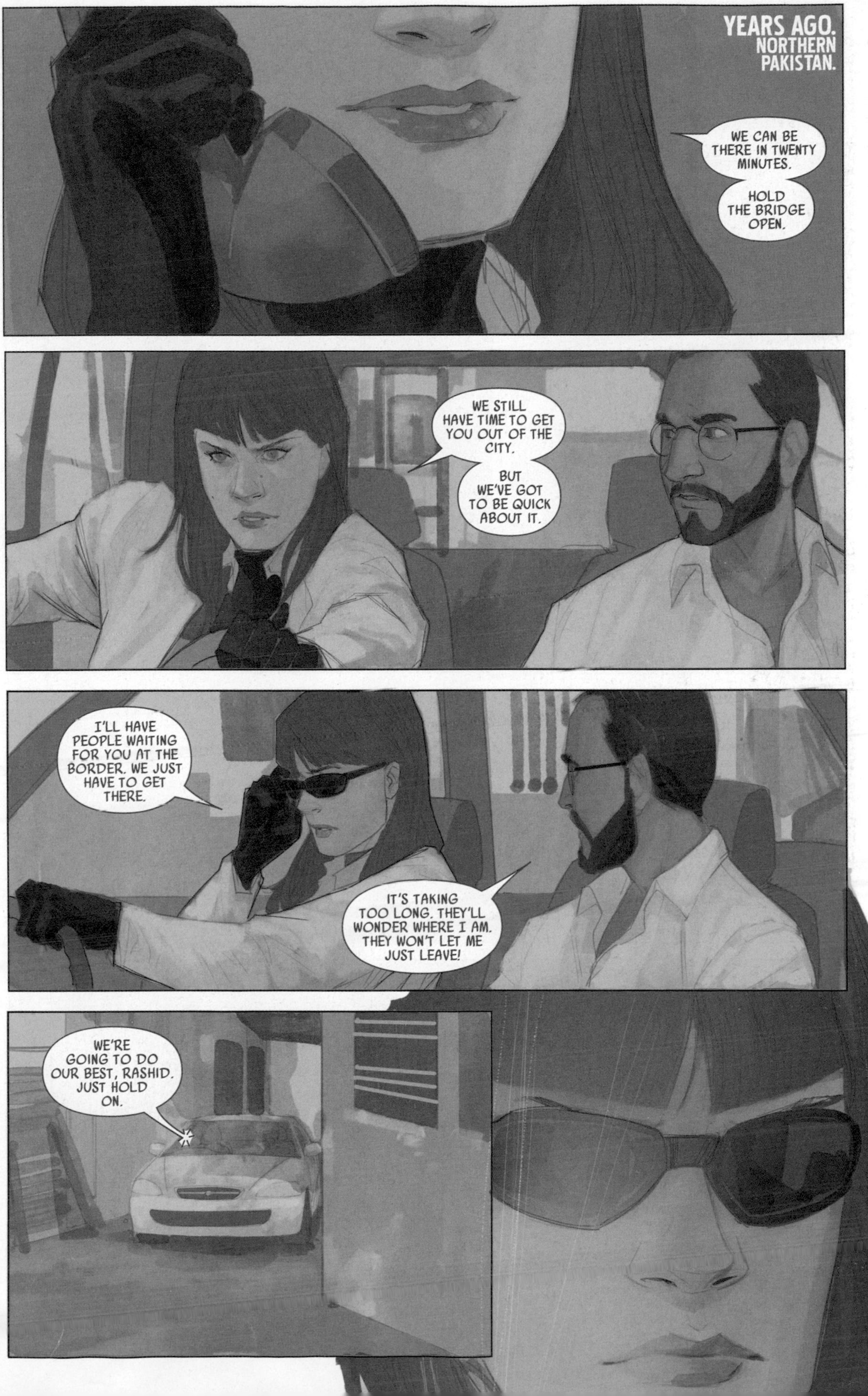
YEARS AGO. NORTHERN PAKISTAN.
WE CAN BE THERE IN TWENTY MINUTES.
HOLD THE BRIDGE OPEN.
WE STILL HAVE TIME TO GET YOU OUT OF THE CITY.
BUT WE'VE GOT TO BE QUICK ABOUT IT.
I'LL HAVE PEOPLE WAITING FOR YOU AT THE BORDER. WE JUST HAVE TO GET THERE.
IT'S TAKING TOO LONG. THEY'LL WONDER WHERE I AM. THEY WON'T LET ME JUST LEAVE!
WE'RE GOING TO DO OUR BEST, RASHID. JUST HOLD ON.

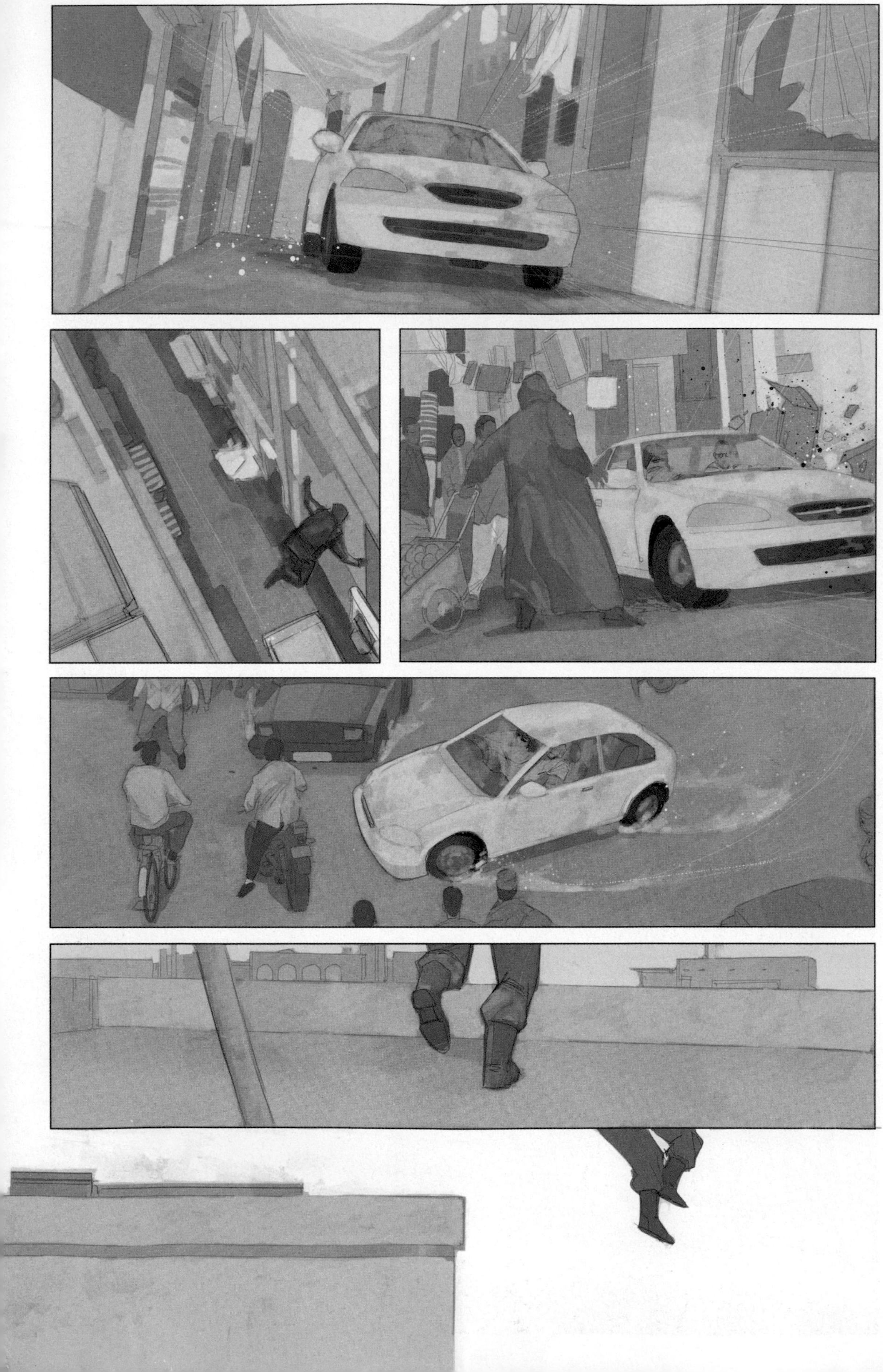

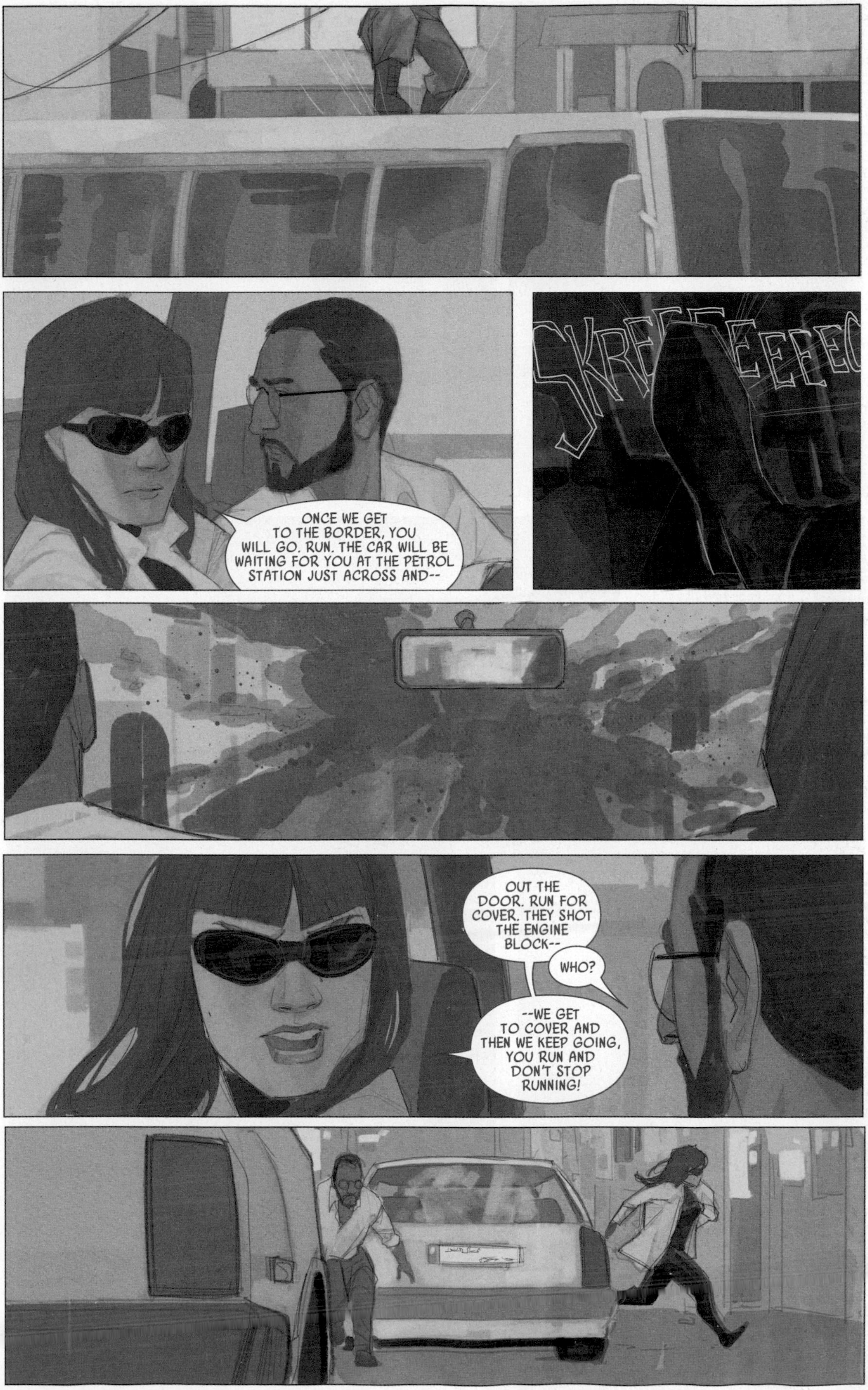
ONCE WE GET TO THE BORDER, YOU WILL GO. RUN. THE CAR WILL BE WAITING FOR YOU AT THE PETROL STATION JUST ACROSS AND--
SKREEEEEEEC
OUT THE DOOR. RUN FOR COVER. THEY SHOT THE ENGINE BLOCK--
WHO?
--WE GET TO COVER AND THEN WE KEEP GOING, YOU RUN AND DON'T STOP RUNNING!

MR. ROSS.

I WAS VERY HAPPY TO HEAR YOU'D BE JOINING US.

IN MY LINE OF WORK, I DON'T GET TO VISIT WITH PEOPLE LIKE YOU VERY OFTEN.

WELL, IT'S BEEN NICE, BUT I'M AFRAID I'LL HAVE TO BE GOING--

OH, DON'T HURRY OFF NOW, ISAIAH. WE'VE ONLY JUST STARTED HERE. AND BESIDES, THERE'S NO POINT IN YOU BEING HERE IF WE HAVEN'T *TOLD* ANYONE ABOUT IT YET, IS THERE?

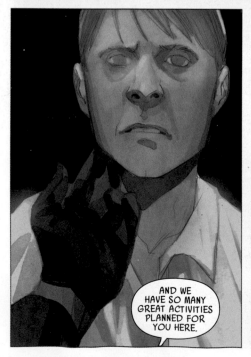

AND WE HAVE SO MANY GREAT ACTIVITIES PLANNED FOR YOU HERE.

ARETA WAS REALLY HOPING TO GET TO SPEND SOME TIME WITH YOU, TOO.

ARE YOU GOING TO TELL ME WHO YOU ARE?

WHY RUIN THE SURPRISE, ISAIAH?

ESPECIALLY WHEN IT'S SO WONDERFUL TO *GET* TO KNOW ONE ANOTHER.

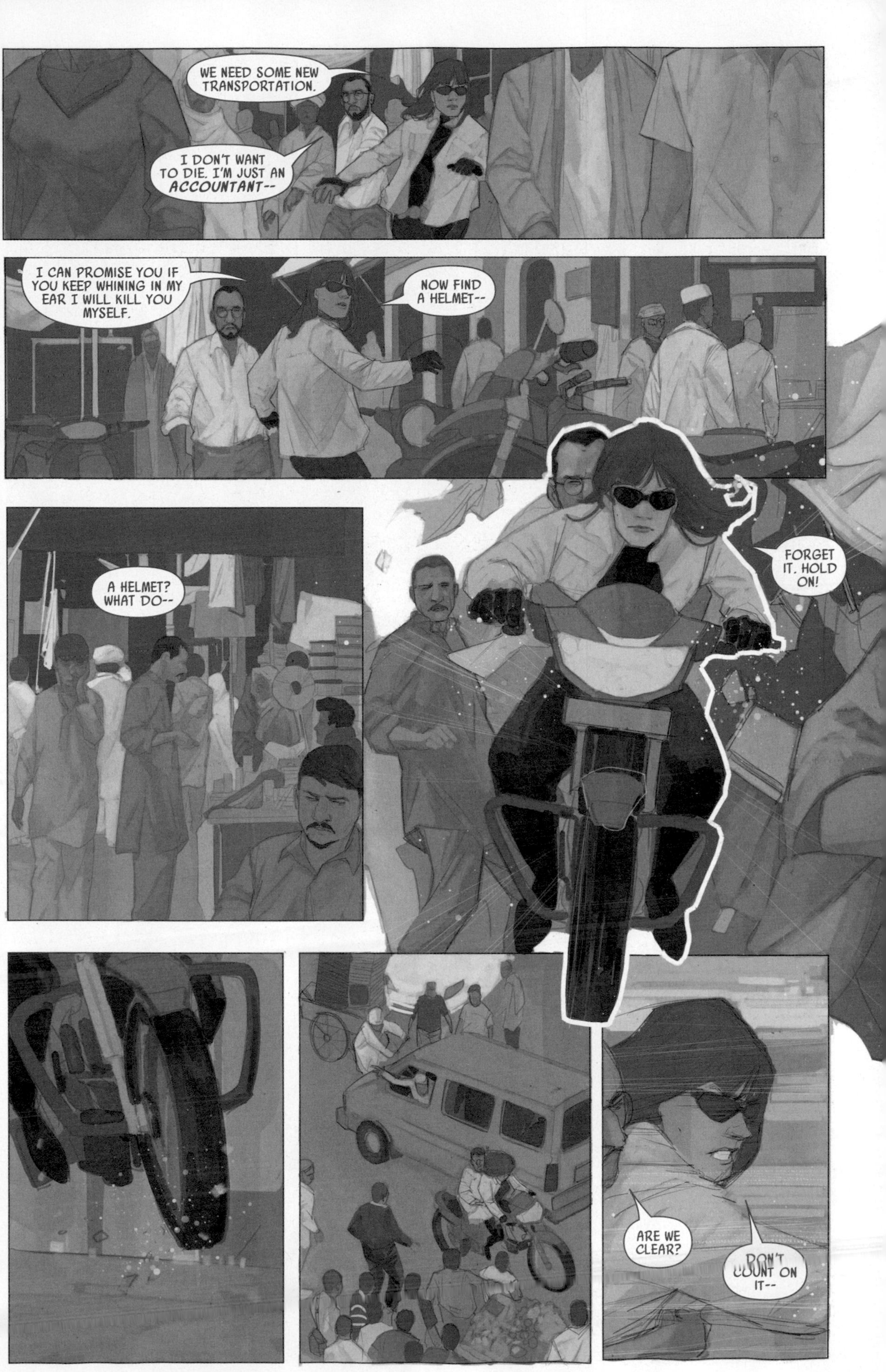
WE NEED SOME NEW TRANSPORTATION.
I DON'T WANT TO DIE. I'M JUST AN ACCOUNTANT--
I CAN PROMISE YOU IF YOU KEEP WHINING IN MY EAR I WILL KILL YOU MYSELF.
NOW FIND A HELMET--
A HELMET? WHAT DO--
FORGET IT. HOLD ON!
ARE WE CLEAR?
DON'T COUNT ON IT--

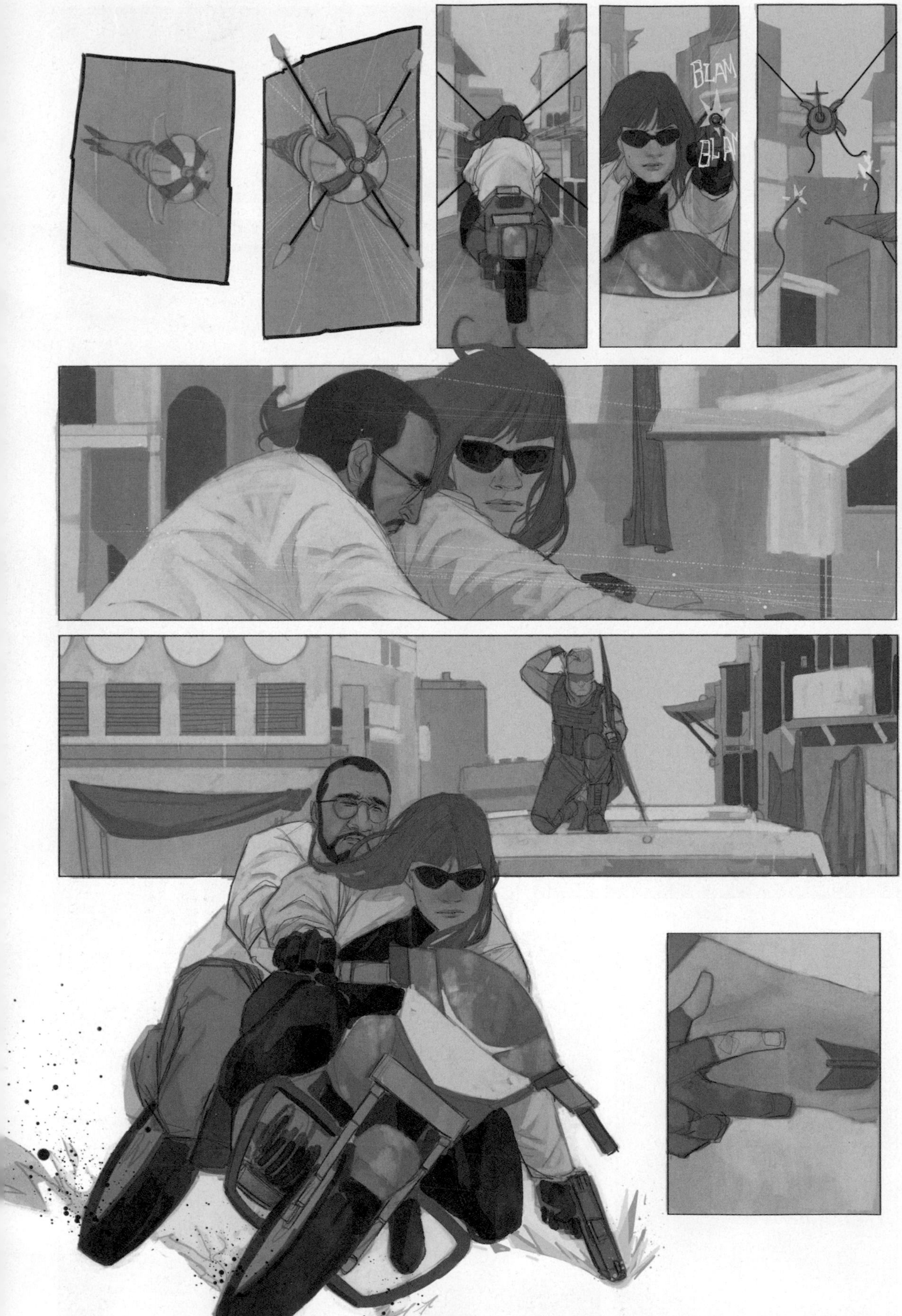
BLAM
BLAM

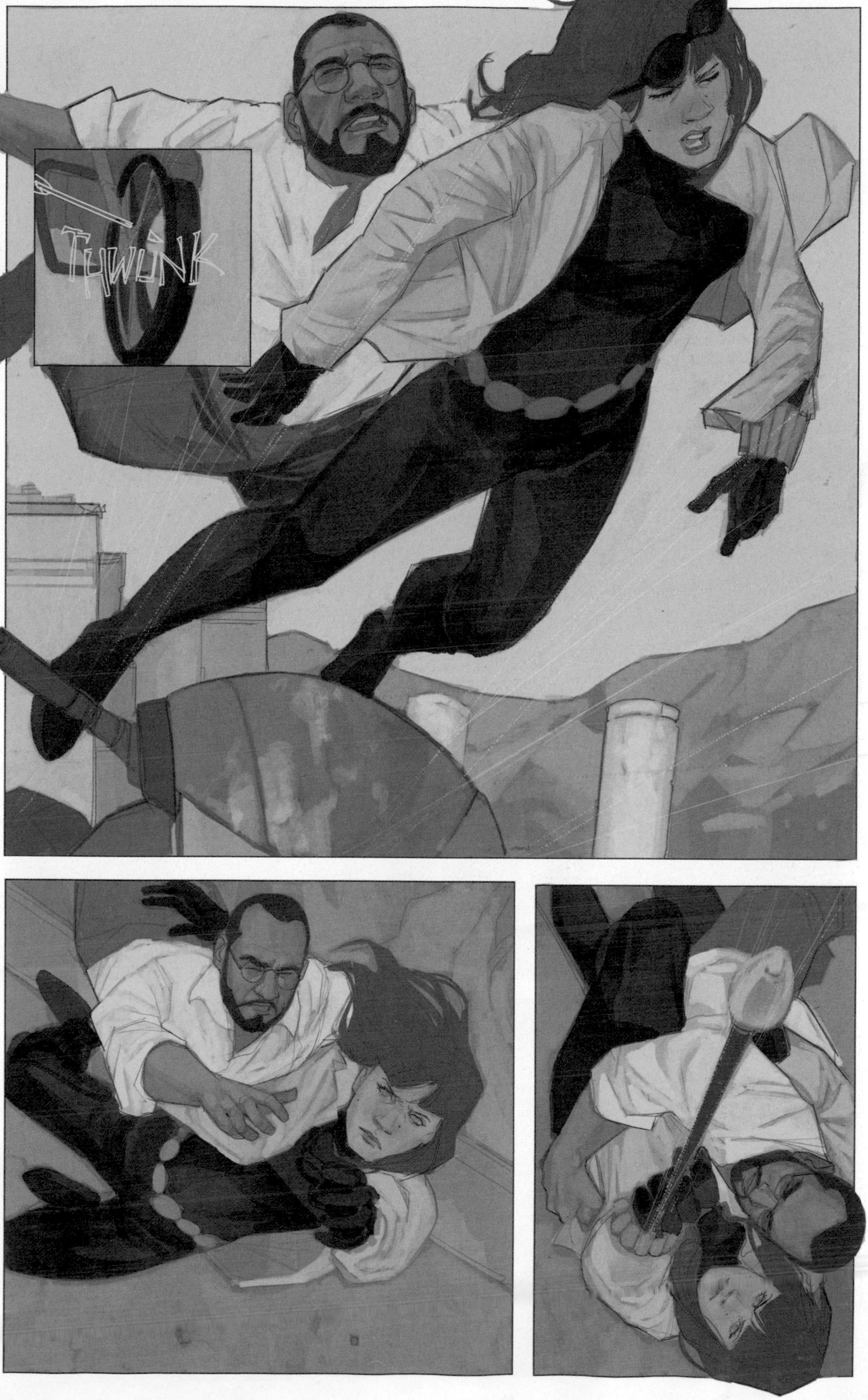
THWINK

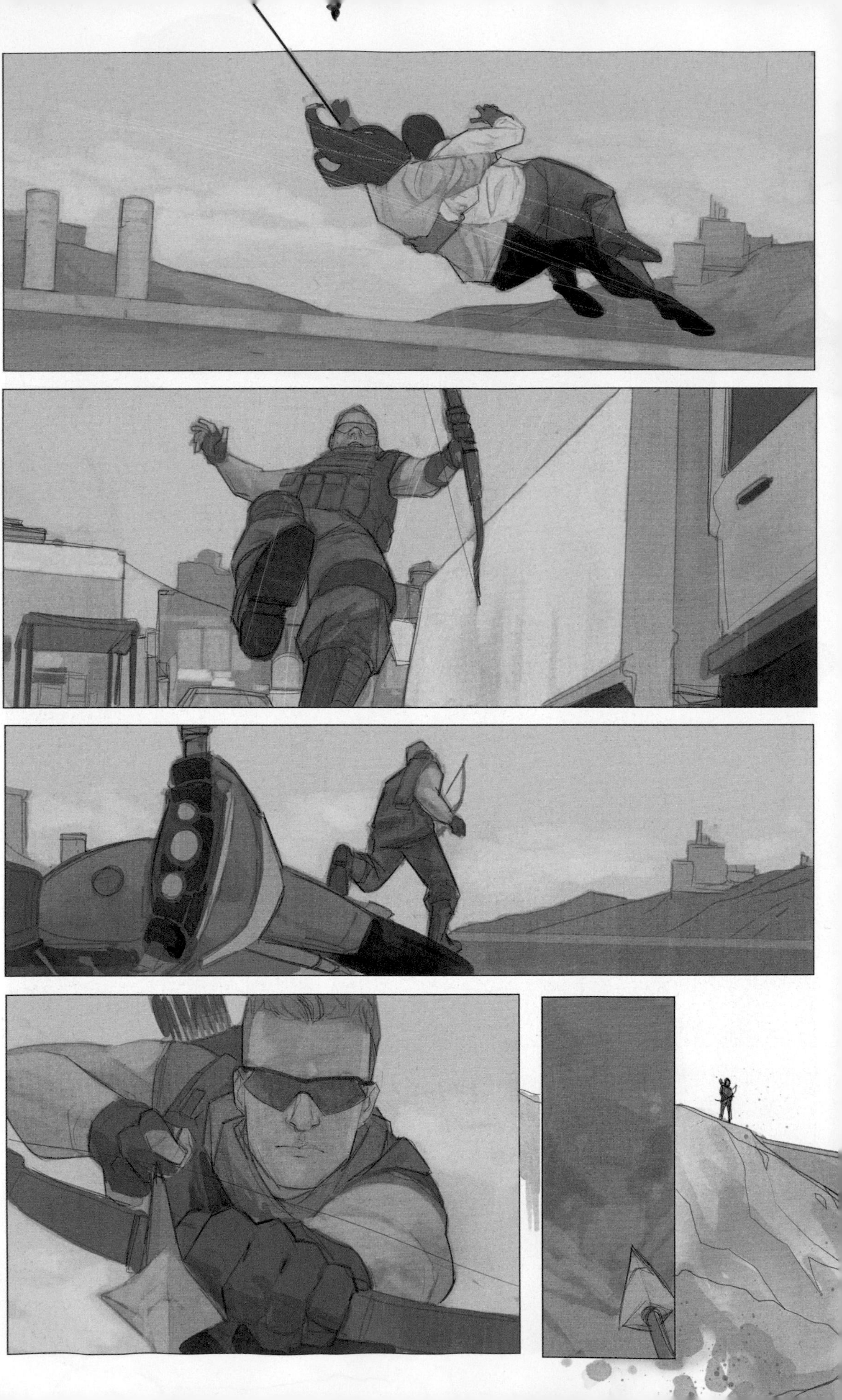

I WAS WONDERING, I MEAN, IF WE'RE GOING TO BE HERE A WHILE...

MAYBE WE COULD ORDER SOME PIZZA...?

BUT PLEASE, NO OLIVES BECAUSE I CAN'T--

ACK--

CK--CK-- CHHK--

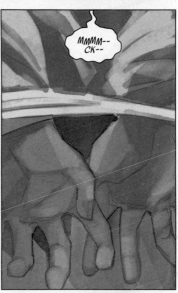

MMMM-- CK--

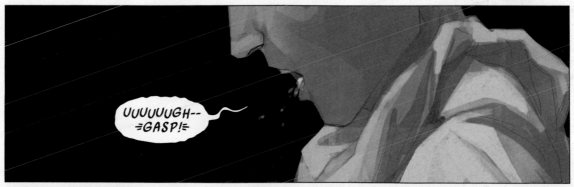

UUUUUUGH-- =GASP!=

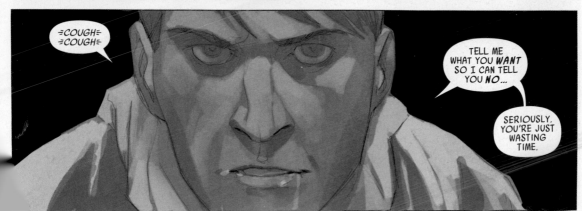

=COUGH= =COUGH=

TELL ME WHAT YOU WANT SO I CAN TELL YOU NO...

SERIOUSLY. YOU'RE JUST WASTING TIME.

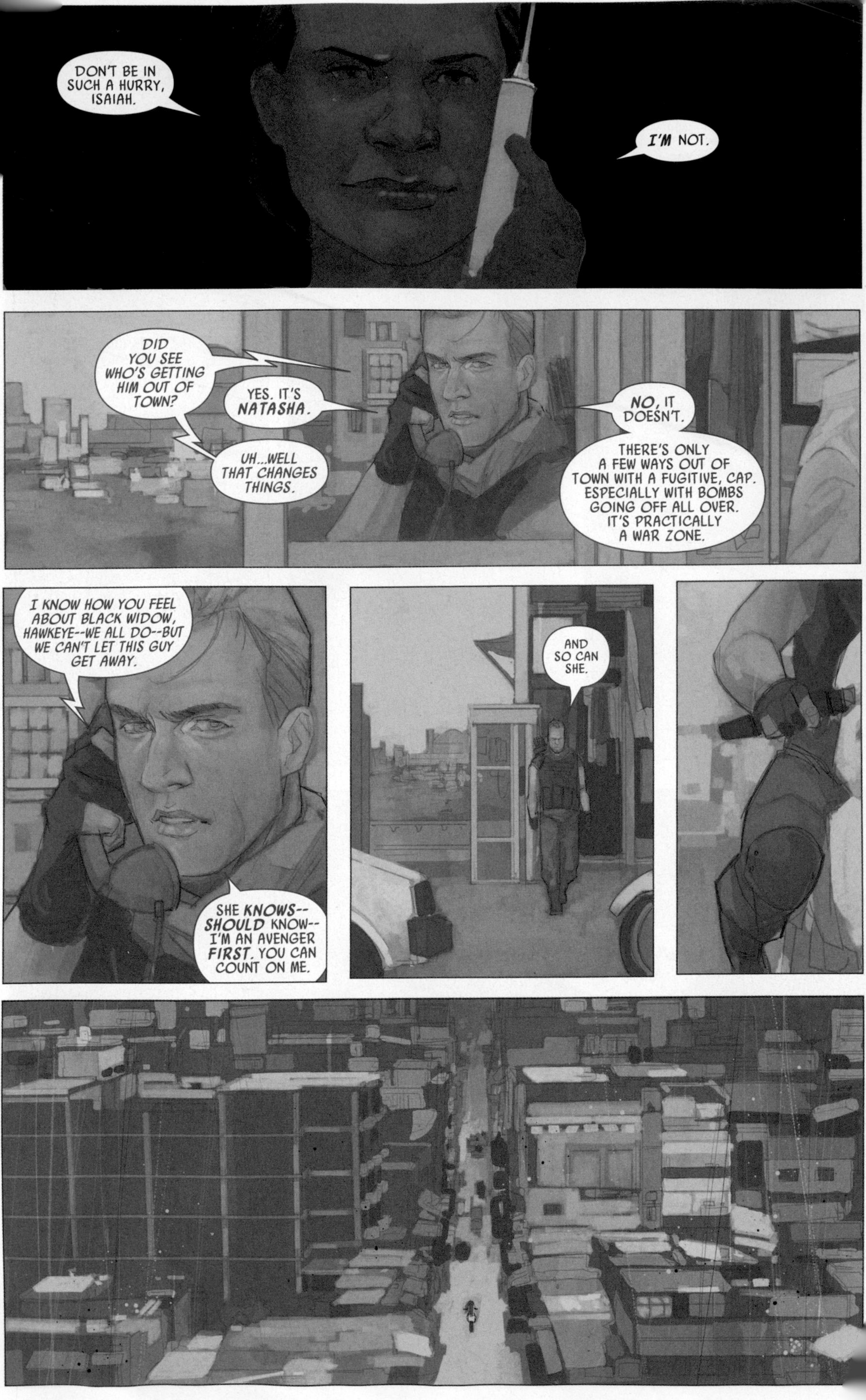
DON'T BE IN SUCH A HURRY, ISAIAH.
I'M NOT.
DID YOU SEE WHO'S GETTING HIM OUT OF TOWN?
YES. IT'S NATASHA.
UH...WELL THAT CHANGES THINGS.
NO, IT DOESN'T.
THERE'S ONLY A FEW WAYS OUT OF TOWN WITH A FUGITIVE, CAP. ESPECIALLY WITH BOMBS GOING OFF ALL OVER. IT'S PRACTICALLY A WAR ZONE.
I KNOW HOW YOU FEEL ABOUT BLACK WIDOW, HAWKEYE--WE ALL DO--BUT WE CAN'T LET THIS GUY GET AWAY.
SHE KNOWS--SHOULD KNOW--I'M AN AVENGER FIRST. YOU CAN COUNT ON ME.
AND SO CAN SHE.

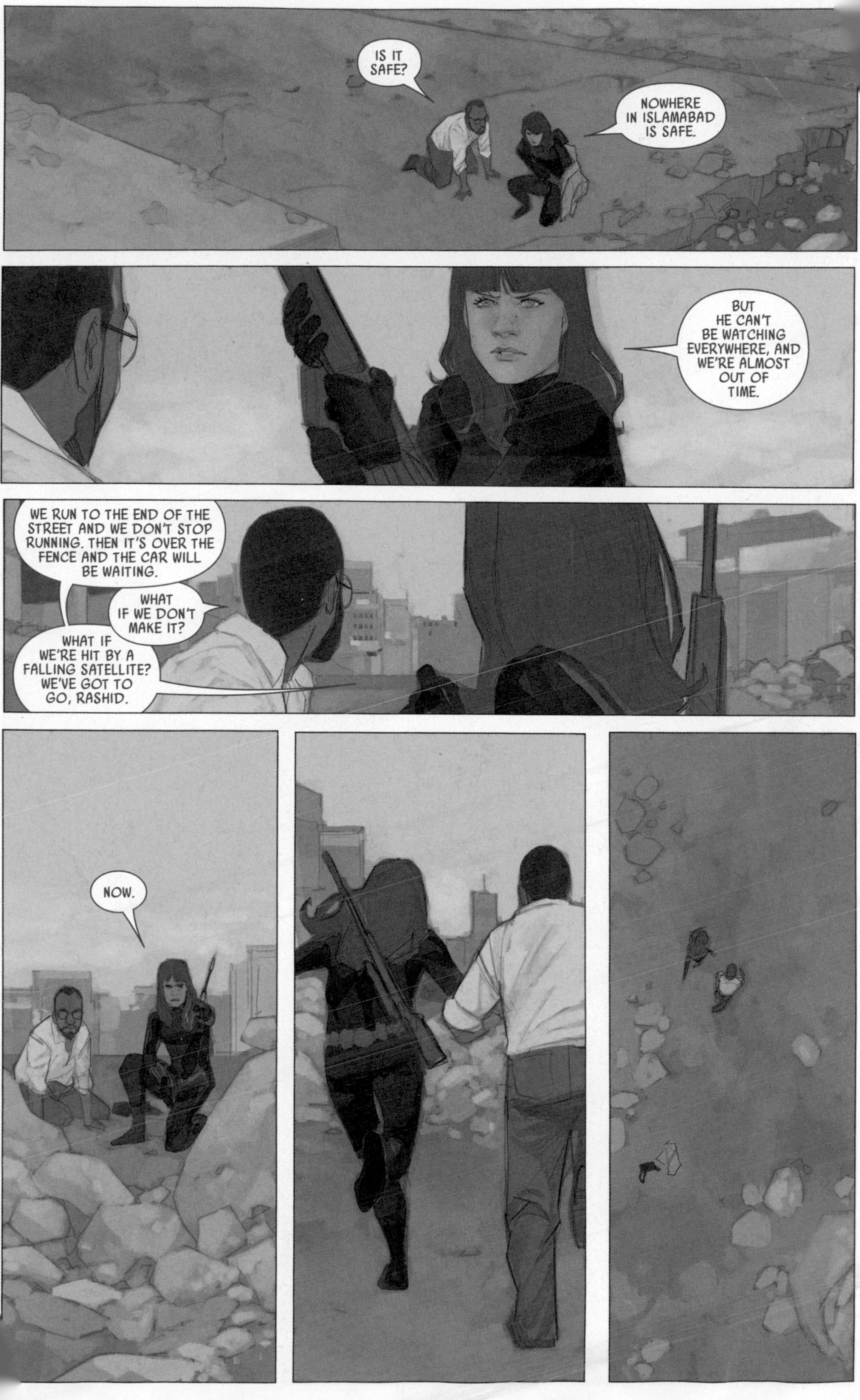
IS IT SAFE?
NOWHERE IN ISLAMABAD IS SAFE.
BUT HE CAN'T BE WATCHING EVERYWHERE, AND WE'RE ALMOST OUT OF TIME.
WE RUN TO THE END OF THE STREET AND WE DON'T STOP RUNNING. THEN IT'S OVER THE FENCE AND THE CAR WILL BE WAITING.
WHAT IF WE DON'T MAKE IT?
WHAT IF WE'RE HIT BY A FALLING SATELLITE? WE'VE GOT TO GO, RASHID.
NOW.

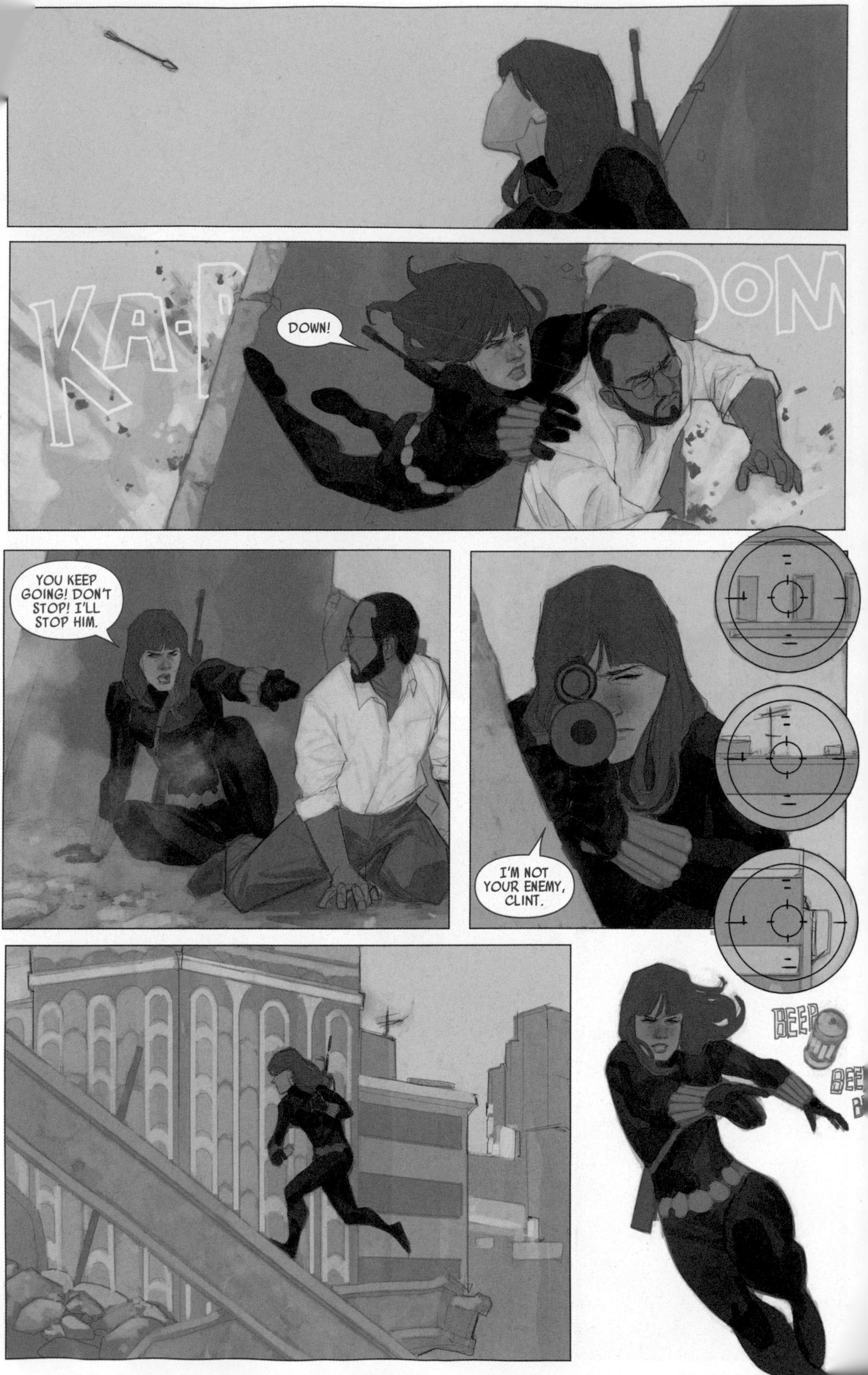
KA-BOOM
DOWN!
YOU KEEP GOING! DON'T STOP! I'LL STOP HIM.
I'M NOT YOUR ENEMY, CLINT.
BEEP

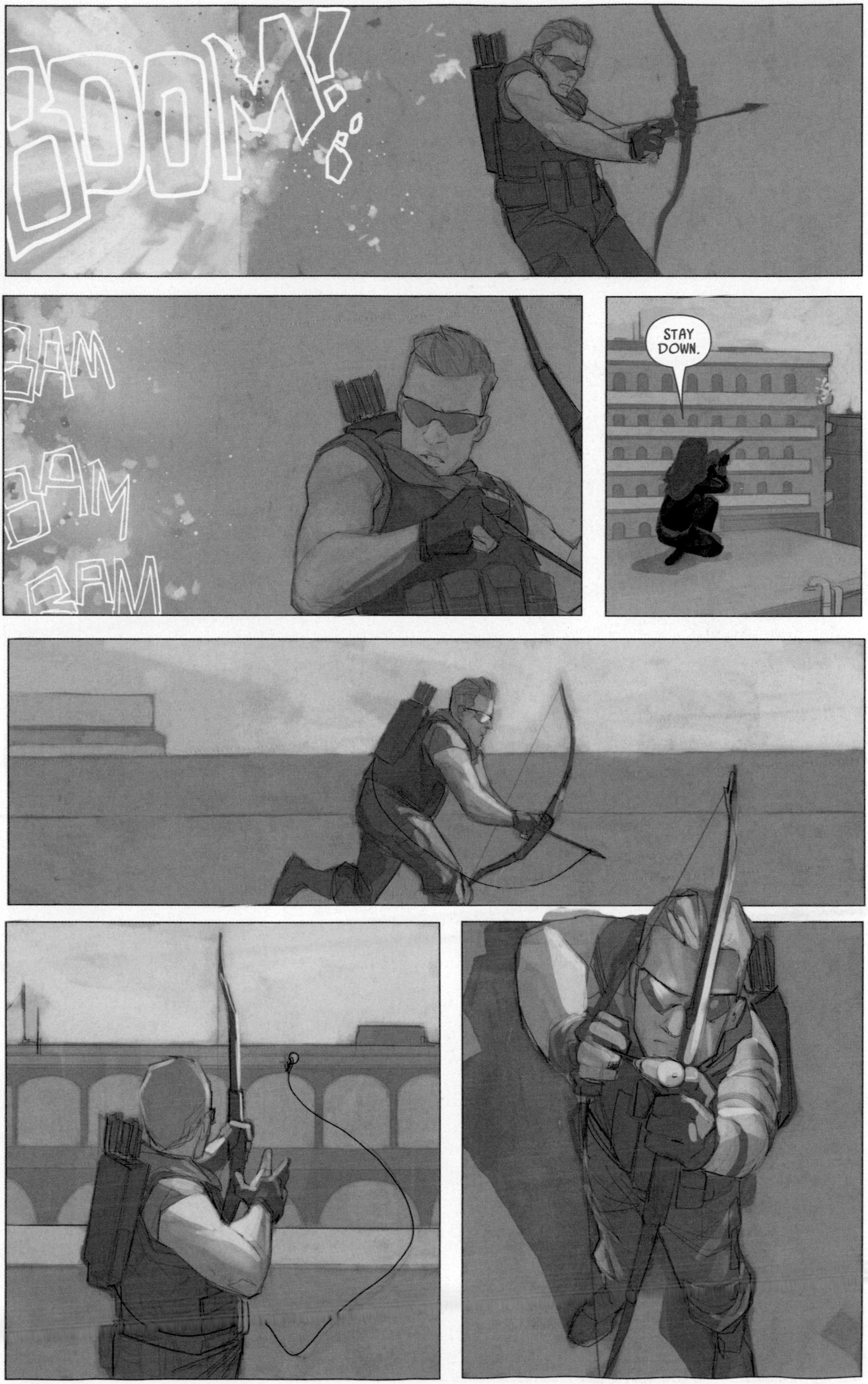
BOOM!
BAM
BAM
BAM
STAY DOWN.

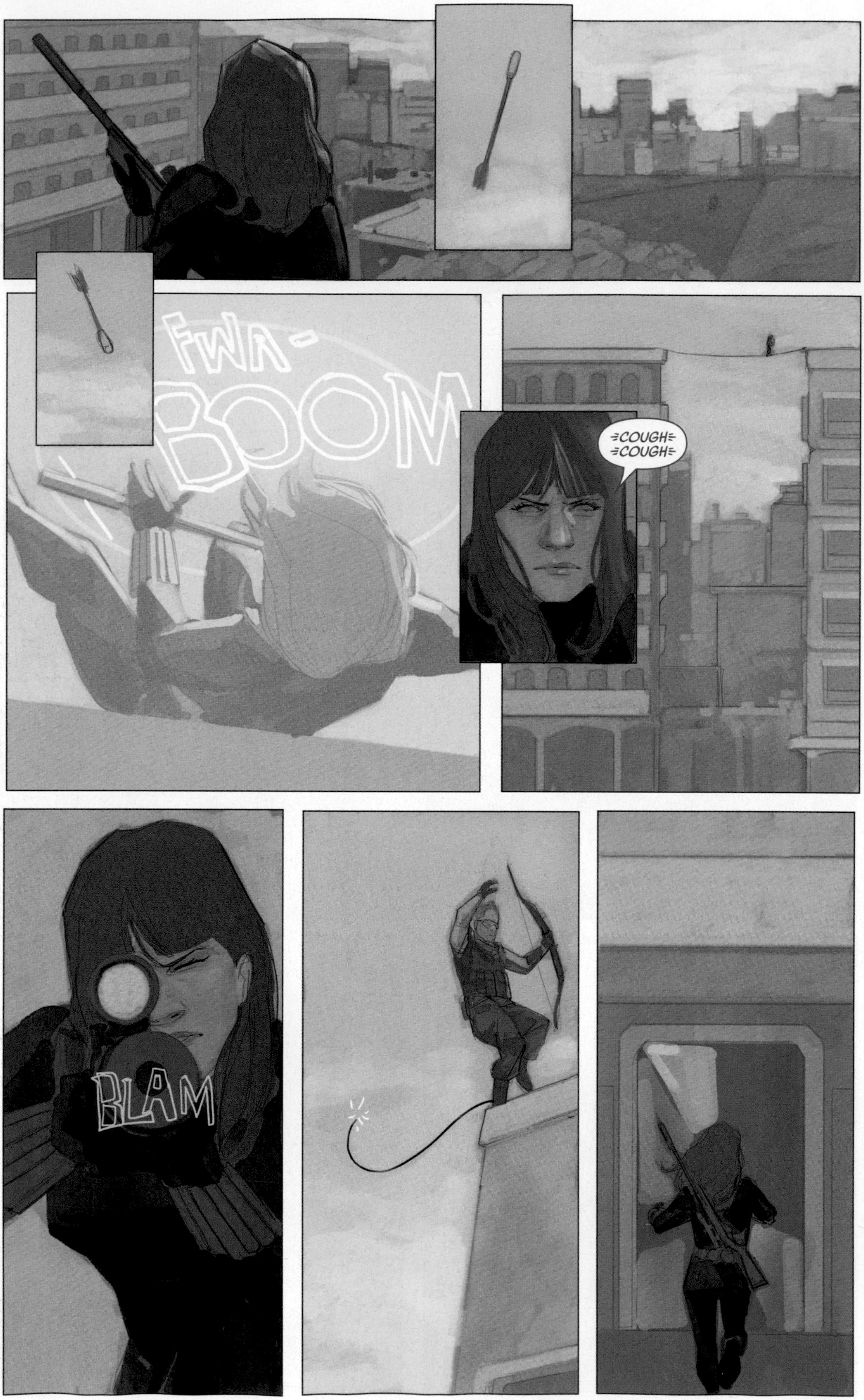
FWA-
BOOM
COUGH COUGH
BLAM

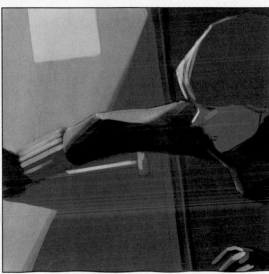

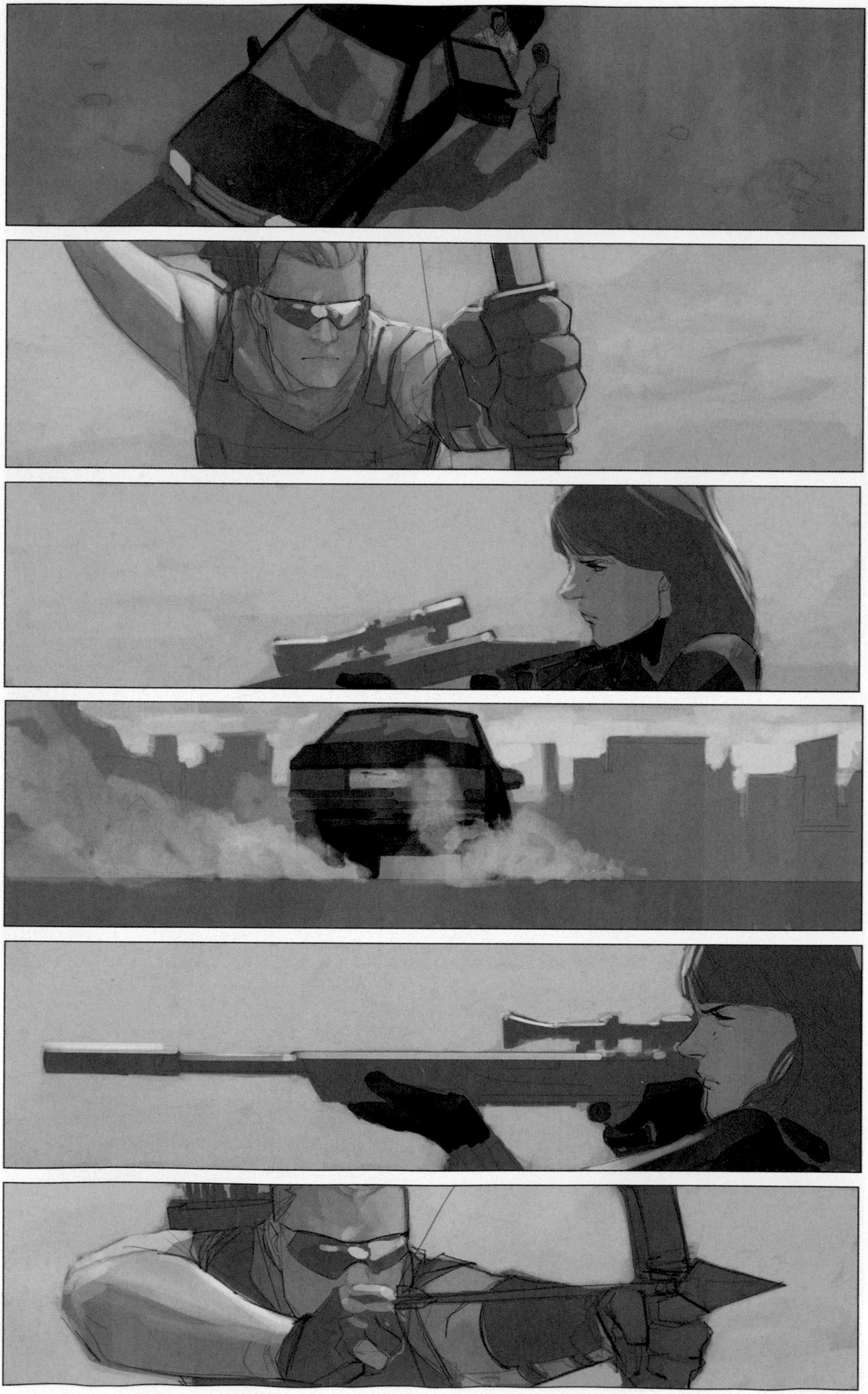

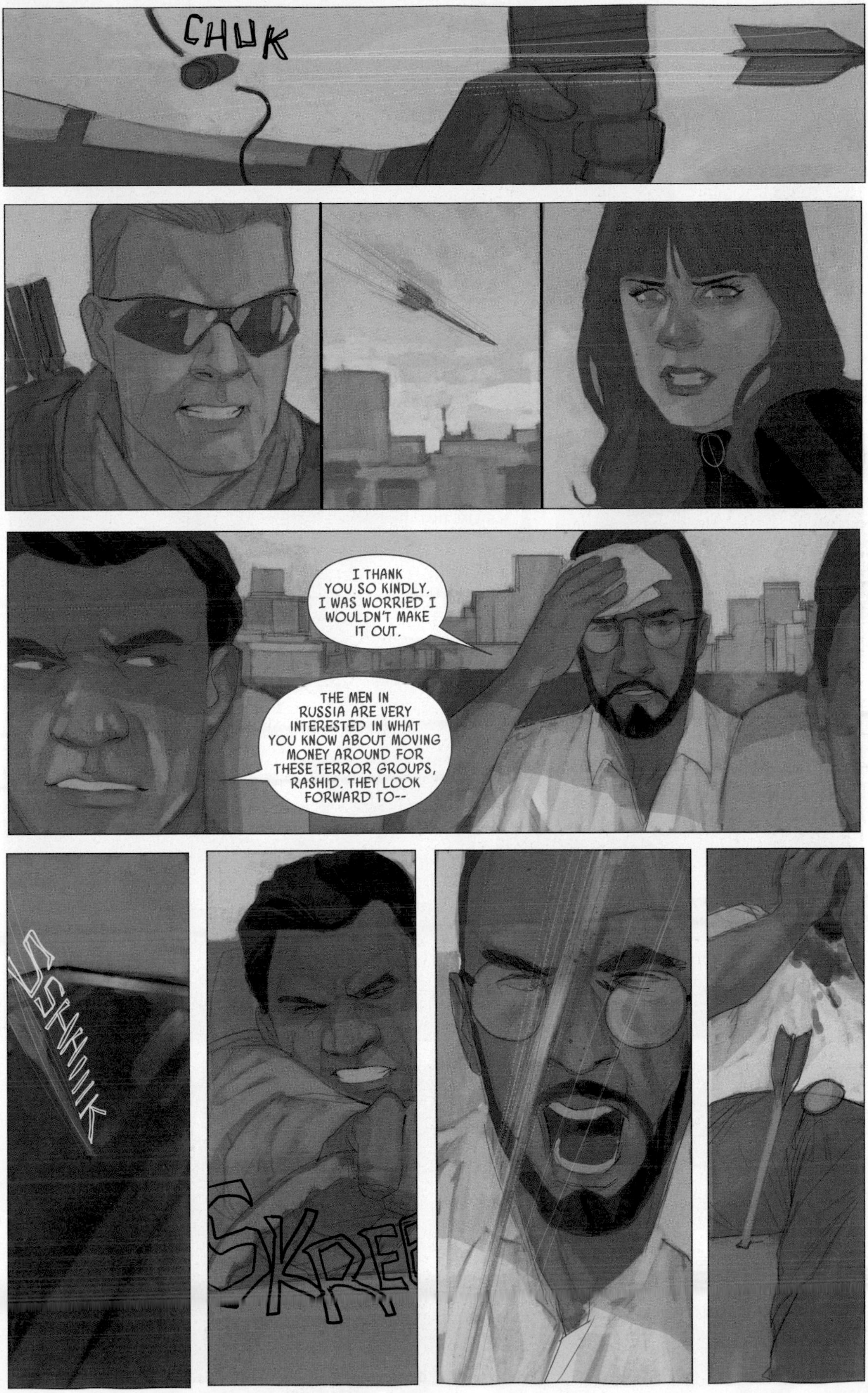
CHUK
I THANK YOU SO KINDLY. I WAS WORRIED I WOULDN'T MAKE IT OUT.
THE MEN IN RUSSIA ARE VERY INTERESTED IN WHAT YOU KNOW ABOUT MOVING MONEY AROUND FOR THESE TERROR GROUPS, RASHID. THEY LOOK FORWARD TO--
SSHHUNK
SKREE

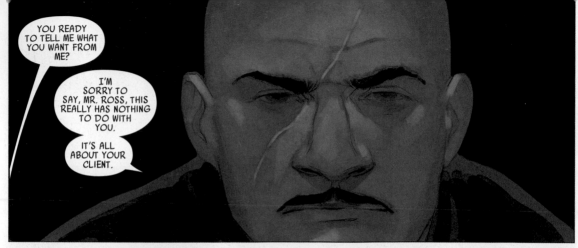

YOU READY TO TELL ME WHAT YOU WANT FROM ME?

I'M SORRY TO SAY, MR. ROSS, THIS REALLY HAS NOTHING TO DO WITH YOU.

IT'S ALL ABOUT YOUR CLIENT.

YOU CAN'T GET TO HER THROUGH ME. I'LL DIE FIRST. SLOWLY.

OH, IT'S NOT LIKE THAT, NOT LIKE THAT AT ALL.

SHE'S JUST BEEN A LITTLE TOO FOCUSED ON MY... *EMPLOYERS* LATELY.

WE THOUGHT SHE COULD USE A DISTRACTION.

I THINK YOU OVERESTIMATE HOW MUCH SHE CARES ABOUT ME.

SHE'S KIND OF A COLD-HEARTED JERK THAT WAY.

I KNOW YOUR CLIENT, ISAIAH. OR I KNEW HER, A LONG TIME AGO.

AND SHE CARES FOR OTHER PEOPLE A GREAT DEAL.

EVEN STRANGERS.

SO, SHOULD WE CALL HER?

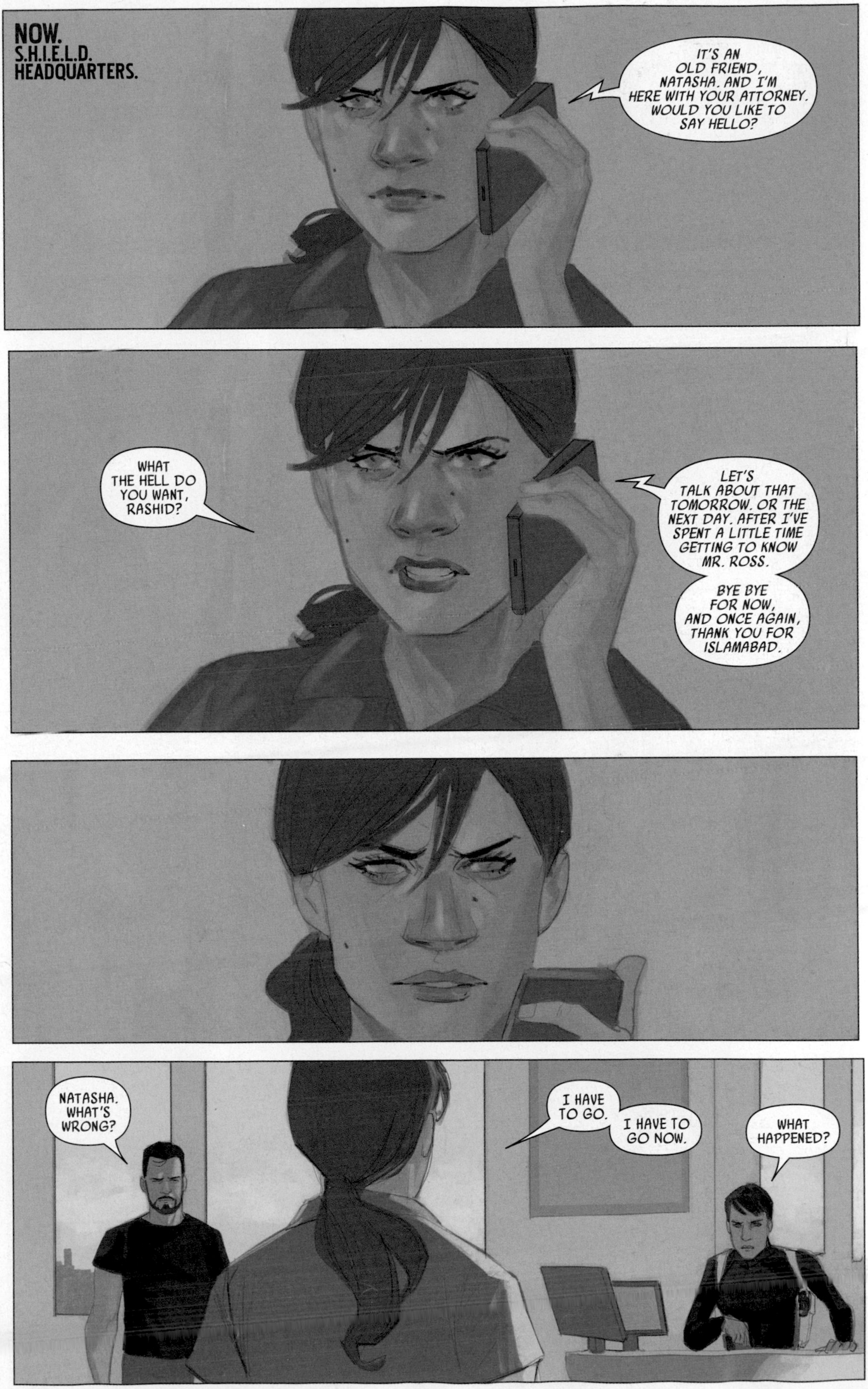
NOW.
S.H.I.E.L.D.
HEADQUARTERS.
IT'S AN OLD FRIEND, NATASHA. AND I'M HERE WITH YOUR ATTORNEY. WOULD YOU LIKE TO SAY HELLO?
WHAT THE HELL DO YOU WANT, RASHID?
LET'S TALK ABOUT THAT TOMORROW. OR THE NEXT DAY. AFTER I'VE SPENT A LITTLE TIME GETTING TO KNOW MR. ROSS.
BYE BYE FOR NOW, AND ONCE AGAIN, THANK YOU FOR ISLAMABAD.
NATASHA. WHAT'S WRONG?
I HAVE TO GO.
I HAVE TO GO NOW.
WHAT HAPPENED?

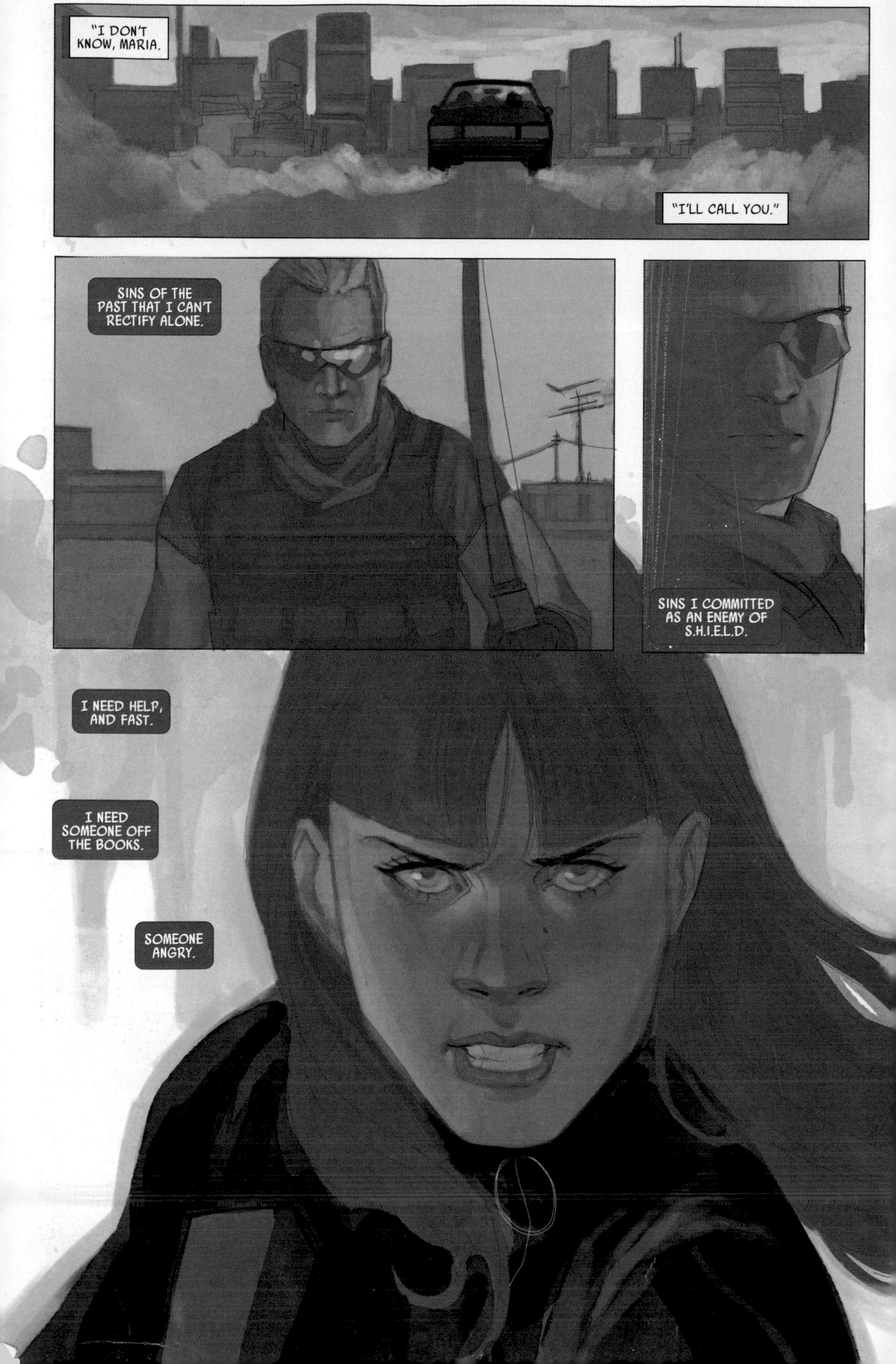
"I DON'T KNOW, MARIA.
"I'LL CALL YOU."
SINS OF THE PAST THAT I CAN'T RECTIFY ALONE.
SINS I COMMITTED AS AN ENEMY OF S.H.I.E.L.D.
I NEED HELP, AND FAST.
I NEED SOMEONE OFF THE BOOKS.
SOMEONE ANGRY.

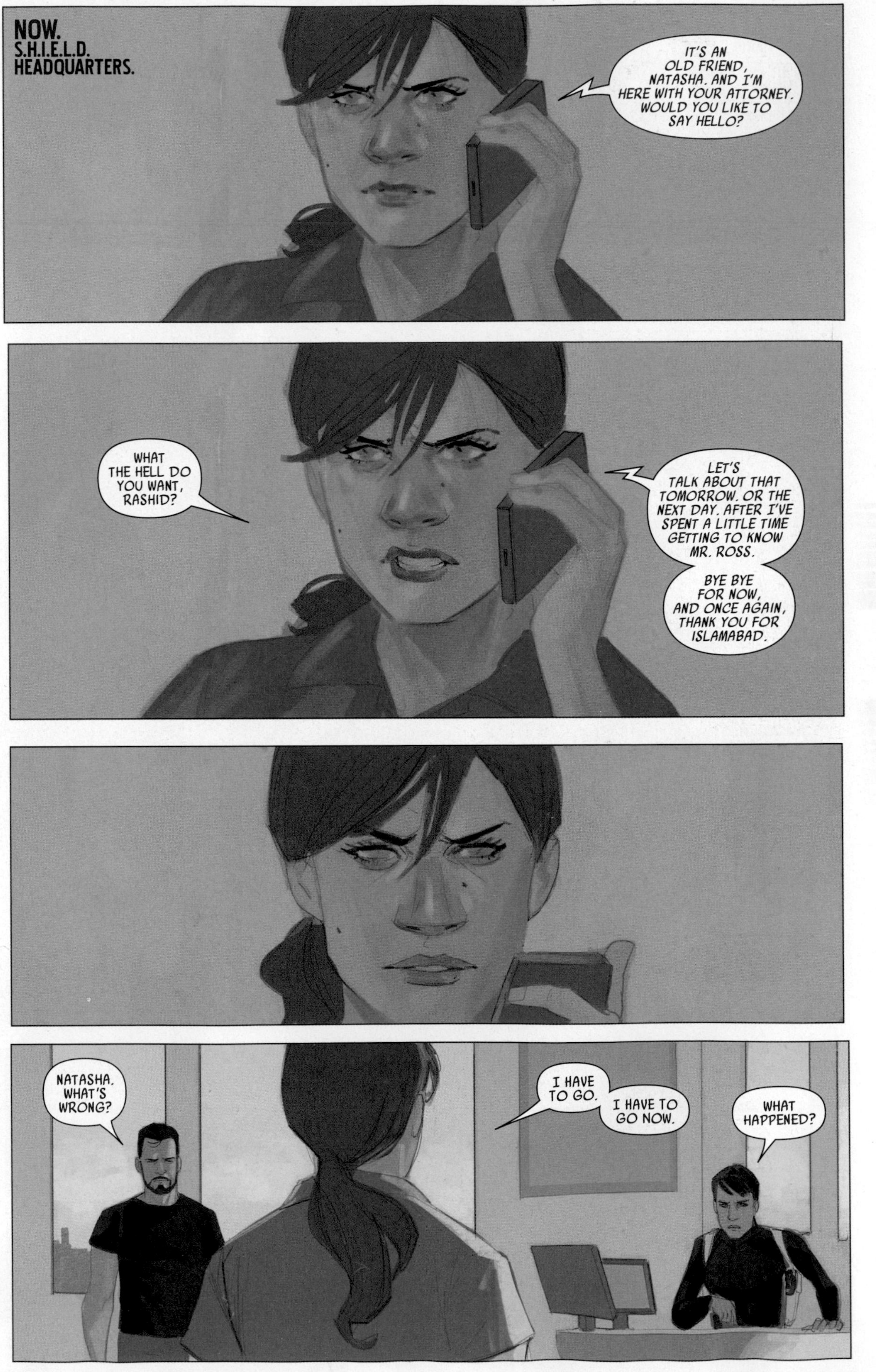
NOW.
S.H.I.E.L.D.
HEADQUARTERS.
IT'S AN OLD FRIEND, NATASHA. AND I'M HERE WITH YOUR ATTORNEY. WOULD YOU LIKE TO SAY HELLO?
WHAT THE HELL DO YOU WANT, RASHID?
LET'S TALK ABOUT THAT TOMORROW. OR THE NEXT DAY. AFTER I'VE SPENT A LITTLE TIME GETTING TO KNOW MR. ROSS.
BYE BYE FOR NOW, AND ONCE AGAIN, THANK YOU FOR ISLAMABAD.
NATASHA. WHAT'S WRONG?
I HAVE TO GO.
I HAVE TO GO NOW.
WHAT HAPPENED?

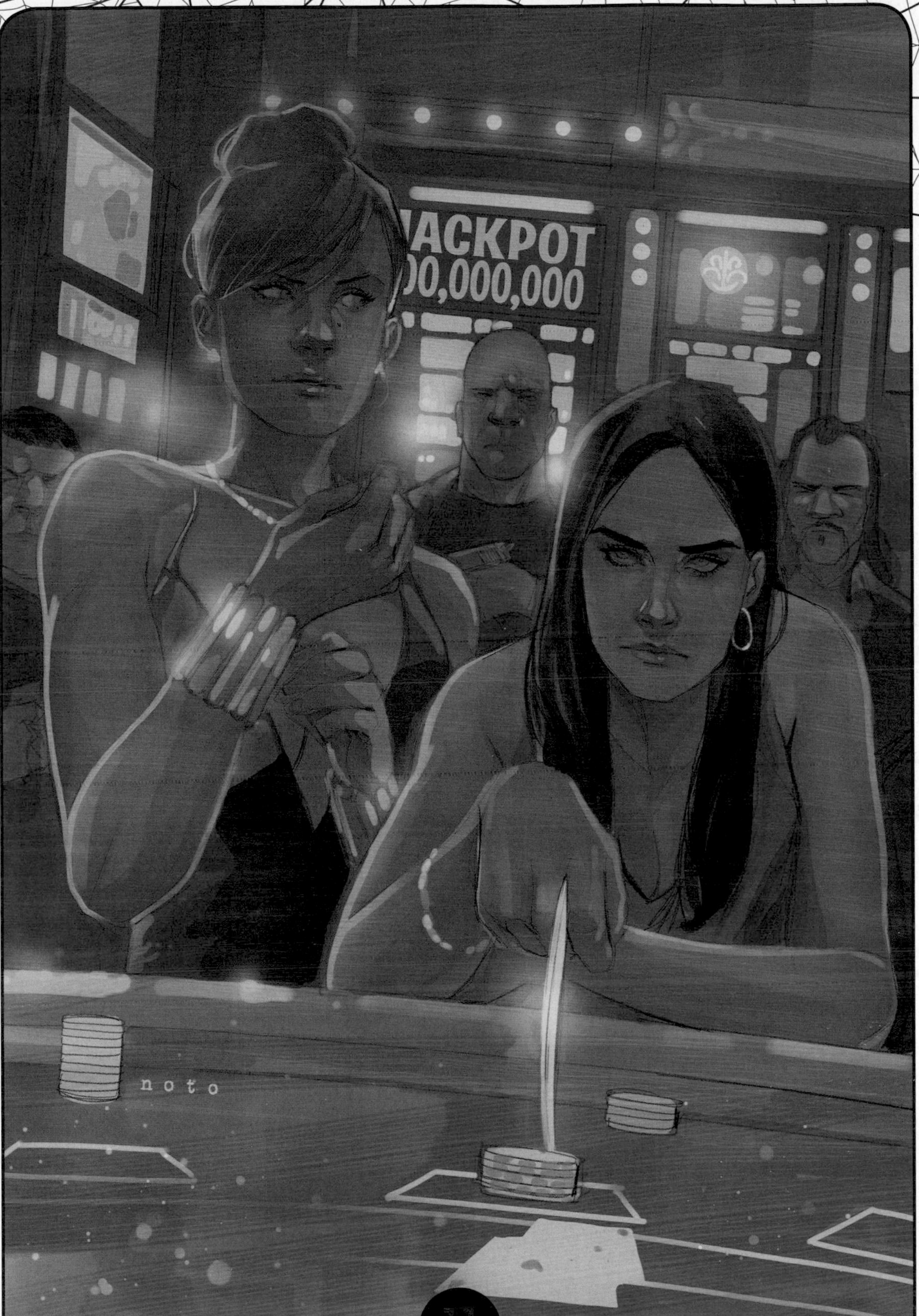
ACKPOT
00,000,000
noto
11

FEMMES FATALES

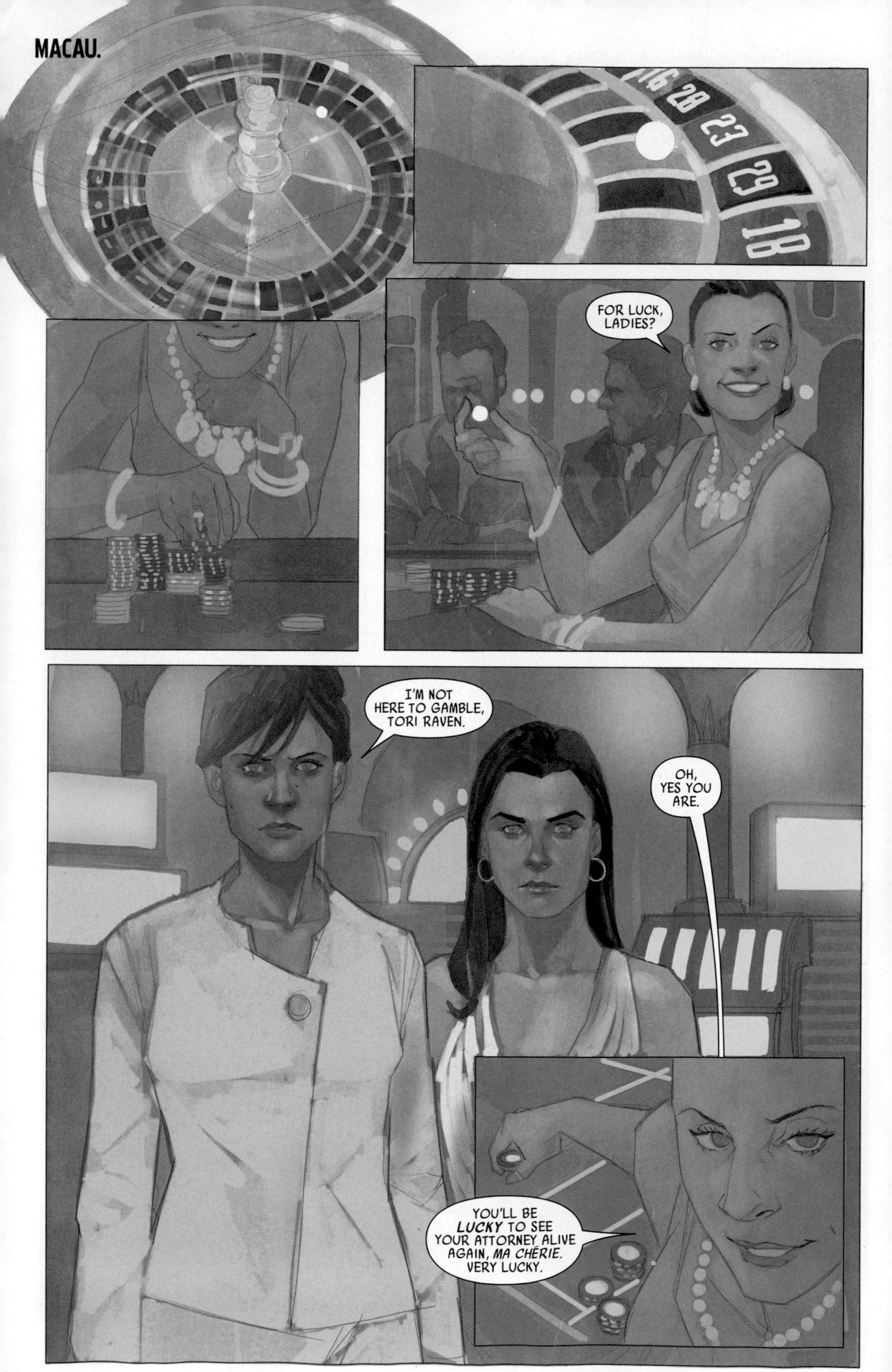
MACAU.
FOR LUCK, LADIES?
I'M NOT HERE TO GAMBLE, TORI RAVEN.
OH, YES YOU ARE.
YOU'LL BE **LUCKY** TO SEE YOUR ATTORNEY ALIVE AGAIN, *MA CHÉRIE*. VERY LUCKY.

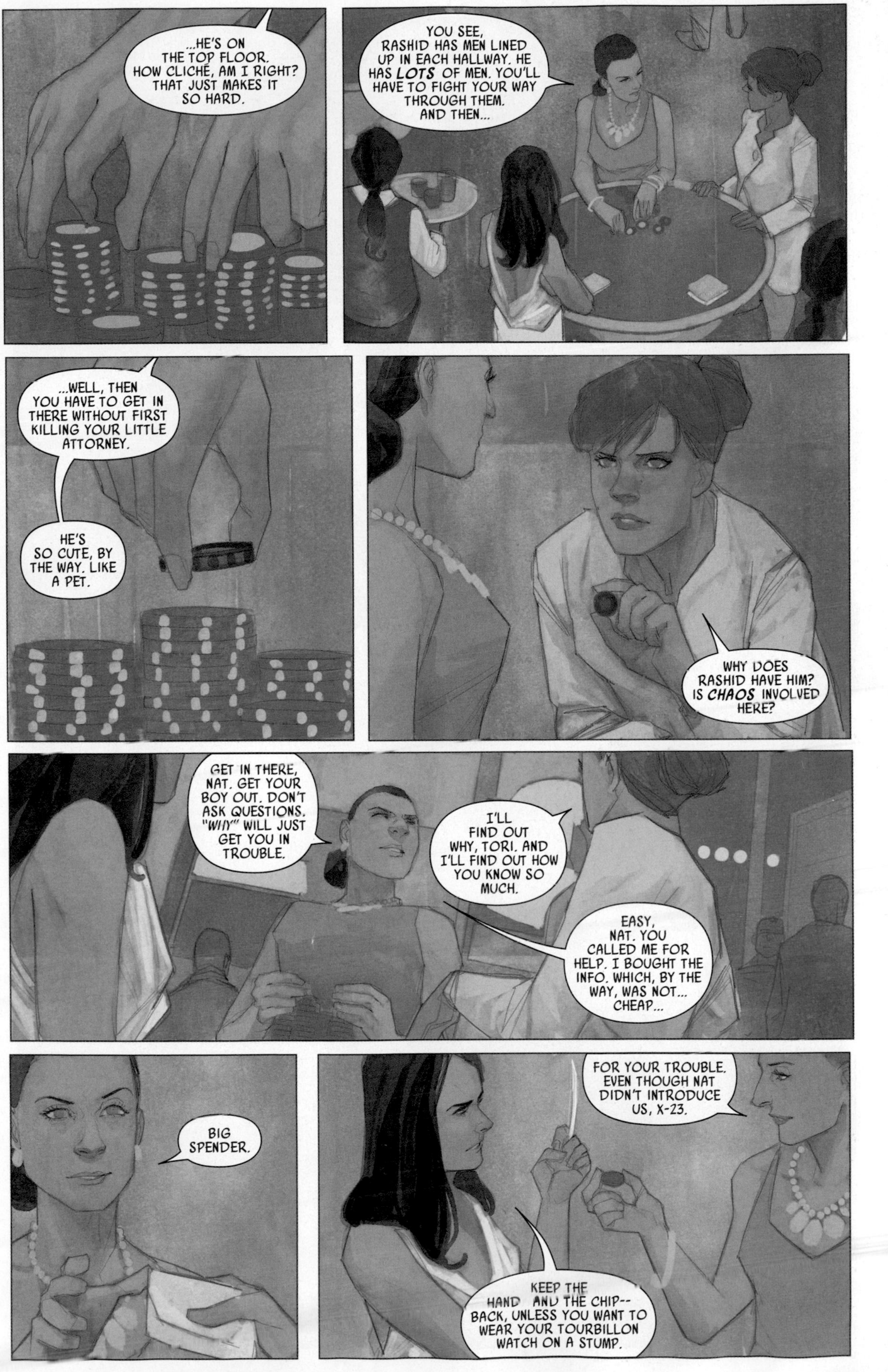
...HE'S ON THE TOP FLOOR. HOW CLICHÉ, AM I RIGHT? THAT JUST MAKES IT SO HARD.
YOU SEE, RASHID HAS MEN LINED UP IN EACH HALLWAY. HE HAS LOTS OF MEN. YOU'LL HAVE TO FIGHT YOUR WAY THROUGH THEM. AND THEN...
...WELL, THEN YOU HAVE TO GET IN THERE WITHOUT FIRST KILLING YOUR LITTLE ATTORNEY.
HE'S SO CUTE, BY THE WAY. LIKE A PET.
WHY DOES RASHID HAVE HIM? IS CHAOS INVOLVED HERE?
GET IN THERE, NAT. GET YOUR BOY OUT. DON'T ASK QUESTIONS. "WHY" WILL JUST GET YOU IN TROUBLE.
I'LL FIND OUT WHY, TORI. AND I'LL FIND OUT HOW YOU KNOW SO MUCH.
EASY, NAT. YOU CALLED ME FOR HELP. I BOUGHT THE INFO. WHICH, BY THE WAY, WAS NOT... CHEAP...
BIG SPENDER.
FOR YOUR TROUBLE. EVEN THOUGH NAT DIDN'T INTRODUCE US, X-23.
KEEP THE HAND AND THE CHIP-- BACK, UNLESS YOU WANT TO WEAR YOUR TOURBILLON WATCH ON A STUMP.

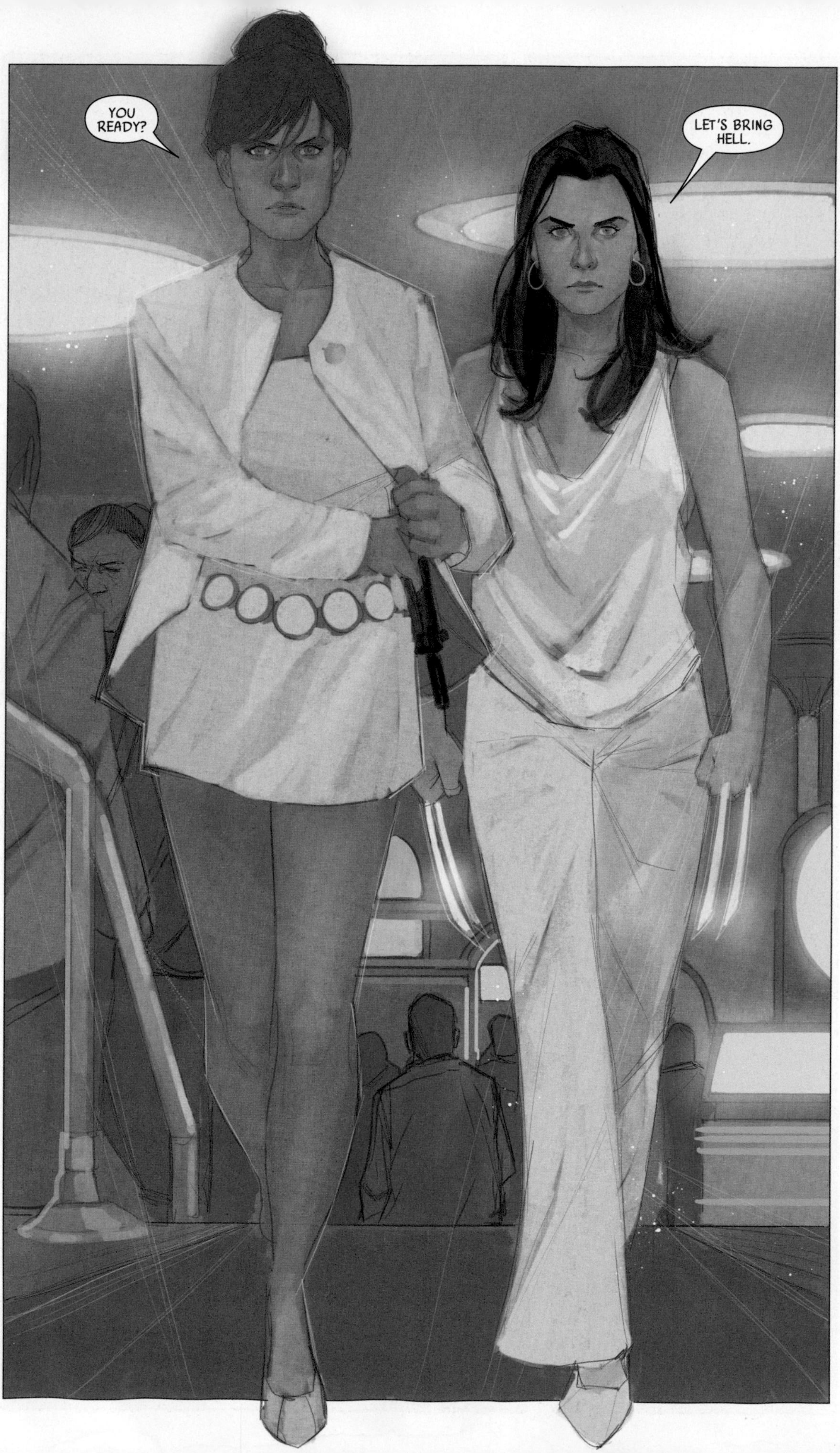
YOU READY?
LET'S BRING HELL.

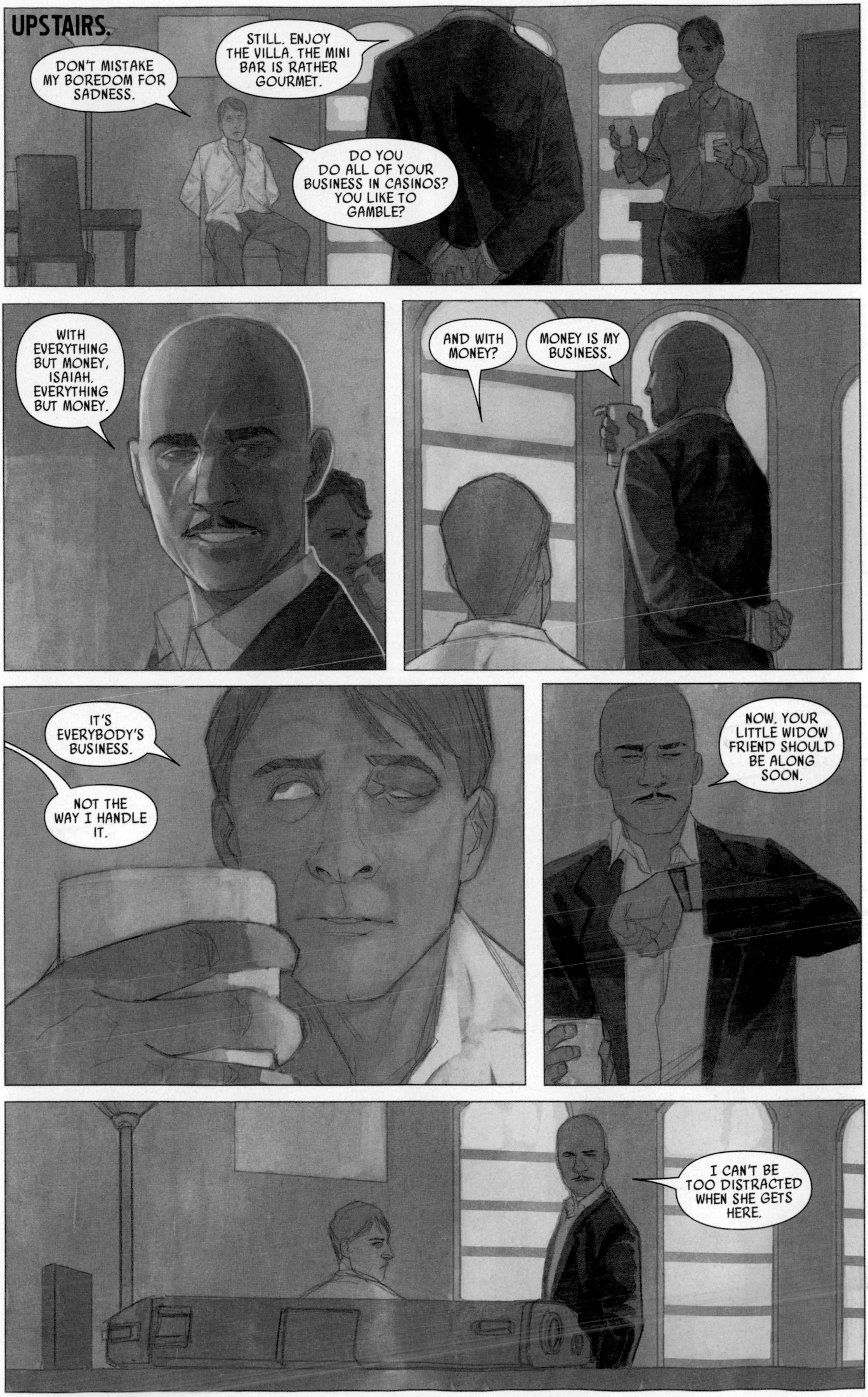
UPSTAIRS.
DON'T MISTAKE MY BOREDOM FOR SADNESS.
STILL. ENJOY THE VILLA. THE MINI BAR IS RATHER GOURMET.
DO YOU DO ALL OF YOUR BUSINESS IN CASINOS? YOU LIKE TO GAMBLE?
WITH EVERYTHING BUT MONEY, ISAIAH. EVERYTHING BUT MONEY.
AND WITH MONEY?
MONEY IS MY BUSINESS.
IT'S EVERYBODY'S BUSINESS.
NOT THE WAY I HANDLE IT.
NOW. YOUR LITTLE WIDOW FRIEND SHOULD BE ALONG SOON.
I CAN'T BE TOO DISTRACTED WHEN SHE GETS HERE.

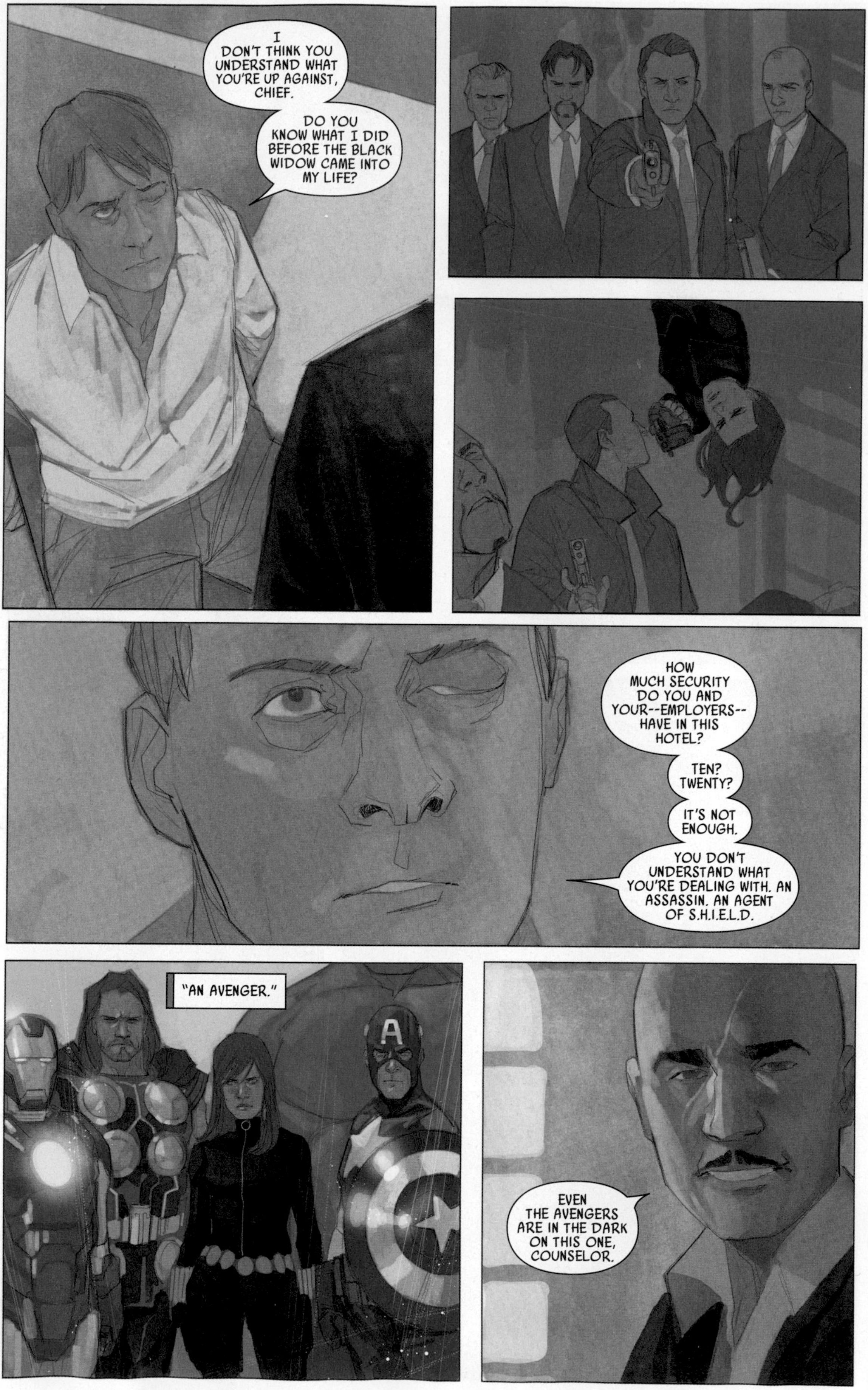
I DON'T THINK YOU UNDERSTAND WHAT YOU'RE UP AGAINST, CHIEF.
DO YOU KNOW WHAT I DID BEFORE THE BLACK WIDOW CAME INTO MY LIFE?
HOW MUCH SECURITY DO YOU AND YOUR--EMPLOYERS--HAVE IN THIS HOTEL?
TEN? TWENTY?
IT'S NOT ENOUGH.
YOU DON'T UNDERSTAND WHAT YOU'RE DEALING WITH. AN ASSASSIN. AN AGENT OF S.H.I.E.L.D.
"AN AVENGER."
EVEN THE AVENGERS ARE IN THE DARK ON THIS ONE, COUNSELOR.

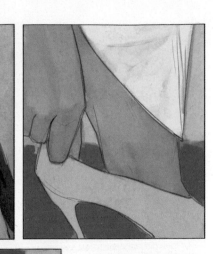

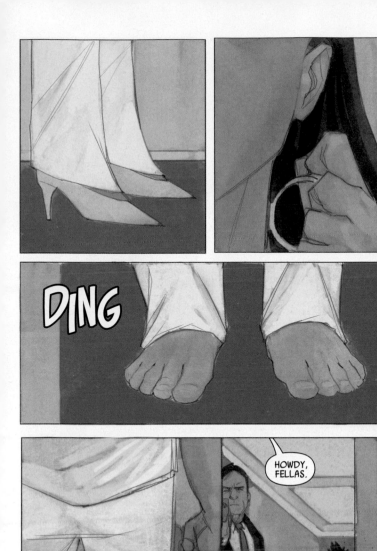

DING

HOWDY, FELLAS.

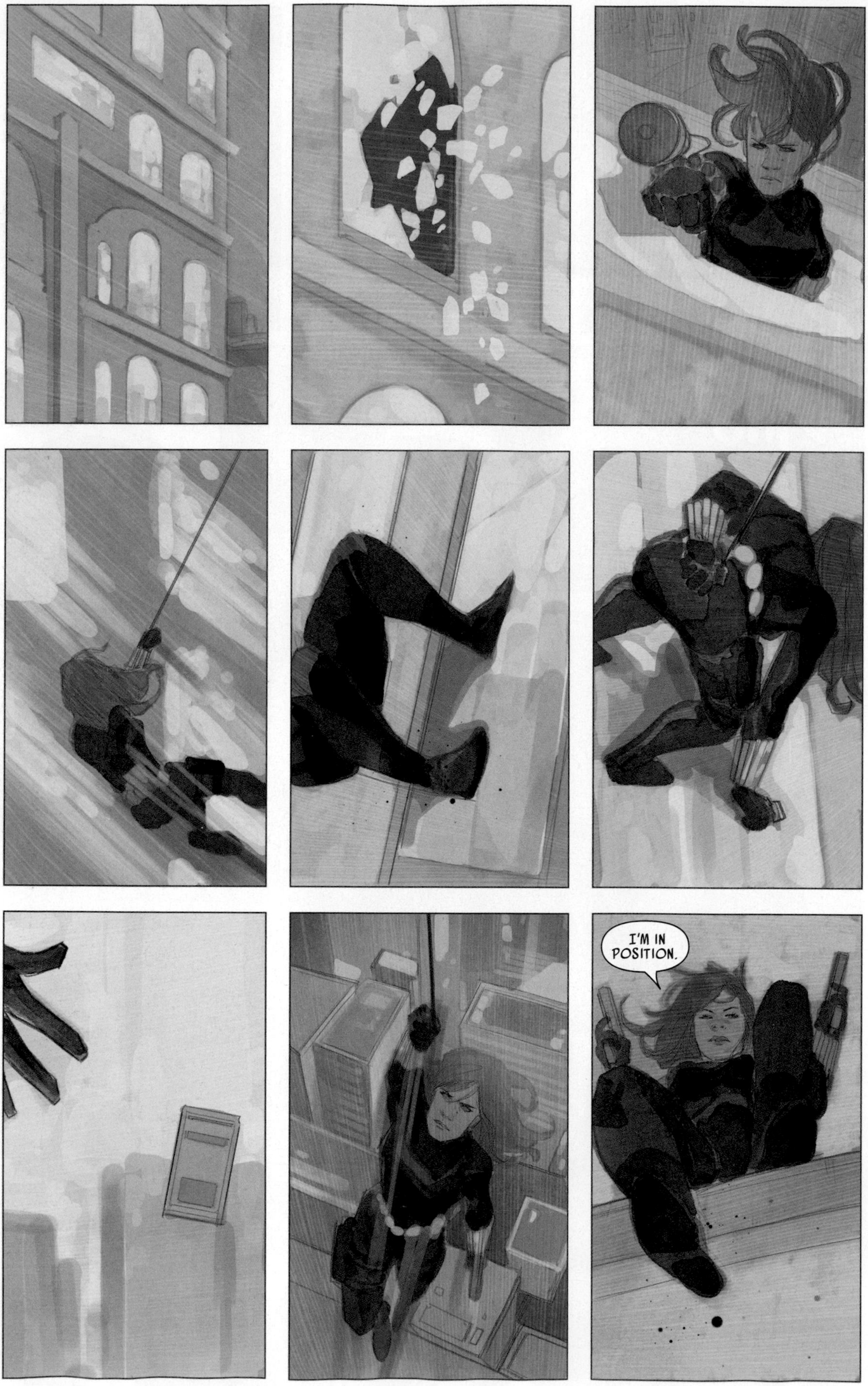
I'M IN POSITION.

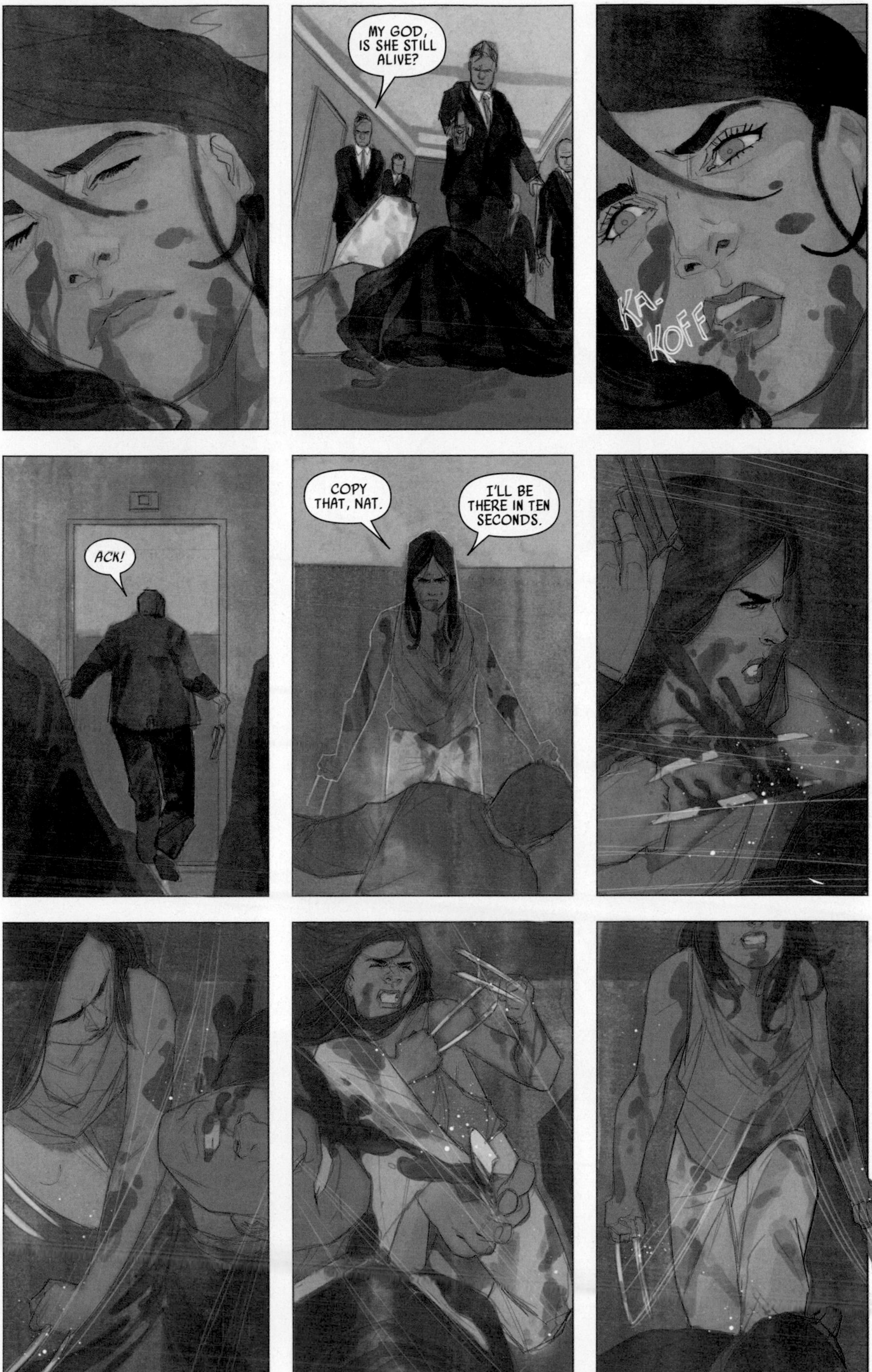

MY GOD, IS SHE STILL ALIVE?
KA-KOFF
ACK!
COPY THAT, NAT.
I'LL BE THERE IN TEN SECONDS.

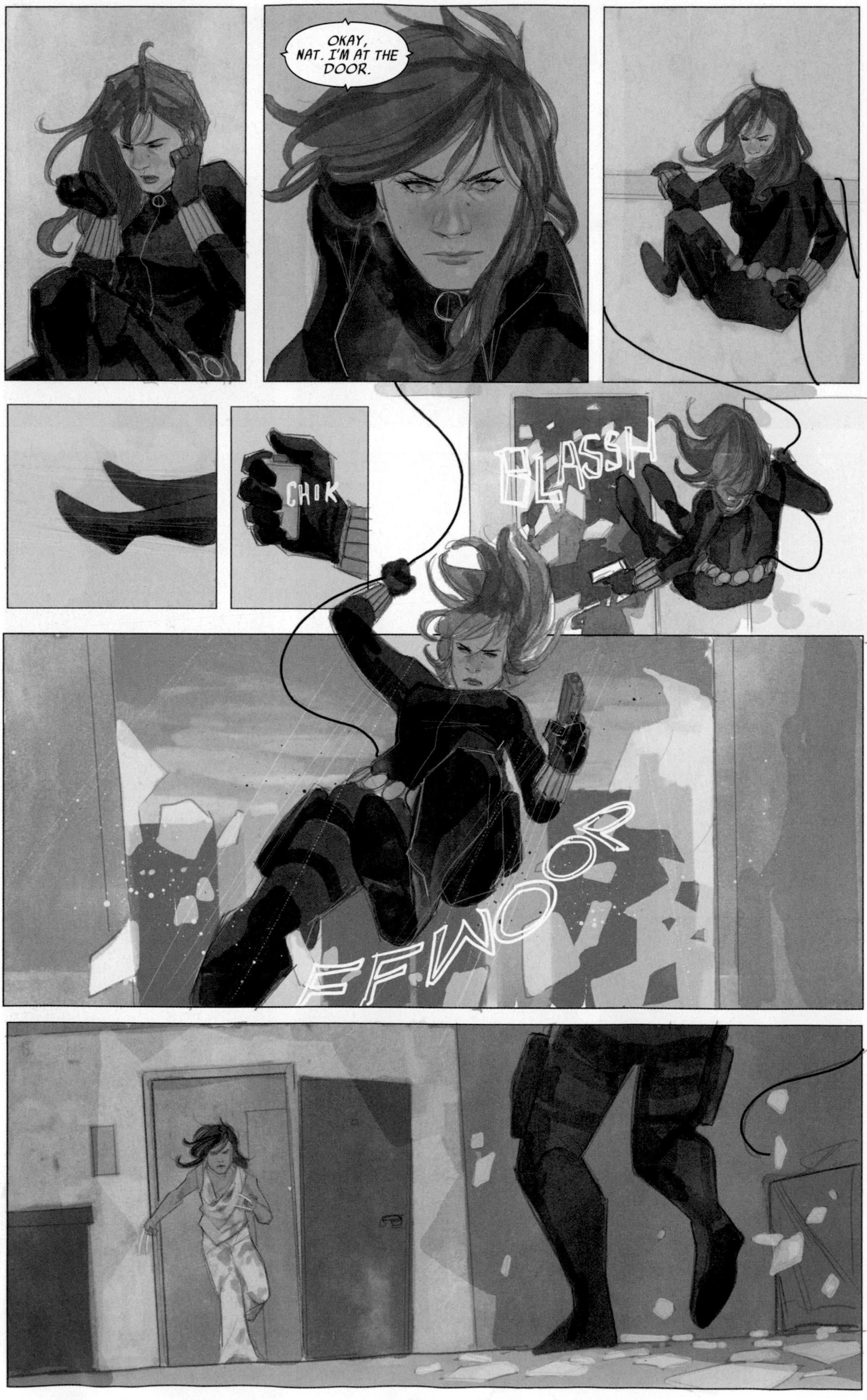
OKAY, NAT. I'M AT THE DOOR.
CHIK
BLASSH
FFWOOOR

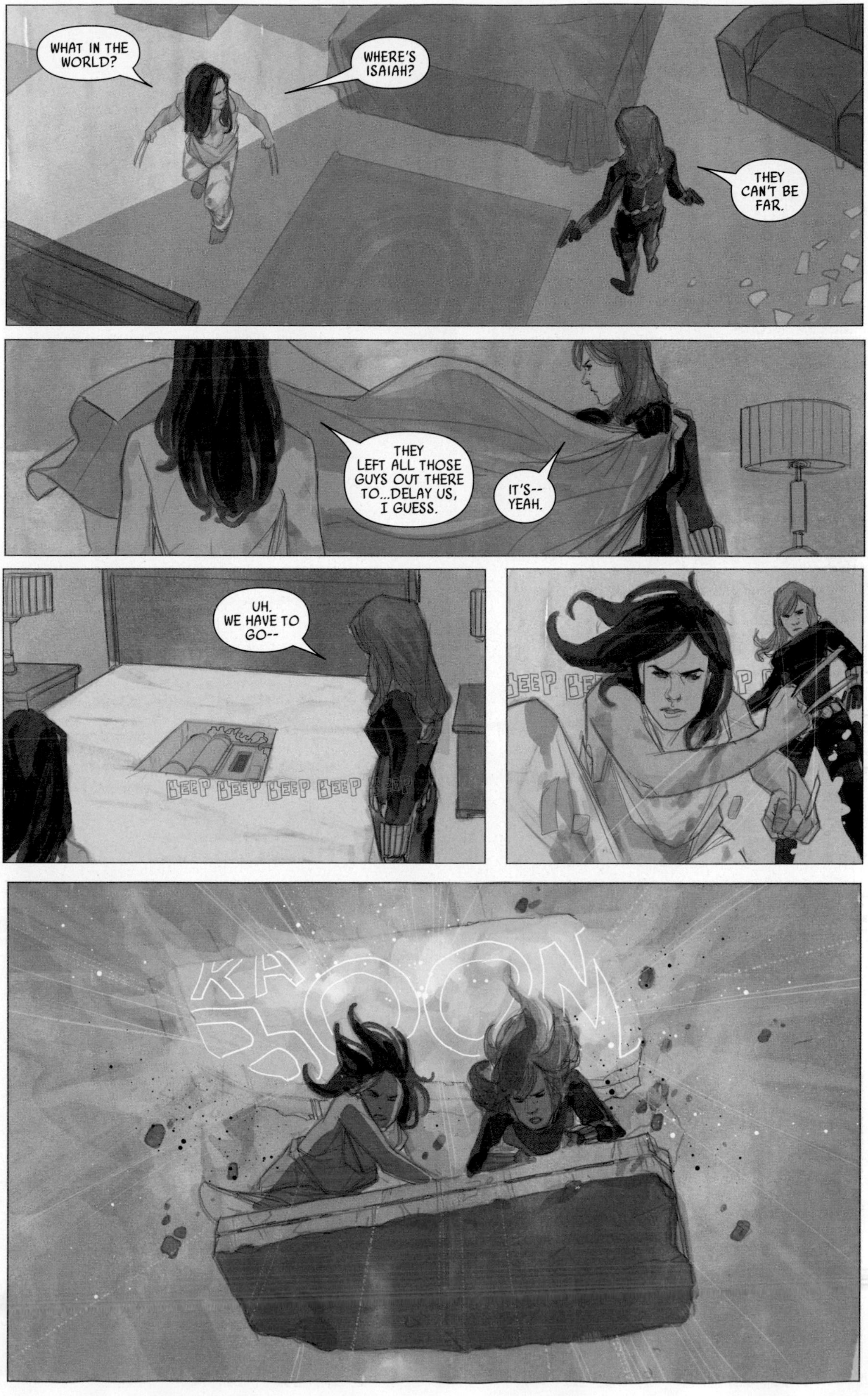
WHAT IN THE WORLD?
WHERE'S ISAIAH?
THEY CAN'T BE FAR.
THEY LEFT ALL THOSE GUYS OUT THERE TO...DELAY US, I GUESS.
IT'S-- YEAH.
UH. WE HAVE TO GO--
BEEP BEEP BEEP BEEP BEEP
KA BOOM

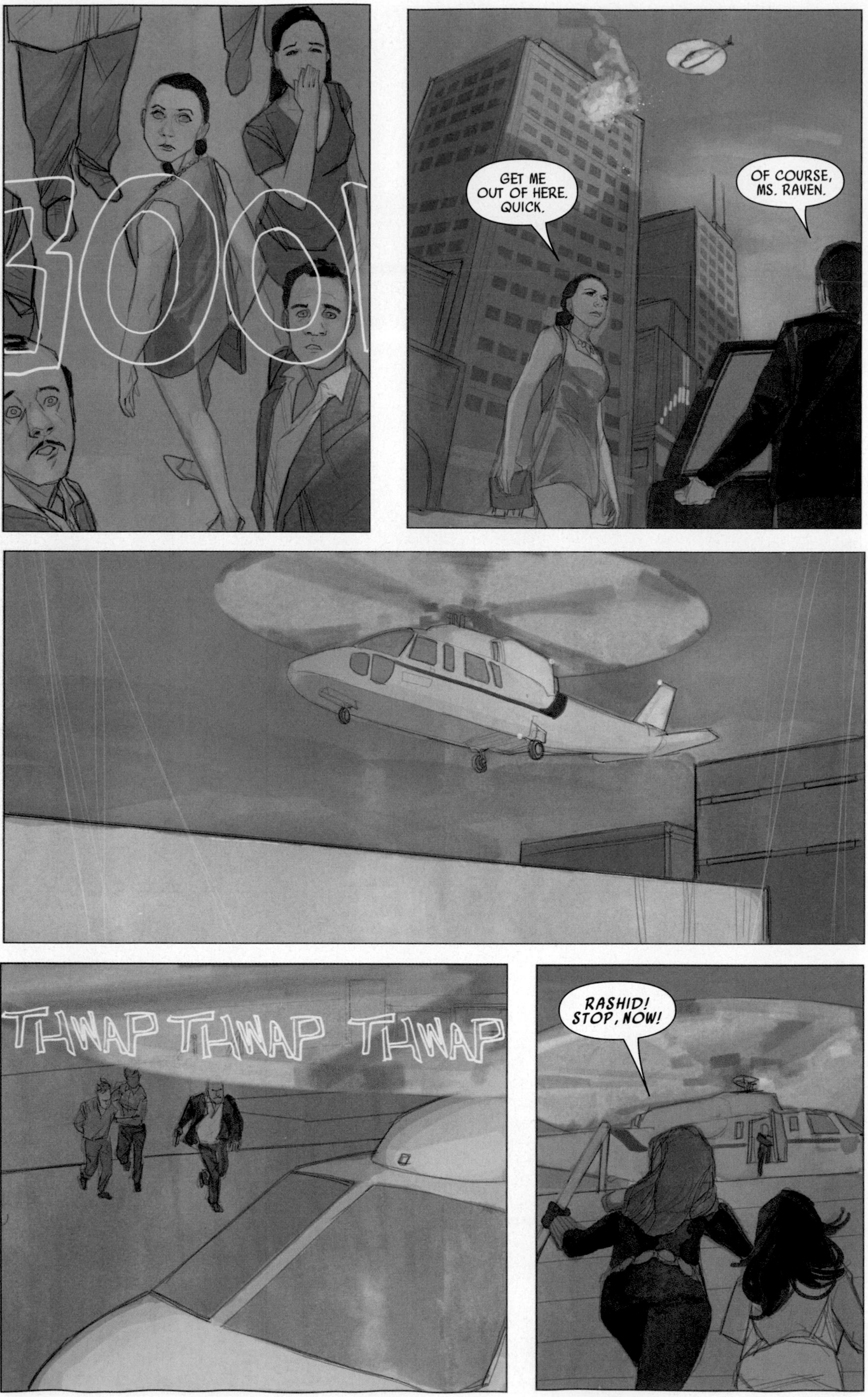
BOOM
GET ME OUT OF HERE. QUICK.
OF COURSE, MS. RAVEN.
THWAP THWAP THWAP
RASHID! STOP, NOW!

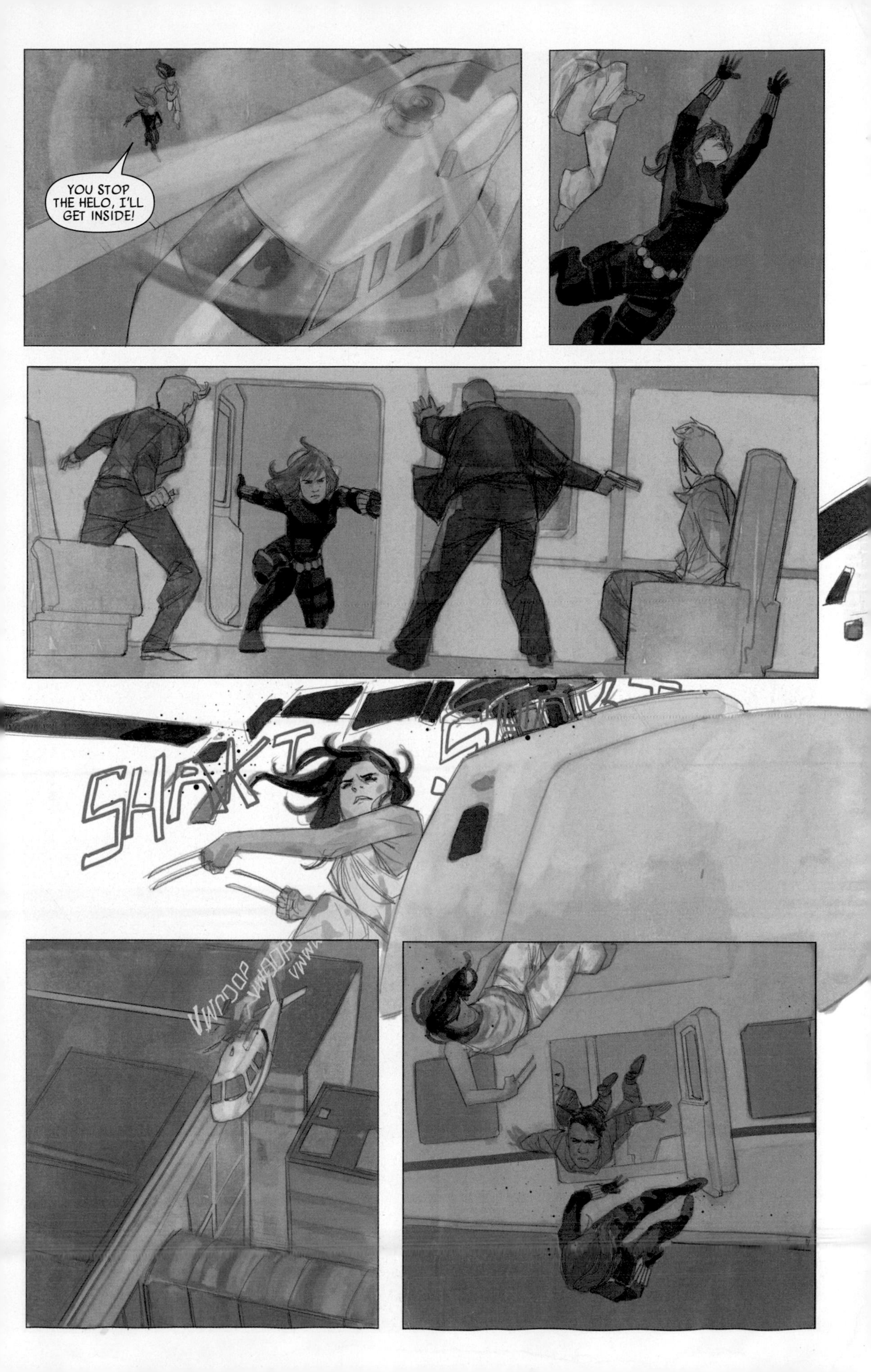
YOU STOP THE HELO, I'LL GET INSIDE!
SHAKT
VWOOP
VWOOP

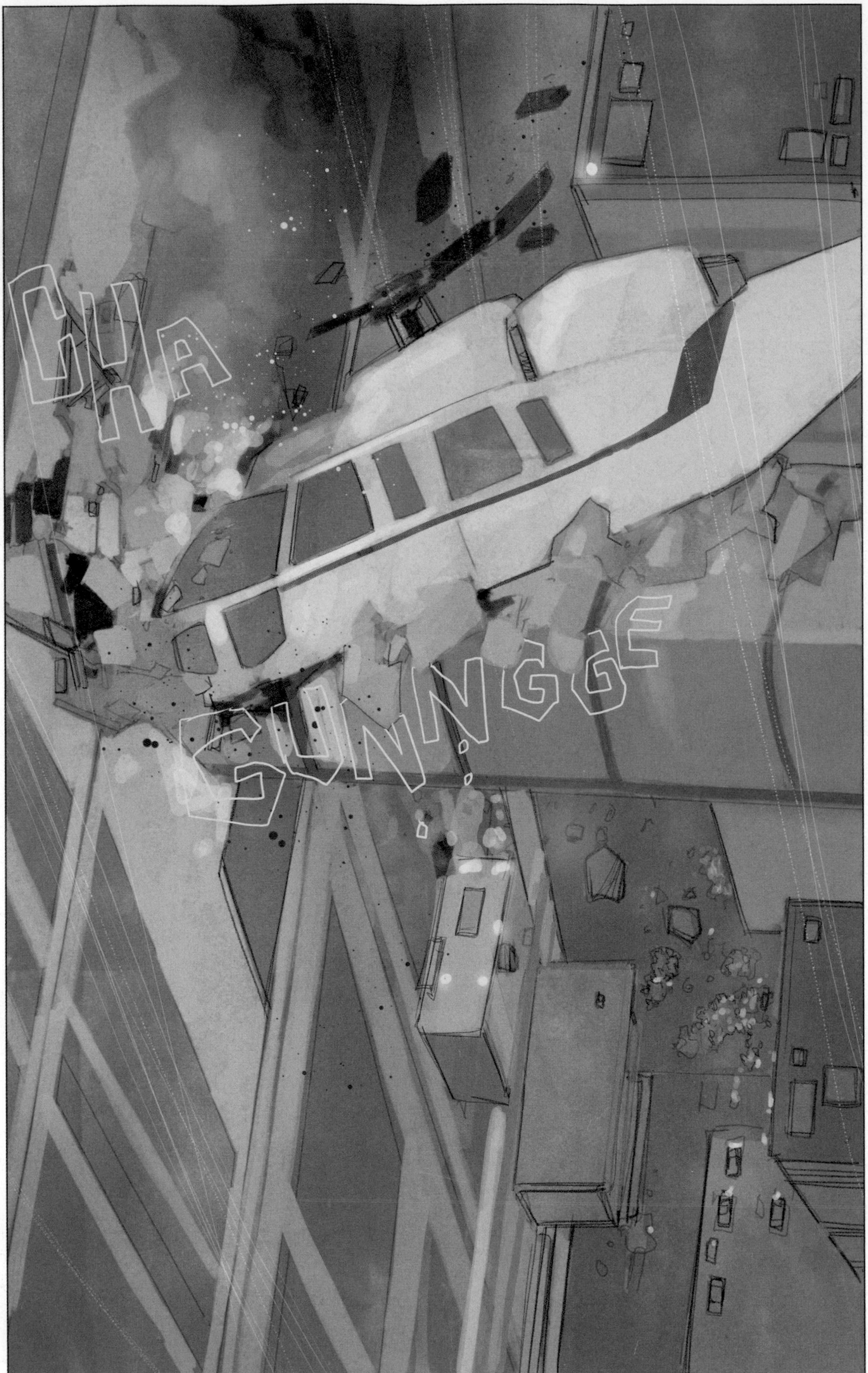
CHA
GUNNGGE

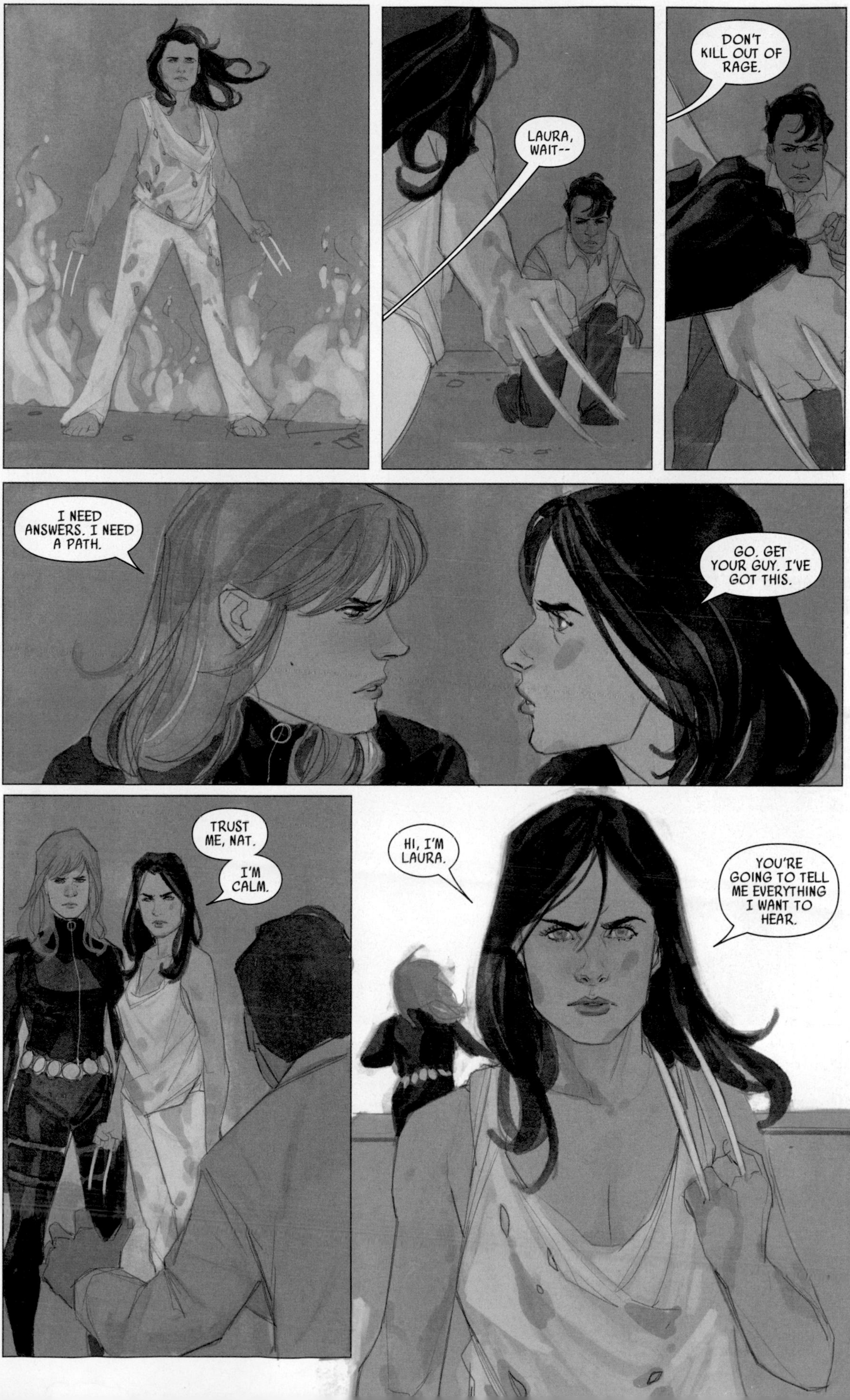
LAURA, WAIT--
DON'T KILL OUT OF RAGE.
I NEED ANSWERS. I NEED A PATH.
GO. GET YOUR GUY. I'VE GOT THIS.
TRUST ME, NAT.
I'M CALM.
HI, I'M LAURA.
YOU'RE GOING TO TELL ME EVERYTHING I WANT TO HEAR.

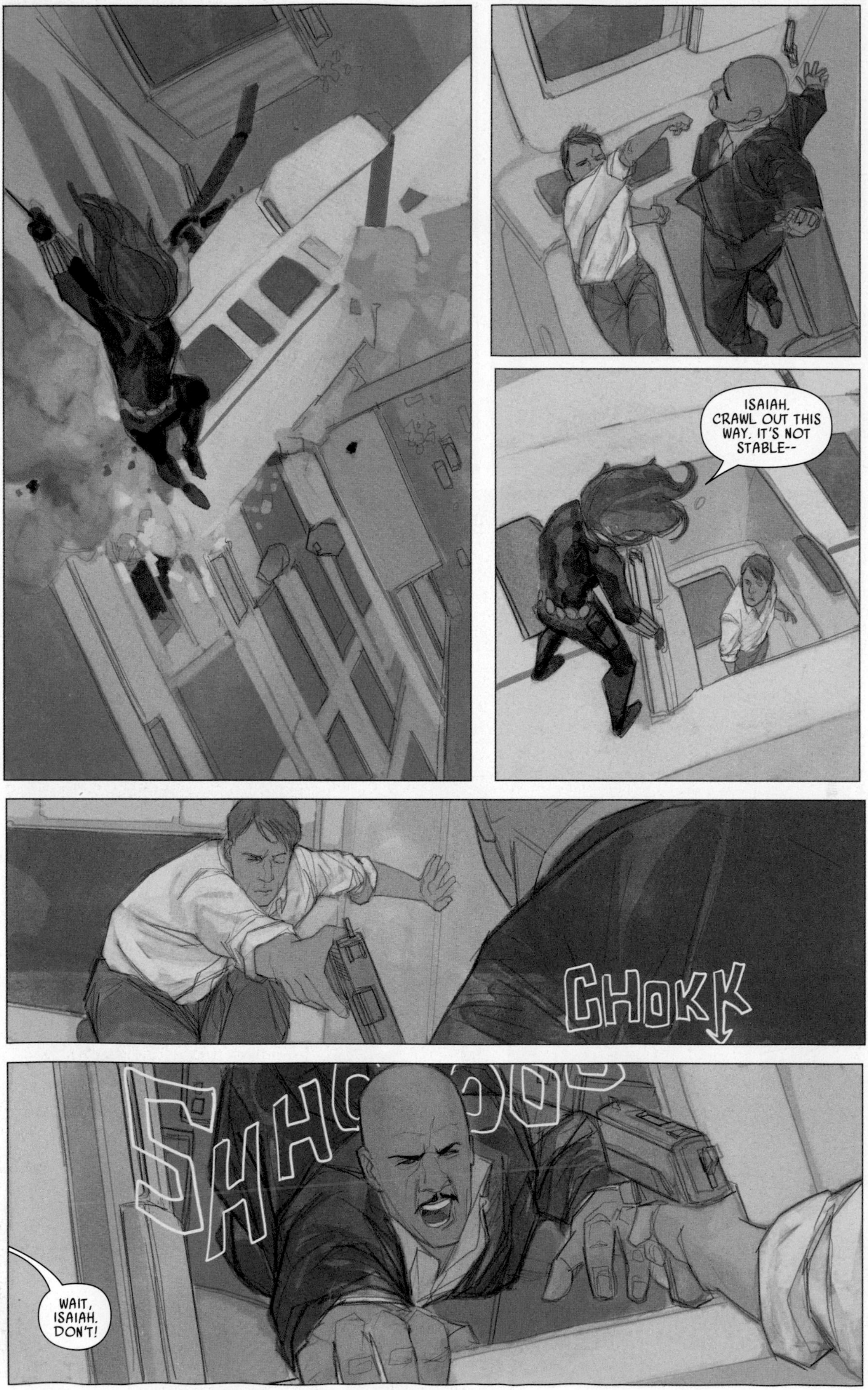

ISAIAH. CRAWL OUT THIS WAY. IT'S NOT STABLE--
CHOKK
WAIT, ISAIAH. DON'T!

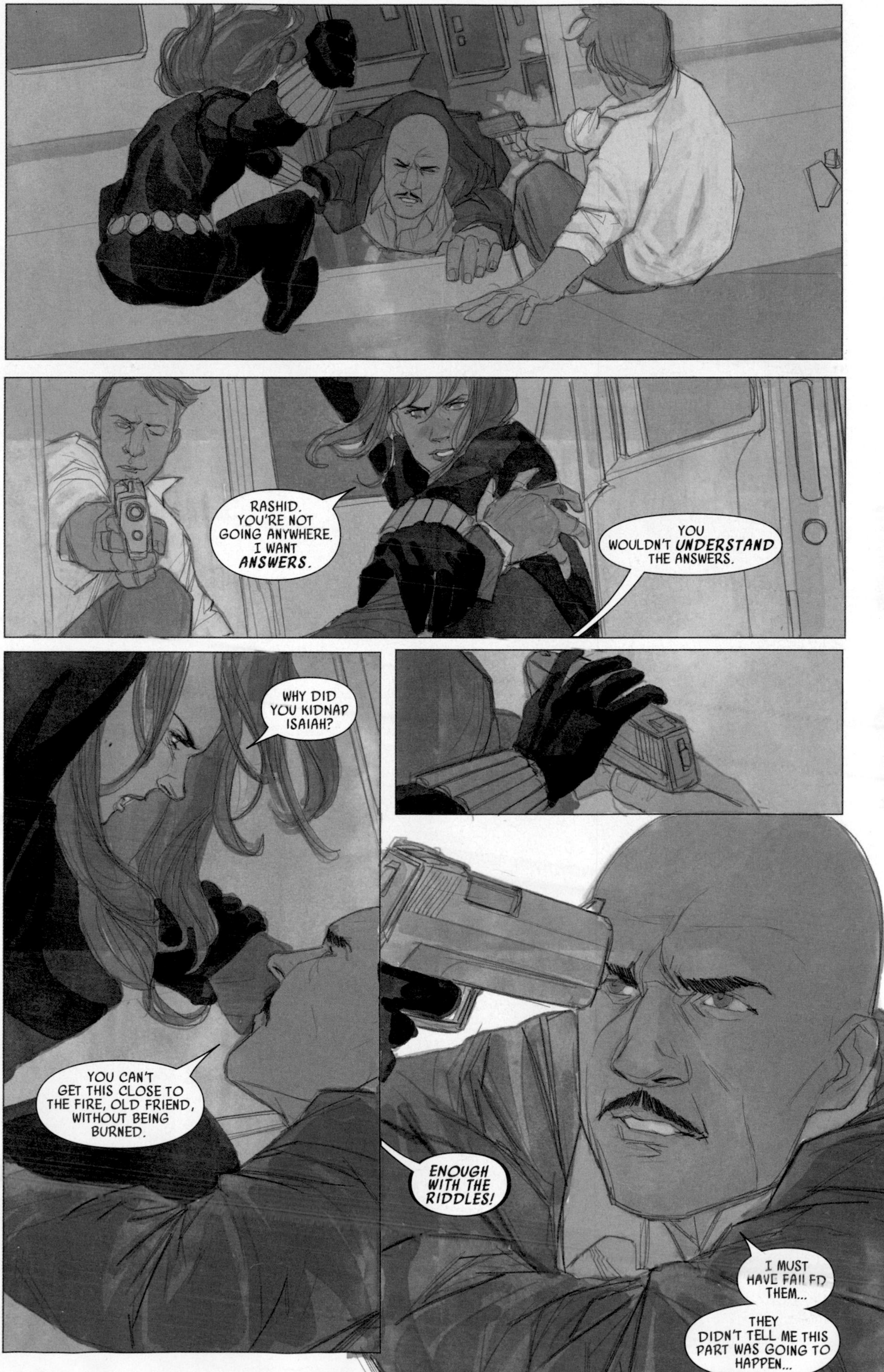
RASHID. YOU'RE NOT GOING ANYWHERE. I WANT ANSWERS.
YOU WOULDN'T UNDERSTAND THE ANSWERS.
WHY DID YOU KIDNAP ISAIAH?
YOU CAN'T GET THIS CLOSE TO THE FIRE, OLD FRIEND, WITHOUT BEING BURNED.
ENOUGH WITH THE RIDDLES!
I MUST HAVE FAILED THEM...
THEY DIDN'T TELL ME THIS PART WAS GOING TO HAPPEN...

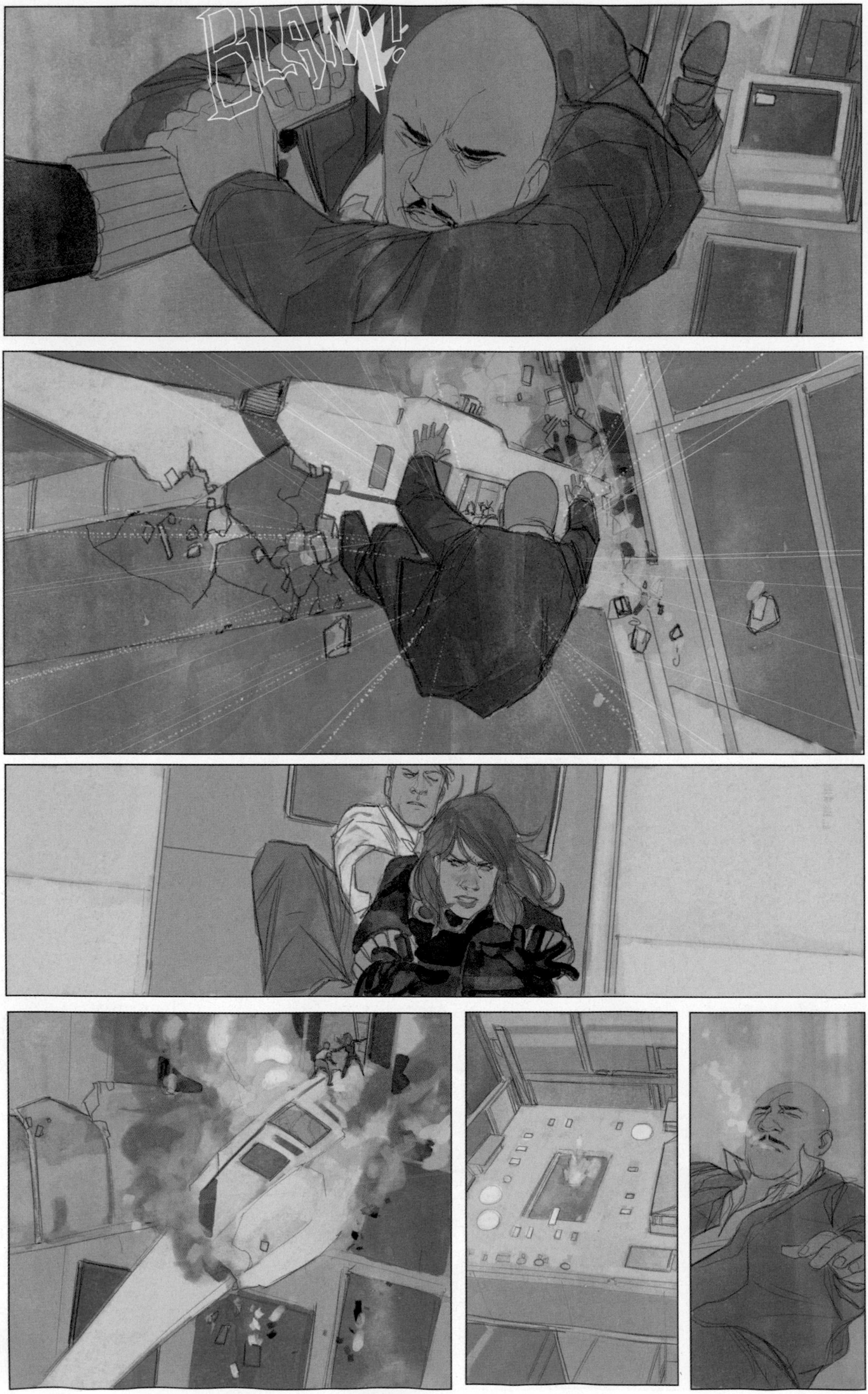
BLAM!

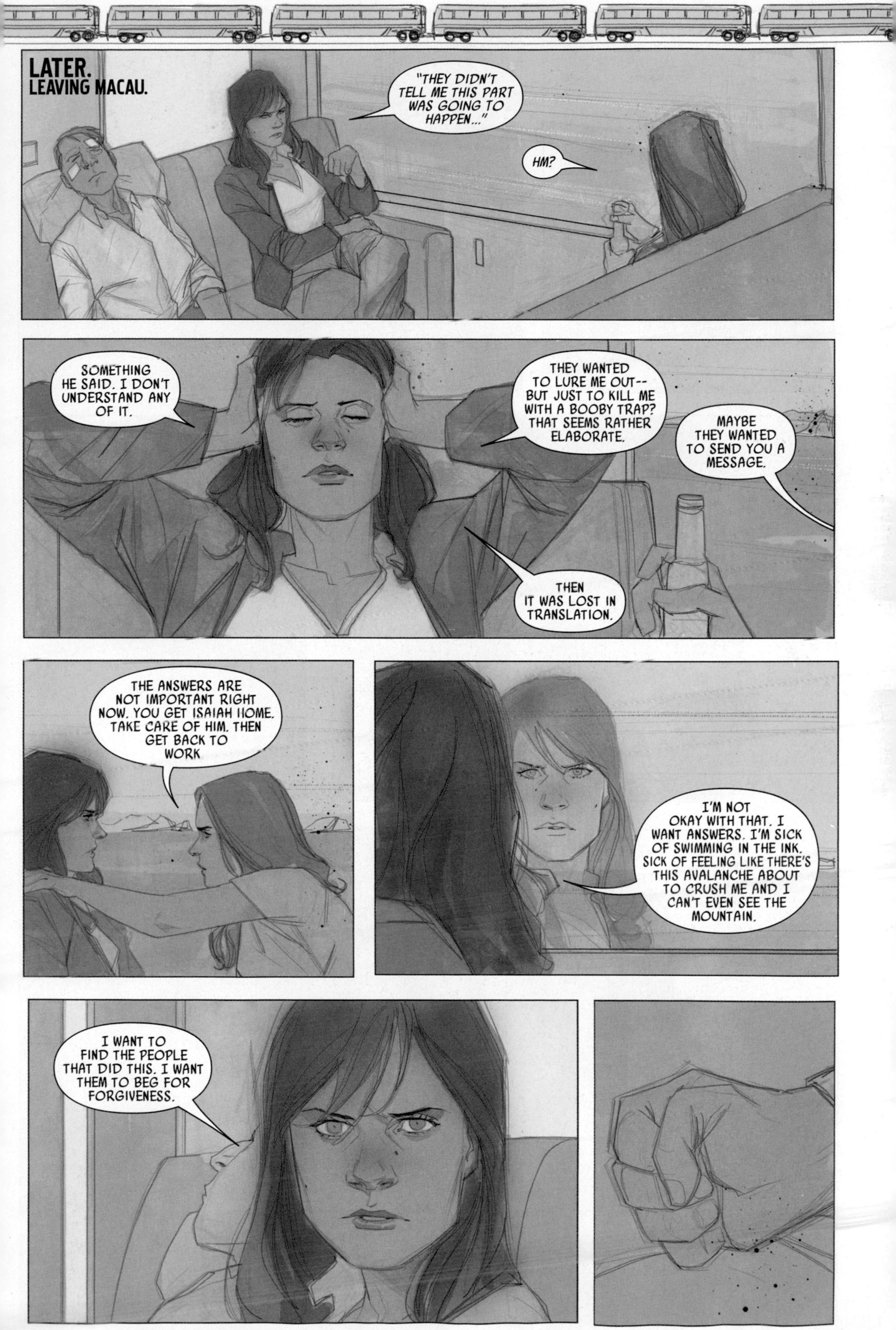
LATER. LEAVING MACAU.
"THEY DIDN'T TELL ME THIS PART WAS GOING TO HAPPEN..."
HM?
SOMETHING HE SAID. I DON'T UNDERSTAND ANY OF IT.
THEY WANTED TO LURE ME OUT-- BUT JUST TO KILL ME WITH A BOOBY TRAP? THAT SEEMS RATHER ELABORATE.
MAYBE THEY WANTED TO SEND YOU A MESSAGE.
THEN IT WAS LOST IN TRANSLATION.
THE ANSWERS ARE NOT IMPORTANT RIGHT NOW. YOU GET ISAIAH HOME. TAKE CARE OF HIM. THEN GET BACK TO WORK
I'M NOT OKAY WITH THAT. I WANT ANSWERS. I'M SICK OF SWIMMING IN THE INK. SICK OF FEELING LIKE THERE'S THIS AVALANCHE ABOUT TO CRUSH ME AND I CAN'T EVEN SEE THE MOUNTAIN.
I WANT TO FIND THE PEOPLE THAT DID THIS. I WANT THEM TO BEG FOR FORGIVENESS.

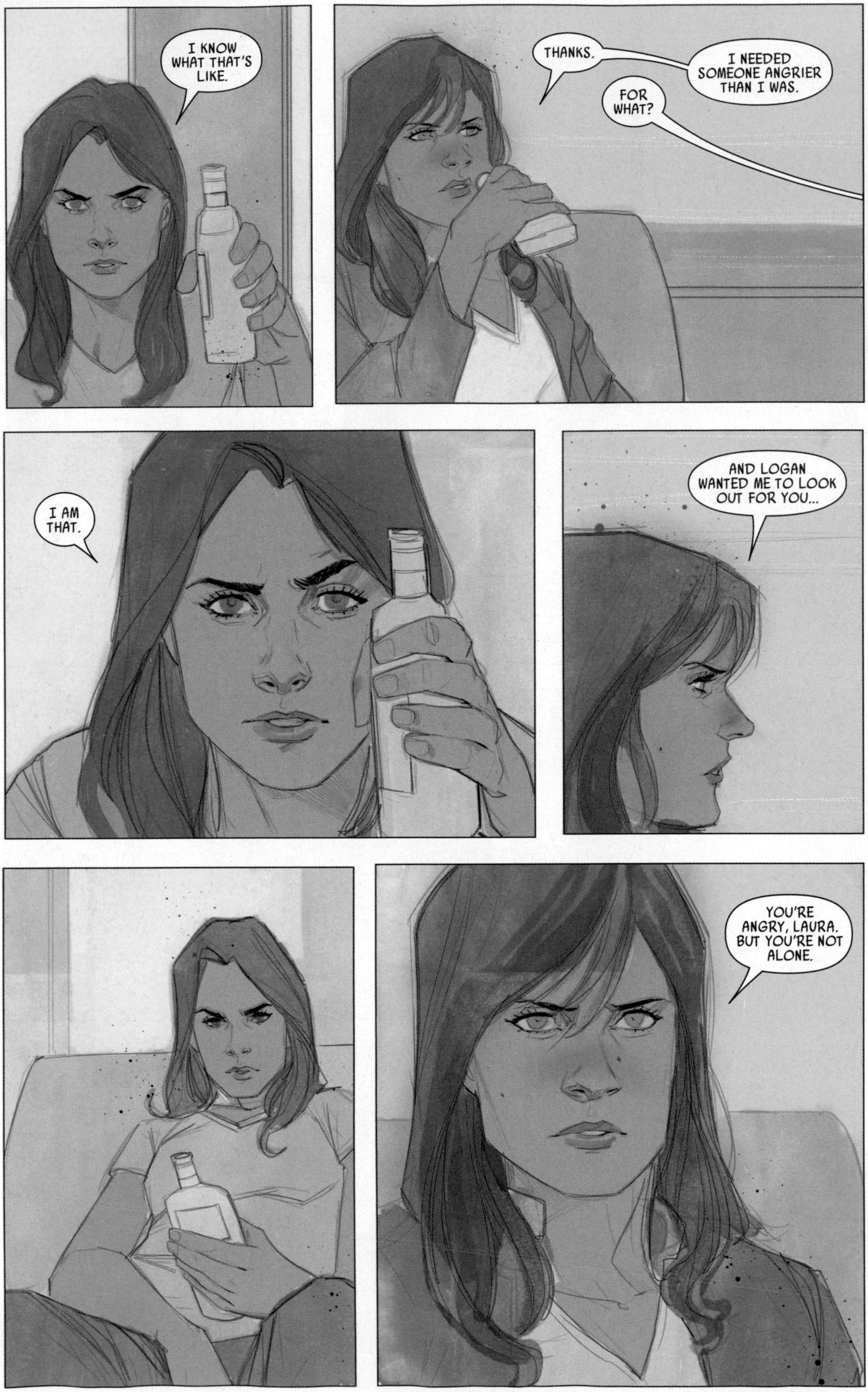
I KNOW WHAT THAT'S LIKE.
THANKS.
I NEEDED SOMEONE ANGRIER THAN I WAS.
FOR WHAT?
I AM THAT.
AND LOGAN WANTED ME TO LOOK OUT FOR YOU...
YOU'RE ANGRY, LAURA. BUT YOU'RE NOT ALONE.

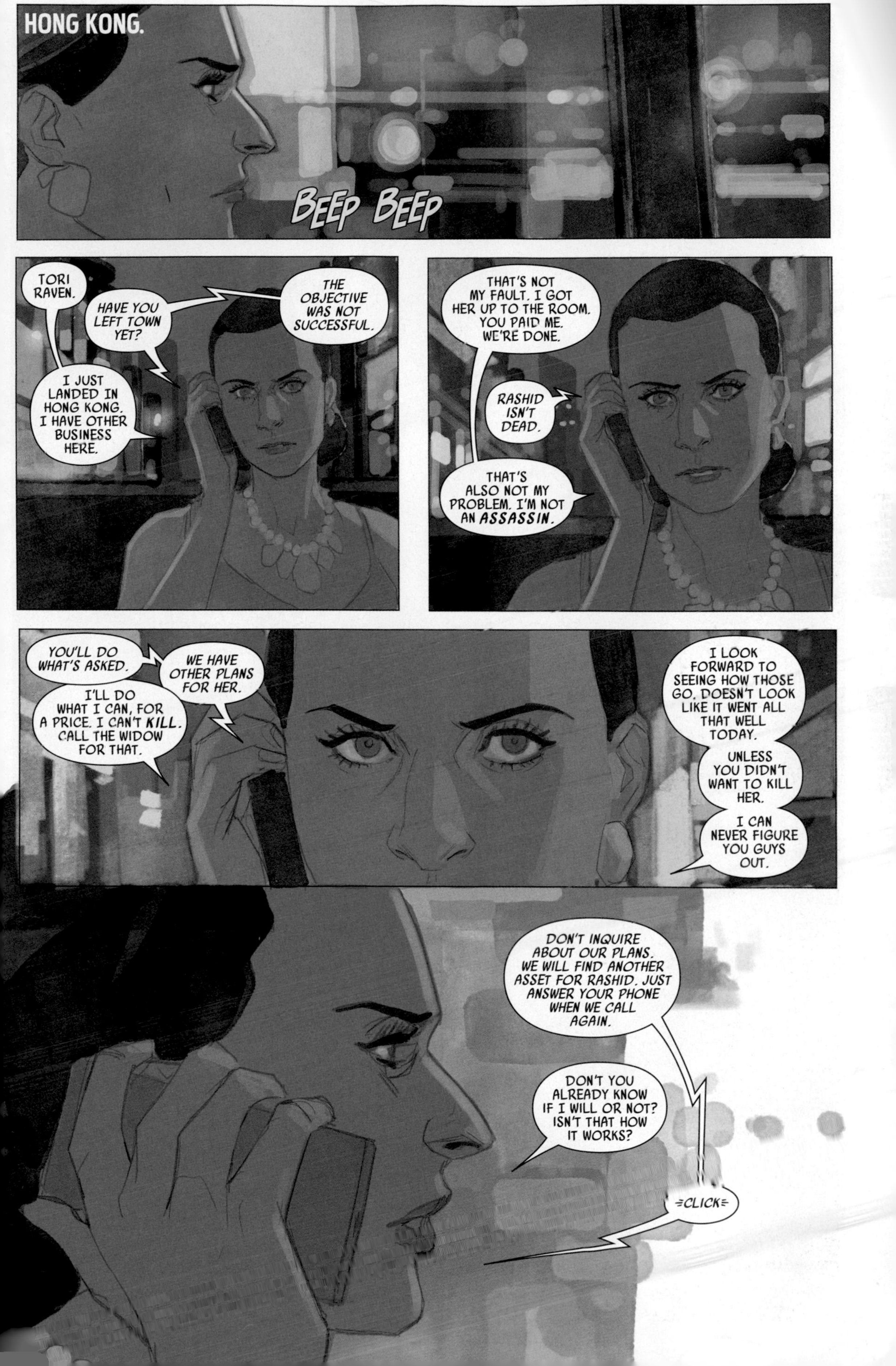
HONG KONG.
BEEP BEEP
TORI RAVEN.
HAVE YOU LEFT TOWN YET?
THE OBJECTIVE WAS NOT SUCCESSFUL.
I JUST LANDED IN HONG KONG. I HAVE OTHER BUSINESS HERE.
THAT'S NOT MY FAULT. I GOT HER UP TO THE ROOM. YOU PAID ME. WE'RE DONE.
RASHID ISN'T DEAD.
THAT'S ALSO NOT MY PROBLEM. I'M NOT AN ASSASSIN.
YOU'LL DO WHAT'S ASKED.
WE HAVE OTHER PLANS FOR HER.
I'LL DO WHAT I CAN, FOR A PRICE. I CAN'T KILL. CALL THE WIDOW FOR THAT.
I LOOK FORWARD TO SEEING HOW THOSE GO. DOESN'T LOOK LIKE IT WENT ALL THAT WELL TODAY.
UNLESS YOU DIDN'T WANT TO KILL HER.
I CAN NEVER FIGURE YOU GUYS OUT.
DON'T INQUIRE ABOUT OUR PLANS. WE WILL FIND ANOTHER ASSET FOR RASHID. JUST ANSWER YOUR PHONE WHEN WE CALL AGAIN.
DON'T YOU ALREADY KNOW IF I WILL OR NOT? ISN'T THAT HOW IT WORKS?
CLICK

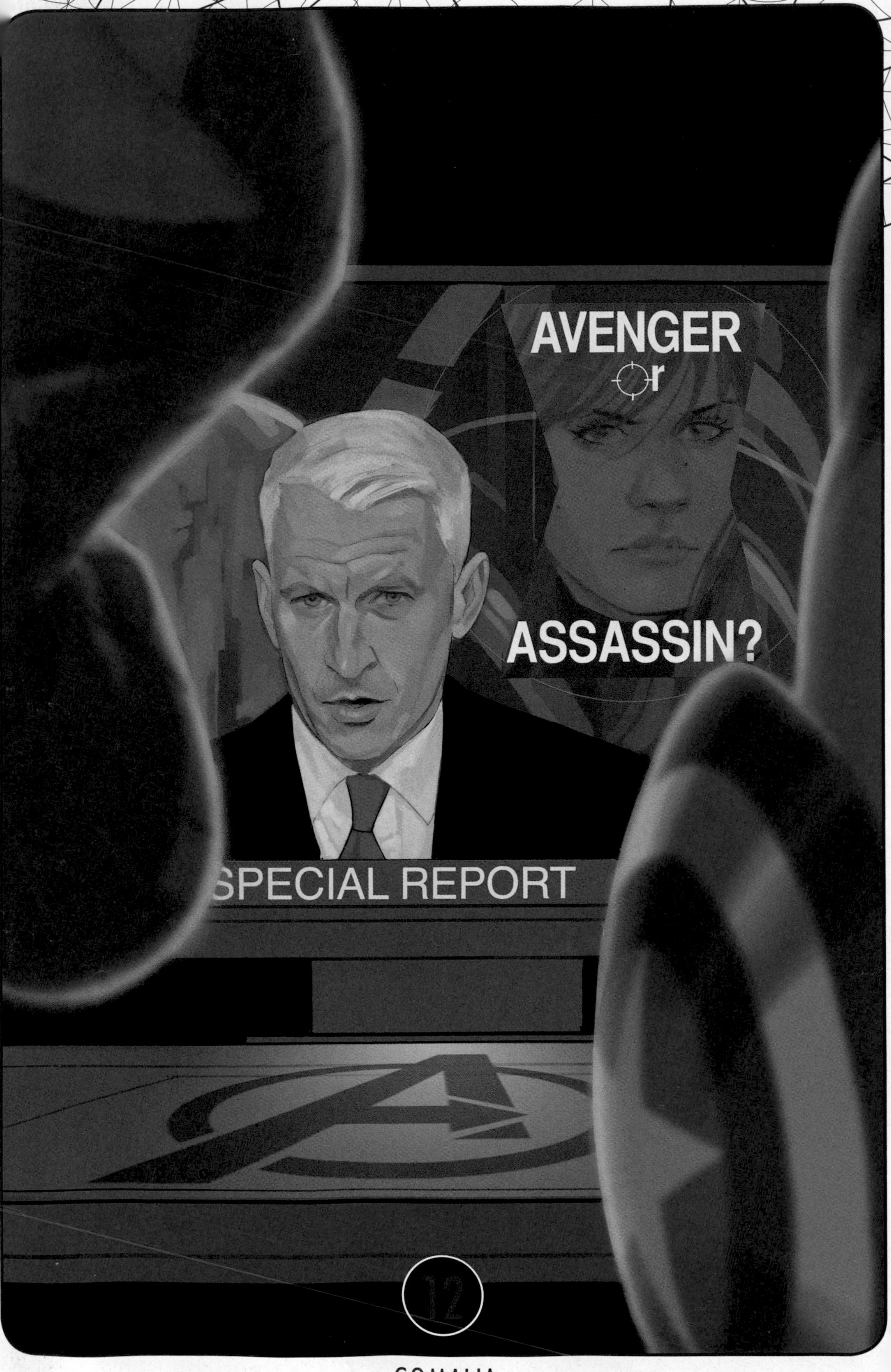
AVENGER
Or
ASSASSIN?
SPECIAL REPORT

SOMALIA

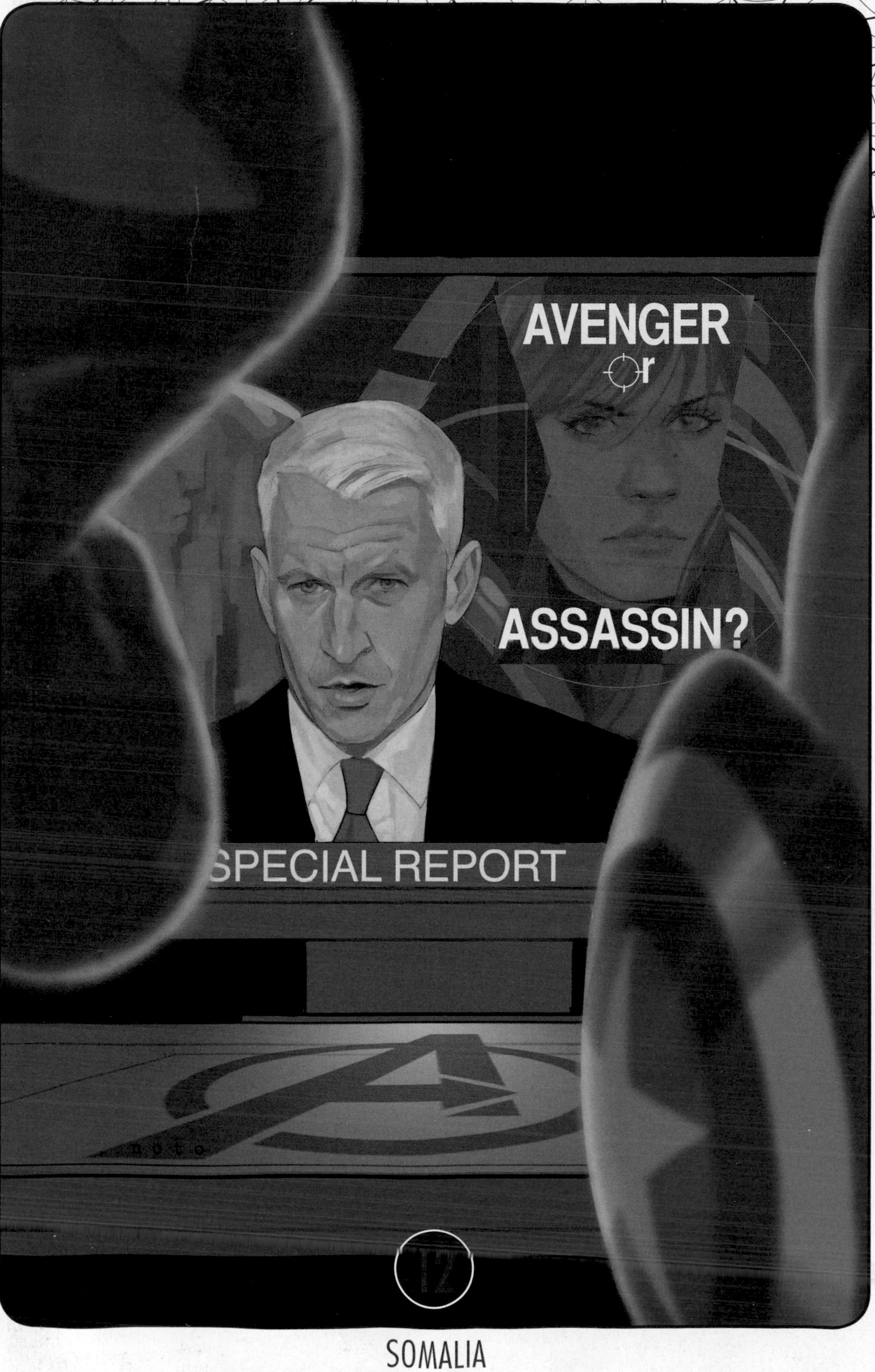
AVENGER
r
ASSASSIN?
SPECIAL REPORT
12

SOMALIA

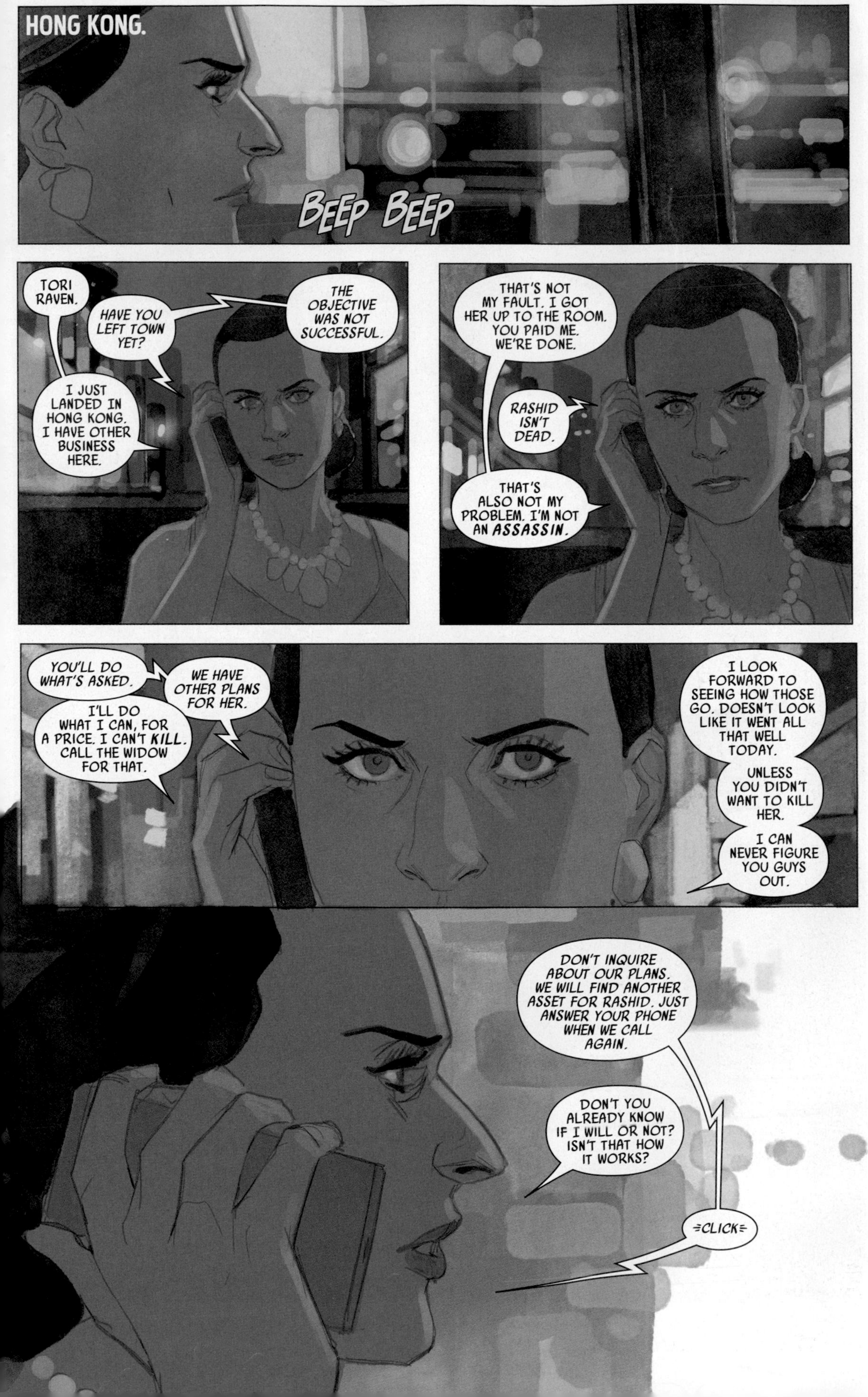
HONG KONG.
BEEP BEEP
TORI RAVEN.
HAVE YOU LEFT TOWN YET?
THE OBJECTIVE WAS NOT SUCCESSFUL.
I JUST LANDED IN HONG KONG. I HAVE OTHER BUSINESS HERE.
THAT'S NOT MY FAULT. I GOT HER UP TO THE ROOM. YOU PAID ME. WE'RE DONE.
RASHID ISN'T DEAD.
THAT'S ALSO NOT MY PROBLEM. I'M NOT AN ASSASSIN.
YOU'LL DO WHAT'S ASKED.
WE HAVE OTHER PLANS FOR HER.
I'LL DO WHAT I CAN, FOR A PRICE. I CAN'T KILL. CALL THE WIDOW FOR THAT.
I LOOK FORWARD TO SEEING HOW THOSE GO. DOESN'T LOOK LIKE IT WENT ALL THAT WELL TODAY.
UNLESS YOU DIDN'T WANT TO KILL HER.
I CAN NEVER FIGURE YOU GUYS OUT.
DON'T INQUIRE ABOUT OUR PLANS. WE WILL FIND ANOTHER ASSET FOR RASHID. JUST ANSWER YOUR PHONE WHEN WE CALL AGAIN.
DON'T YOU ALREADY KNOW IF I WILL OR NOT? ISN'T THAT HOW IT WORKS?
CLICK

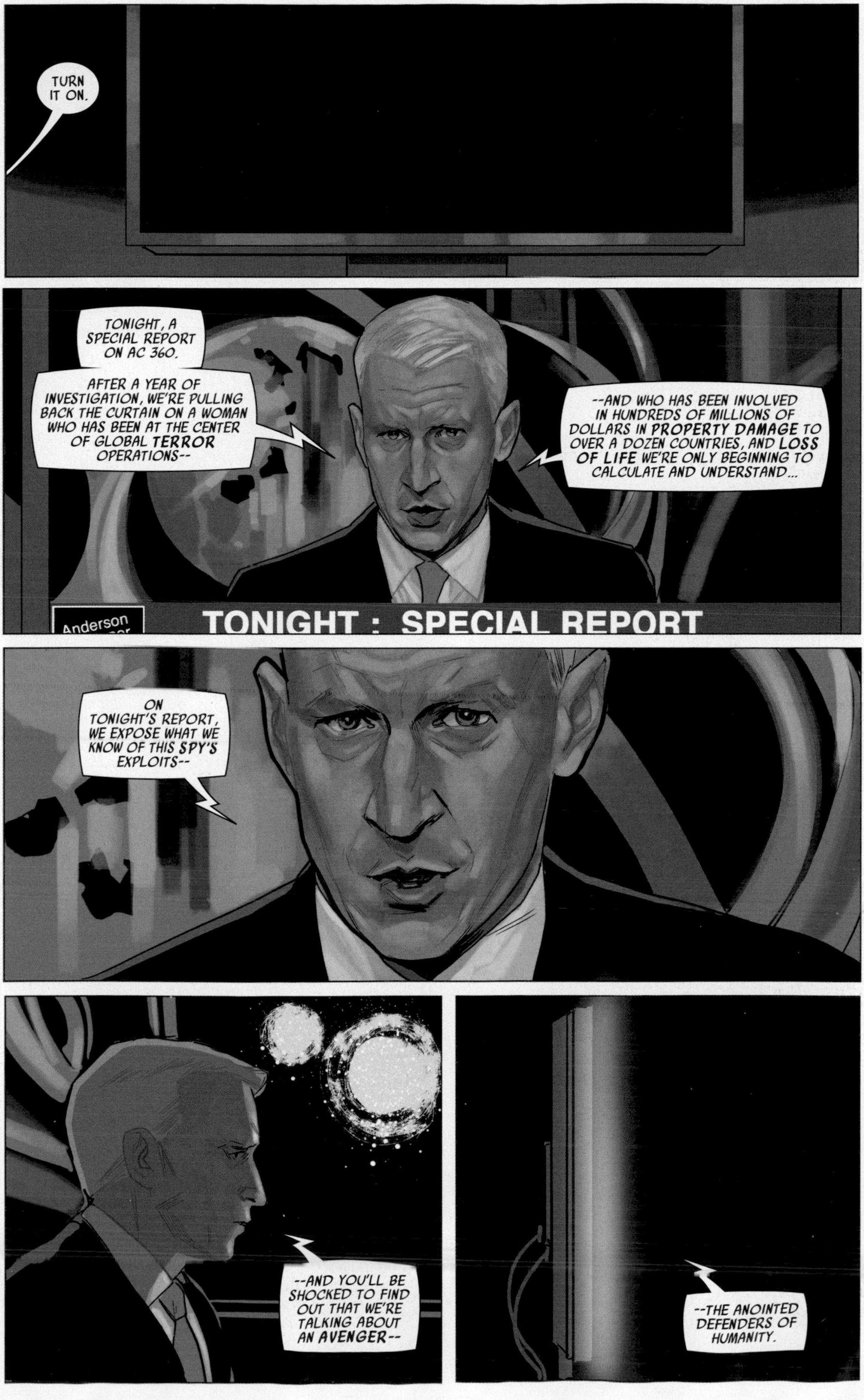
TURN IT ON.
TONIGHT, A SPECIAL REPORT ON AC 360.
AFTER A YEAR OF INVESTIGATION, WE'RE PULLING BACK THE CURTAIN ON A WOMAN WHO HAS BEEN AT THE CENTER OF GLOBAL TERROR OPERATIONS--
--AND WHO HAS BEEN INVOLVED IN HUNDREDS OF MILLIONS OF DOLLARS IN PROPERTY DAMAGE TO OVER A DOZEN COUNTRIES, AND LOSS OF LIFE WE'RE ONLY BEGINNING TO CALCULATE AND UNDERSTAND...
Anderson
TONIGHT : SPECIAL REPORT
ON TONIGHT'S REPORT, WE EXPOSE WHAT WE KNOW OF THIS SPY'S EXPLOITS--
--AND YOU'LL BE SHOCKED TO FIND OUT THAT WE'RE TALKING ABOUT AN AVENGER--
--THE ANOINTED DEFENDERS OF HUMANITY.

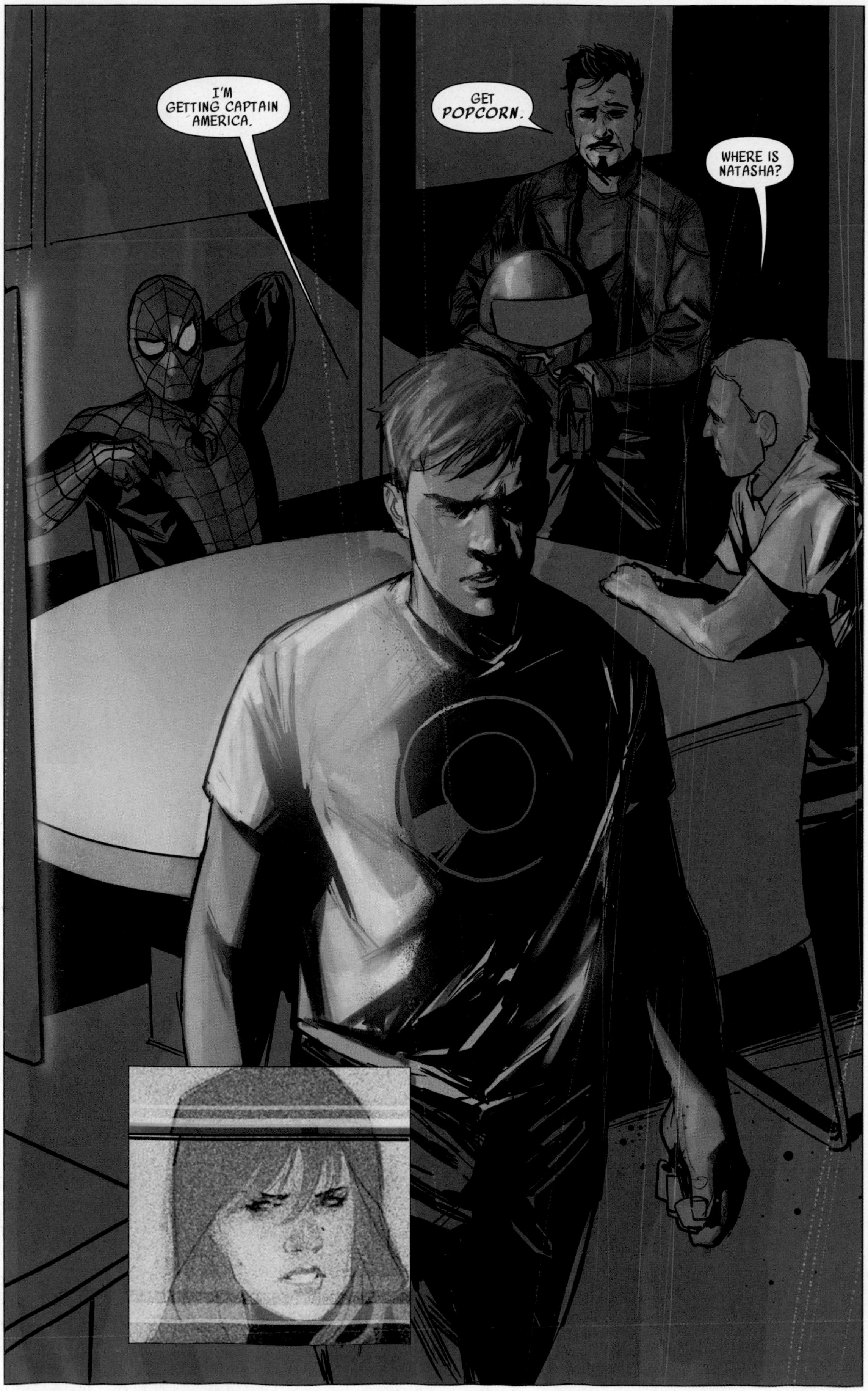
I'M GETTING CAPTAIN AMERICA.
GET POPCORN.
WHERE IS NATASHA?

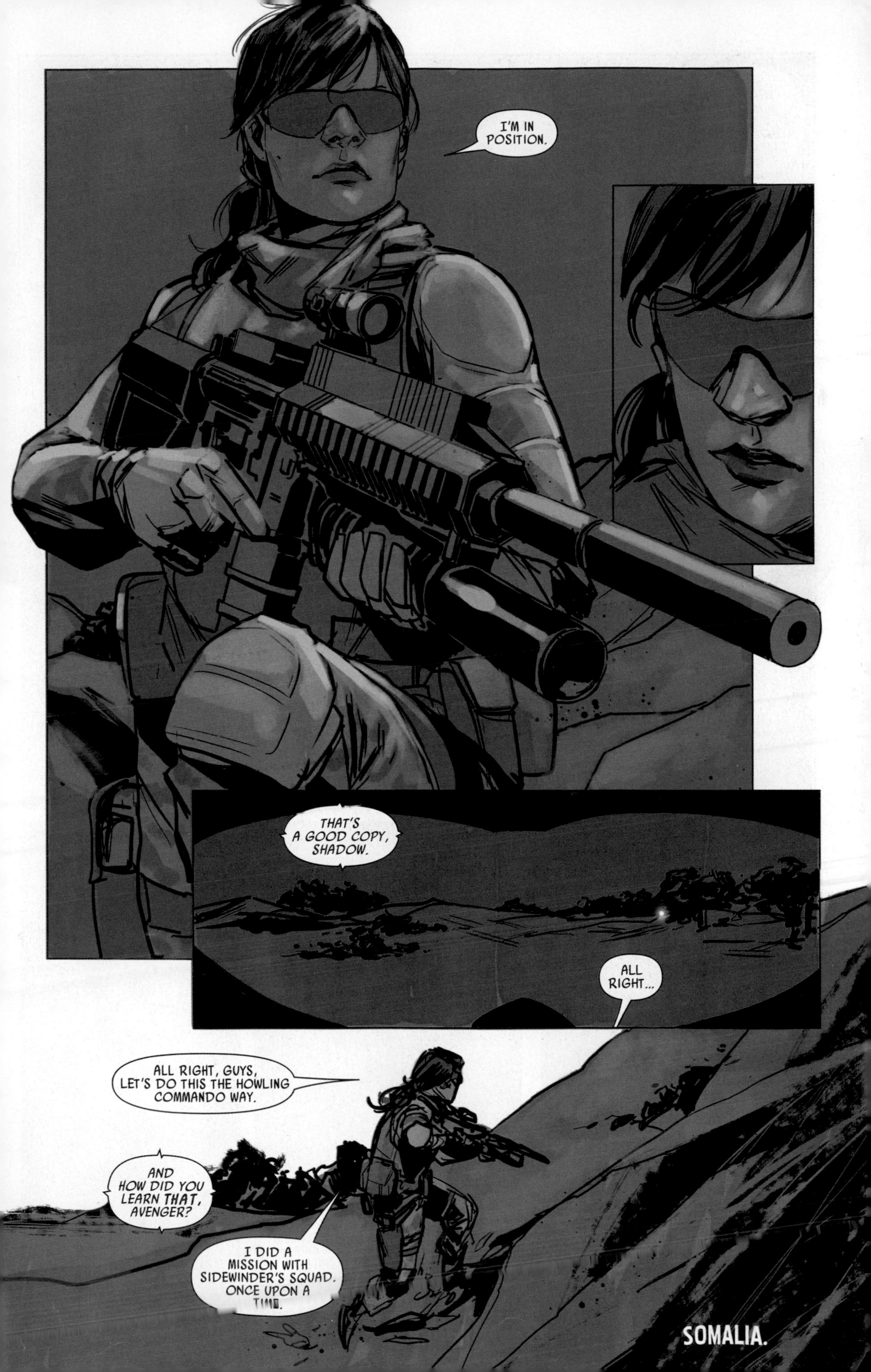
I'M IN POSITION.
THAT'S A GOOD COPY, SHADOW.
ALL RIGHT...
ALL RIGHT, GUYS, LET'S DO THIS THE HOWLING COMMANDO WAY.
AND HOW DID YOU LEARN THAT, AVENGER?
I DID A MISSION WITH SIDEWINDER'S SQUAD. ONCE UPON A TIME.
SOMALIA.

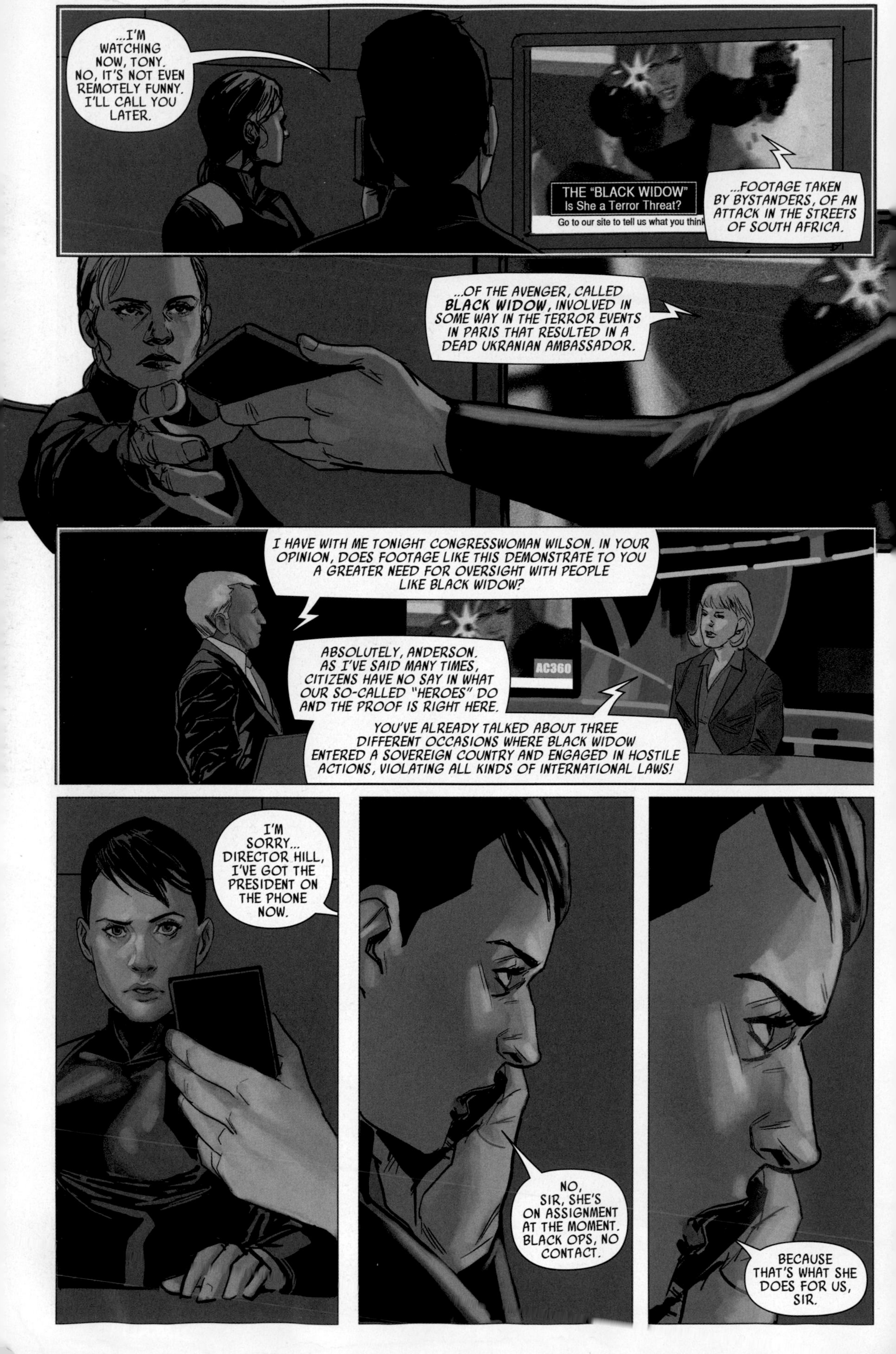
...I'M WATCHING NOW, TONY. NO, IT'S NOT EVEN REMOTELY FUNNY. I'LL CALL YOU LATER.
THE "BLACK WIDOW" Is She a Terror Threat?
Go to our site to tell us what you think
...FOOTAGE TAKEN BY BYSTANDERS, OF AN ATTACK IN THE STREETS OF SOUTH AFRICA.
...OF THE AVENGER, CALLED BLACK WIDOW, INVOLVED IN SOME WAY IN THE TERROR EVENTS IN PARIS THAT RESULTED IN A DEAD UKRANIAN AMBASSADOR.
I HAVE WITH ME TONIGHT CONGRESSWOMAN WILSON. IN YOUR OPINION, DOES FOOTAGE LIKE THIS DEMONSTRATE TO YOU A GREATER NEED FOR OVERSIGHT WITH PEOPLE LIKE BLACK WIDOW?
AC360
ABSOLUTELY, ANDERSON. AS I'VE SAID MANY TIMES, CITIZENS HAVE NO SAY IN WHAT OUR SO-CALLED "HEROES" DO AND THE PROOF IS RIGHT HERE.
YOU'VE ALREADY TALKED ABOUT THREE DIFFERENT OCCASIONS WHERE BLACK WIDOW ENTERED A SOVEREIGN COUNTRY AND ENGAGED IN HOSTILE ACTIONS, VIOLATING ALL KINDS OF INTERNATIONAL LAWS!
I'M SORRY... DIRECTOR HILL, I'VE GOT THE PRESIDENT ON THE PHONE NOW.
NO, SIR, SHE'S ON ASSIGNMENT AT THE MOMENT. BLACK OPS, NO CONTACT.
BECAUSE THAT'S WHAT SHE DOES FOR US, SIR.

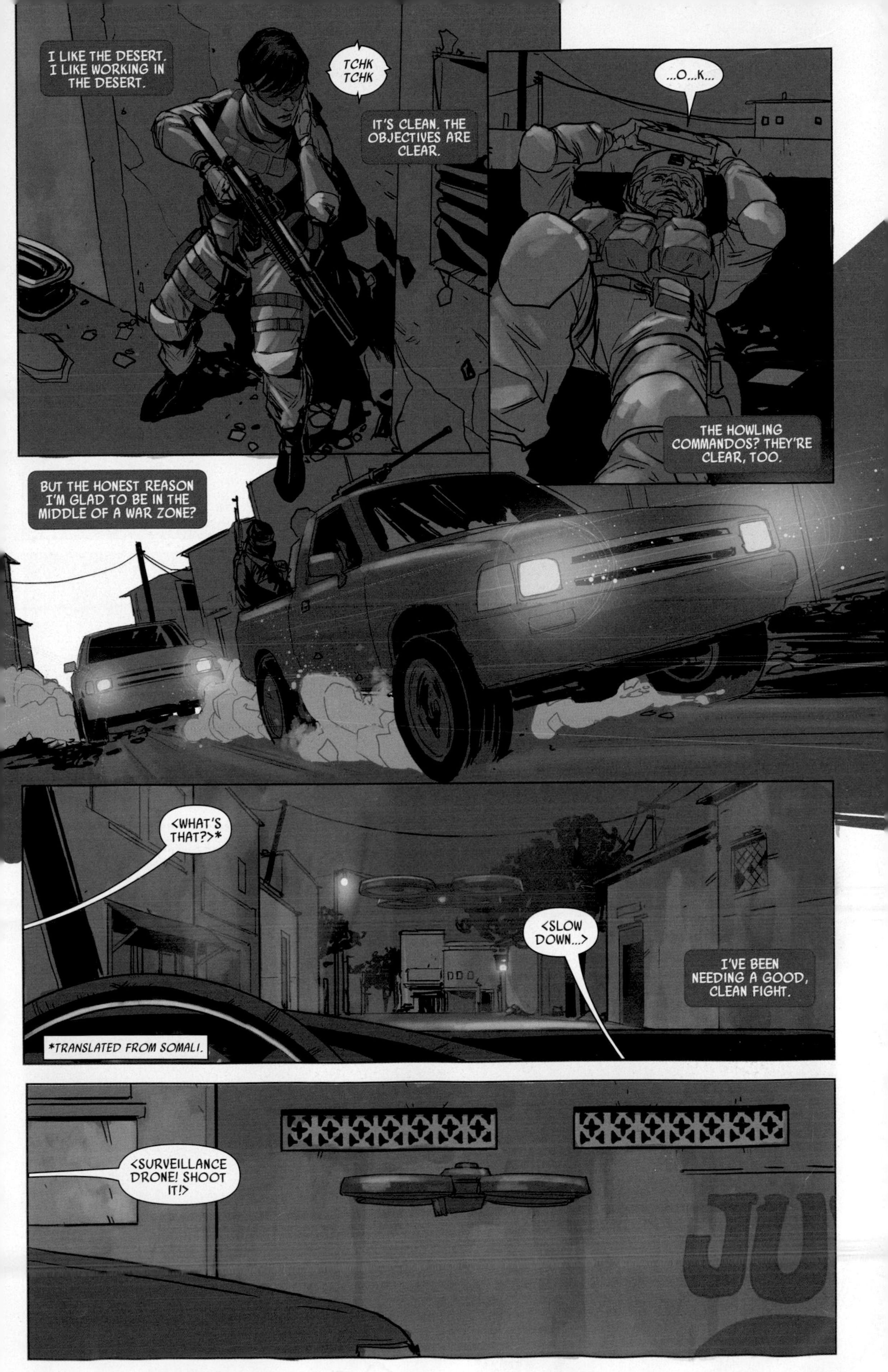
I LIKE THE DESERT. I LIKE WORKING IN THE DESERT.
TCHK TCHK
IT'S CLEAN. THE OBJECTIVES ARE CLEAR.
...O...K...
THE HOWLING COMMANDOS? THEY'RE CLEAR, TOO.
BUT THE HONEST REASON I'M GLAD TO BE IN THE MIDDLE OF A WAR ZONE?
<WHAT'S THAT?>*
<SLOW DOWN...>
I'VE BEEN NEEDING A GOOD, CLEAN FIGHT.
*TRANSLATED FROM SOMALI.
<SURVEILLANCE DRONE! SHOOT IT!>
JU

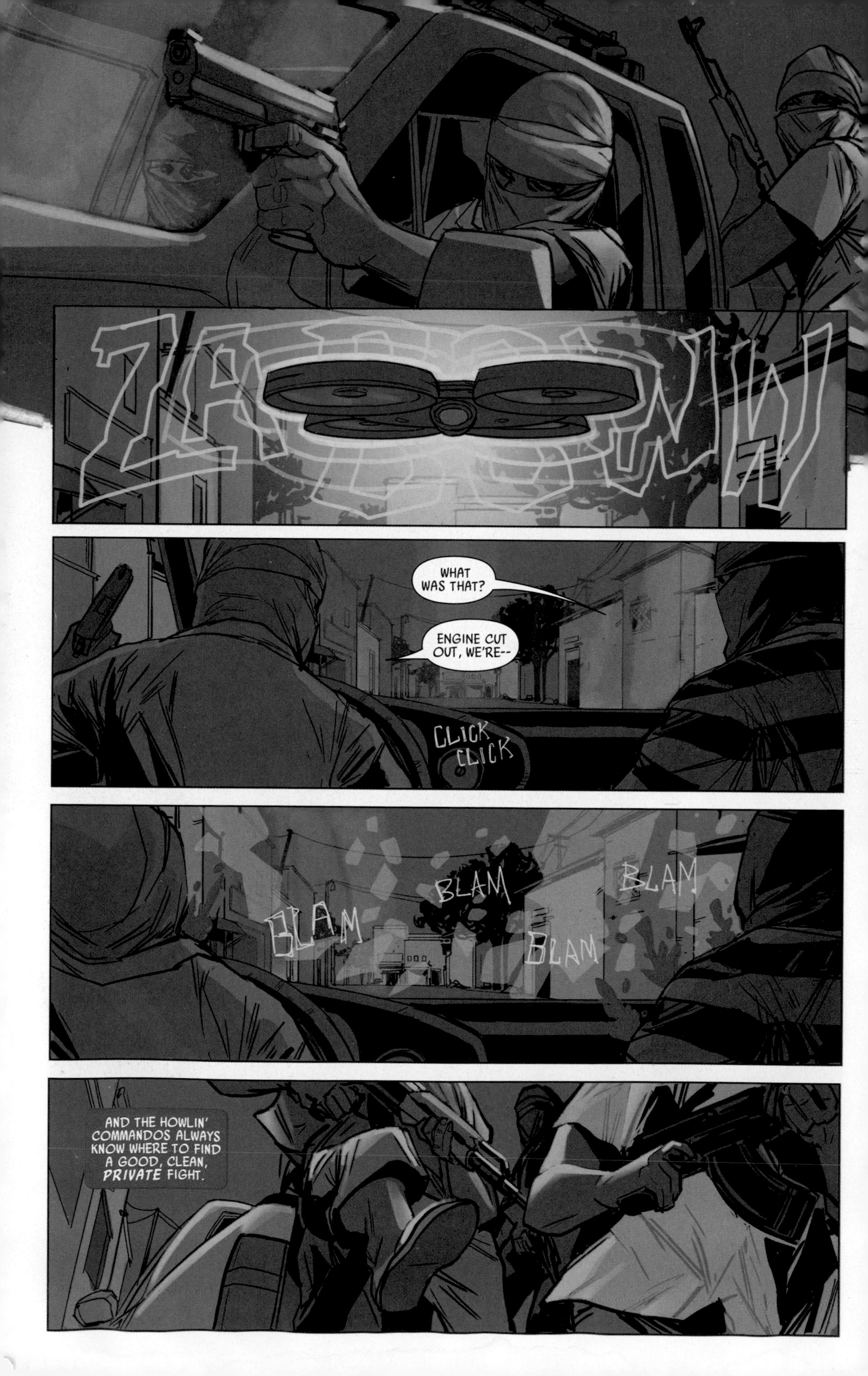
WHAT WAS THAT?
ENGINE CUT OUT, WE'RE--
CLICK CLICK
BLAM
BLAM
BLAM
BLAM
AND THE HOWLIN' COMMANDOS ALWAYS KNOW WHERE TO FIND A GOOD, CLEAN, *PRIVATE* FIGHT.

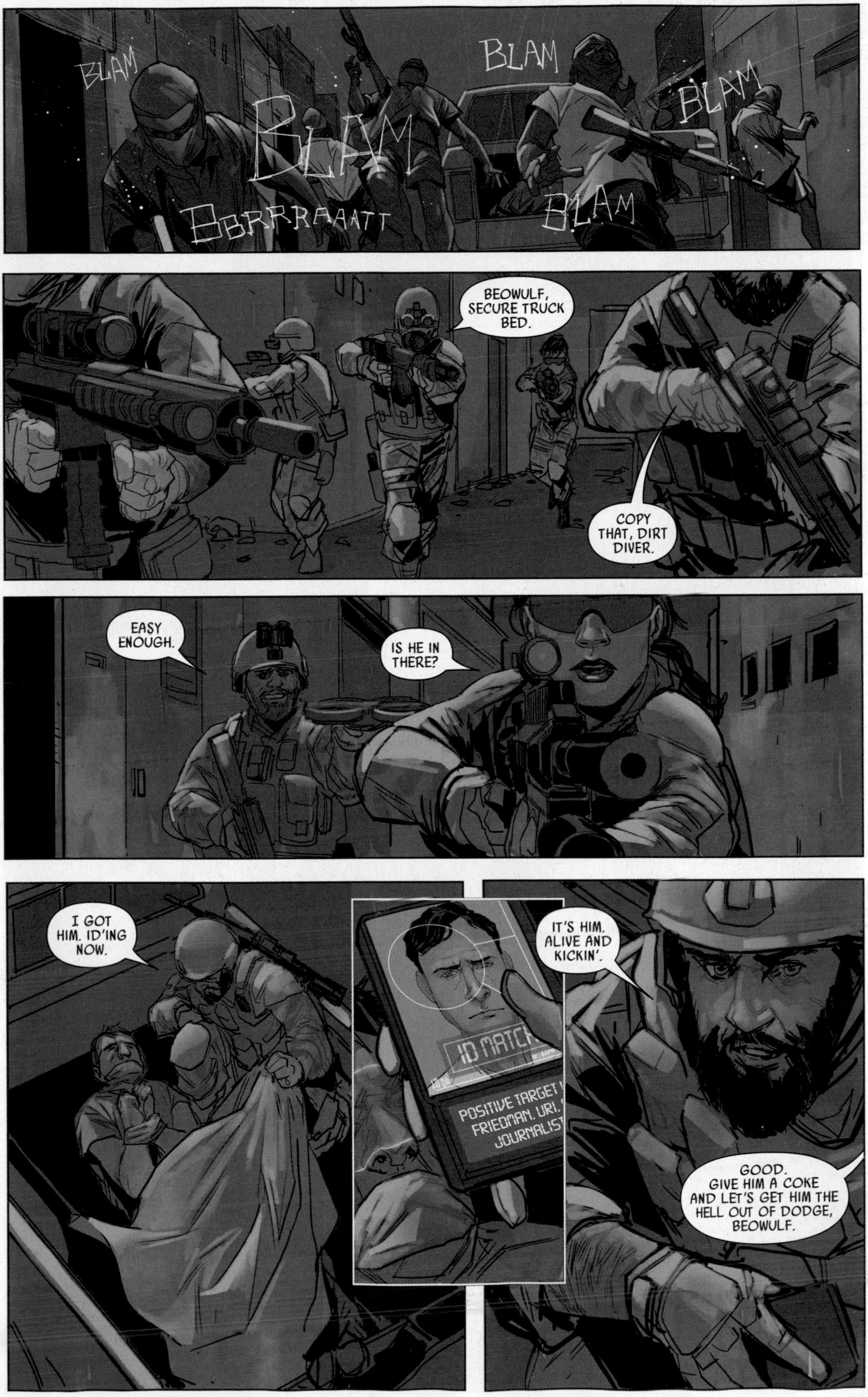
BLAM
BLAM
BLAM
BLAM
BBRRRAAATT
BLAM
BEOWULF, SECURE TRUCK BED.
COPY THAT, DIRT DIVER.
EASY ENOUGH.
IS HE IN THERE?
I GOT HIM. ID'ING NOW.
ID MATCH
POSITIVE TARGET
FRIEDMAN, URI
JOURNALIST
IT'S HIM. ALIVE AND KICKIN'.
GOOD. GIVE HIM A COKE AND LET'S GET HIM THE HELL OUT OF DODGE, BEOWULF.

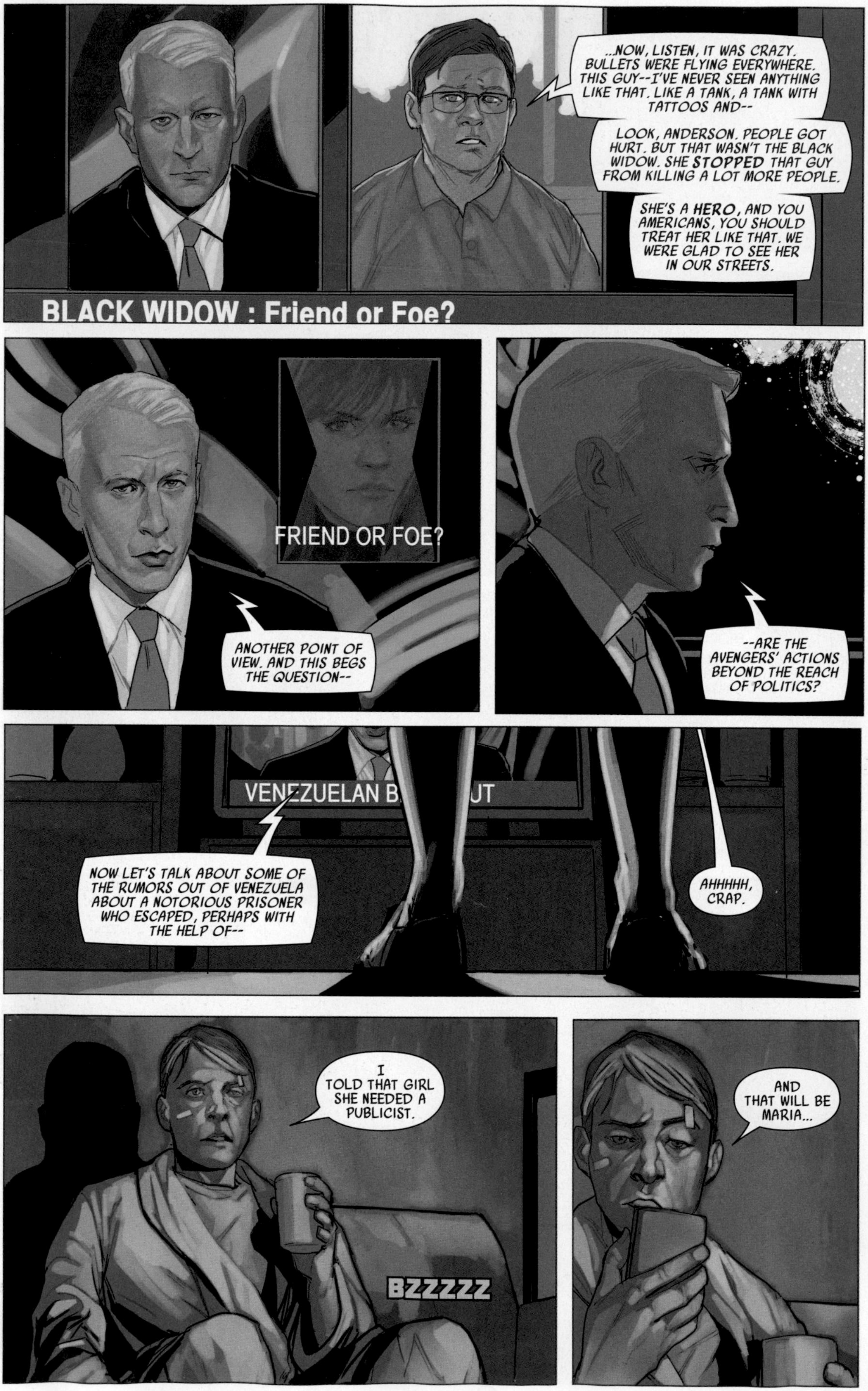
...NOW, LISTEN, IT WAS CRAZY. BULLETS WERE FLYING EVERYWHERE. THIS GUY--I'VE NEVER SEEN ANYTHING LIKE THAT. LIKE A TANK, A TANK WITH TATTOOS AND--
LOOK, ANDERSON. PEOPLE GOT HURT. BUT THAT WASN'T THE BLACK WIDOW. SHE STOPPED THAT GUY FROM KILLING A LOT MORE PEOPLE.
SHE'S A HERO, AND YOU AMERICANS, YOU SHOULD TREAT HER LIKE THAT. WE WERE GLAD TO SEE HER IN OUR STREETS.
BLACK WIDOW : Friend or Foe?
FRIEND OR FOE?
ANOTHER POINT OF VIEW. AND THIS BEGS THE QUESTION--
--ARE THE AVENGERS' ACTIONS BEYOND THE REACH OF POLITICS?
NOW LET'S TALK ABOUT SOME OF THE RUMORS OUT OF VENEZUELA ABOUT A NOTORIOUS PRISONER WHO ESCAPED, PERHAPS WITH THE HELP OF--
AHHHHH, CRAP.
I TOLD THAT GIRL SHE NEEDED A PUBLICIST.
BZZZZZ
AND THAT WILL BE MARIA...

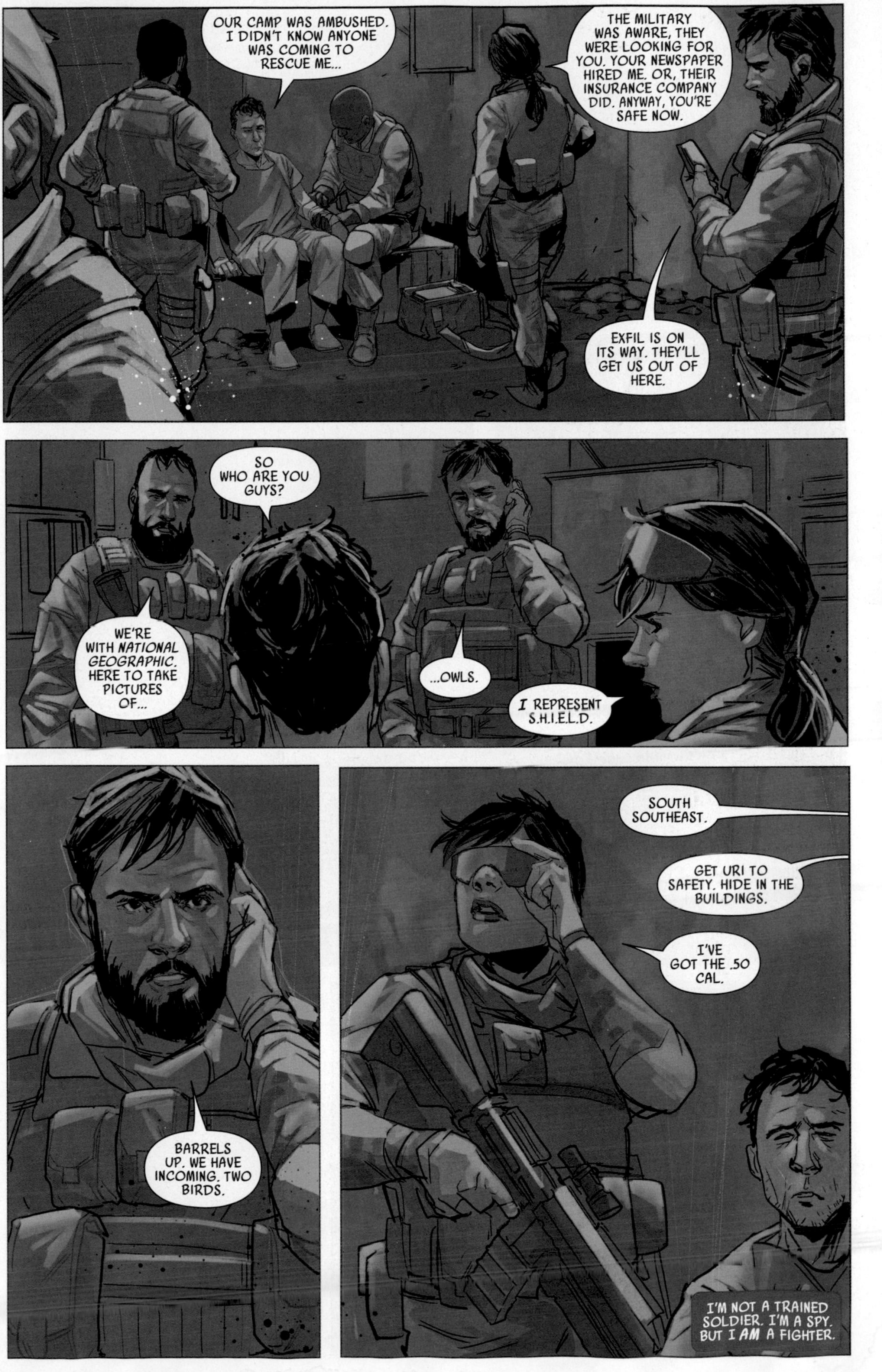
OUR CAMP WAS AMBUSHED. I DIDN'T KNOW ANYONE WAS COMING TO RESCUE ME...
THE MILITARY WAS AWARE, THEY WERE LOOKING FOR YOU. YOUR NEWSPAPER HIRED ME. OR, THEIR INSURANCE COMPANY DID. ANYWAY, YOU'RE SAFE NOW.
EXFIL IS ON ITS WAY. THEY'LL GET US OUT OF HERE.
SO WHO ARE YOU GUYS?
WE'RE WITH NATIONAL GEOGRAPHIC. HERE TO TAKE PICTURES OF...
...OWLS.
I REPRESENT S.H.I.E.L.D.
BARRELS UP. WE HAVE INCOMING. TWO BIRDS.
SOUTH SOUTHEAST.
GET URI TO SAFETY. HIDE IN THE BUILDINGS.
I'VE GOT THE .50 CAL.
I'M NOT A TRAINED SOLDIER. I'M A SPY. BUT I AM A FIGHTER.

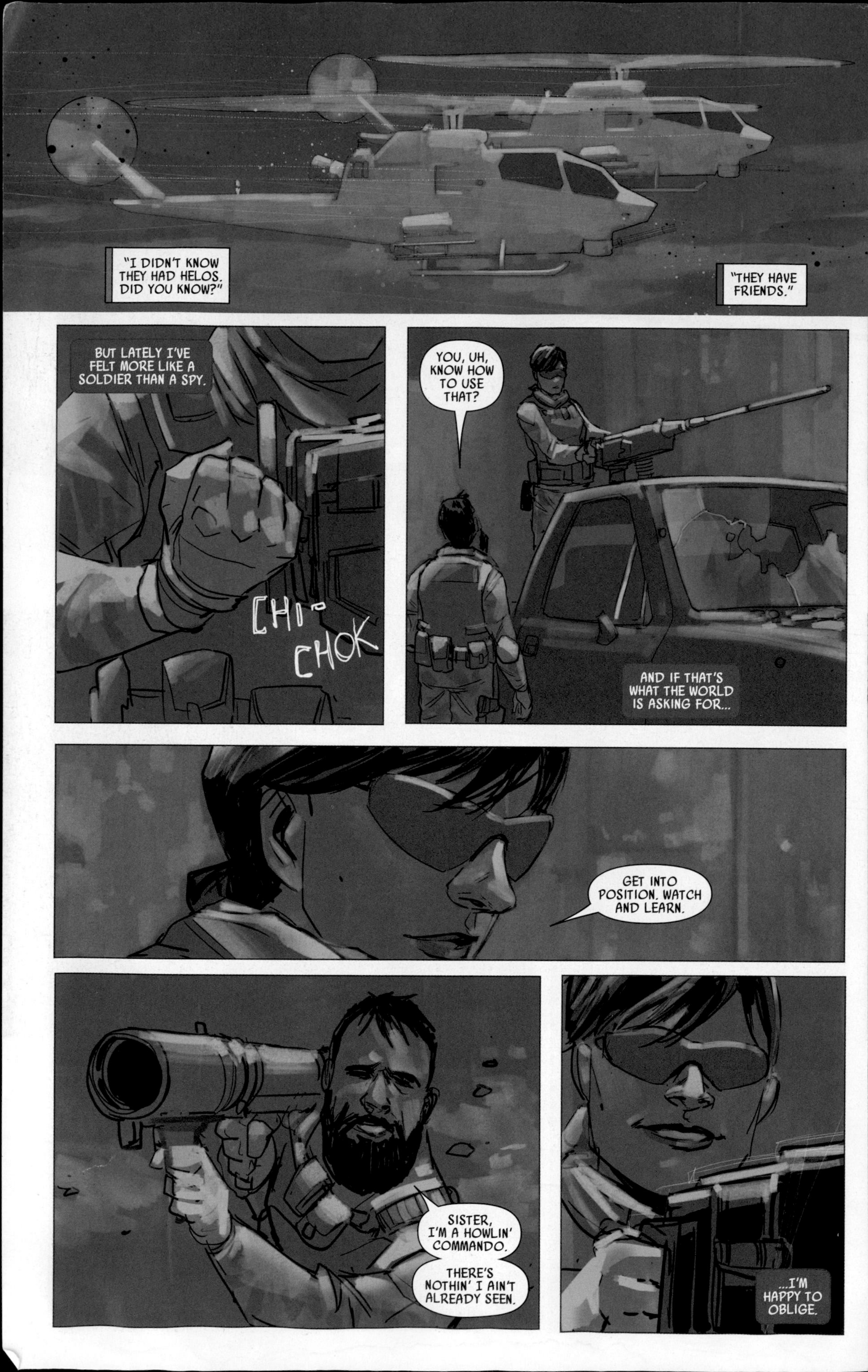
"I DIDN'T KNOW THEY HAD HELOS. DID YOU KNOW?"
"THEY HAVE FRIENDS."
BUT LATELY I'VE FELT MORE LIKE A SOLDIER THAN A SPY.
CHI-CHOK
YOU, UH, KNOW HOW TO USE THAT?
AND IF THAT'S WHAT THE WORLD IS ASKING FOR...
GET INTO POSITION. WATCH AND LEARN.
SISTER, I'M A HOWLIN' COMMANDO.
THERE'S NOTHIN' I AIN'T ALREADY SEEN.
...I'M HAPPY TO OBLIGE.

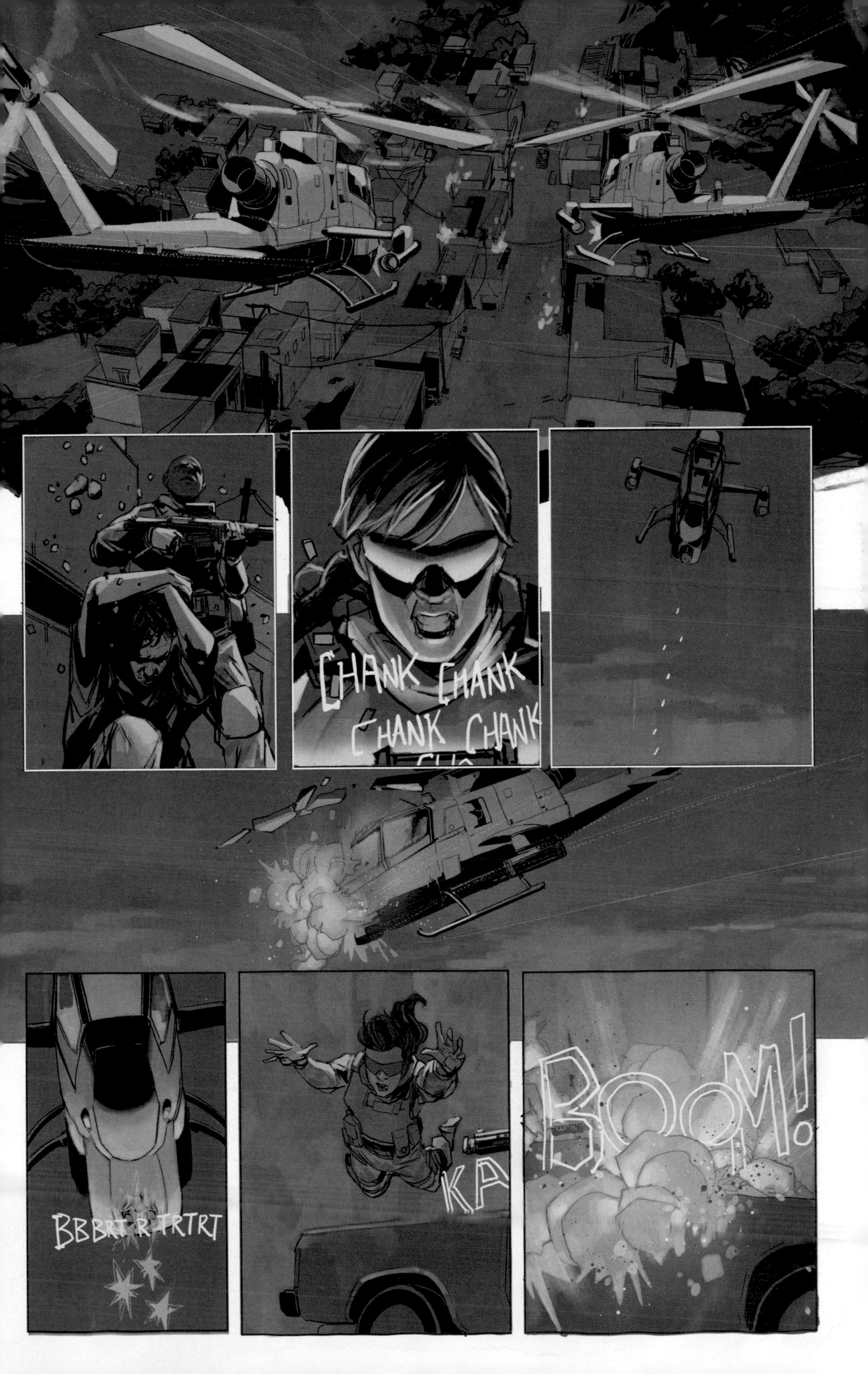
CHANK CHANK
CHANK CHANK
BBBRT R TRTRT
KA
BOOM!

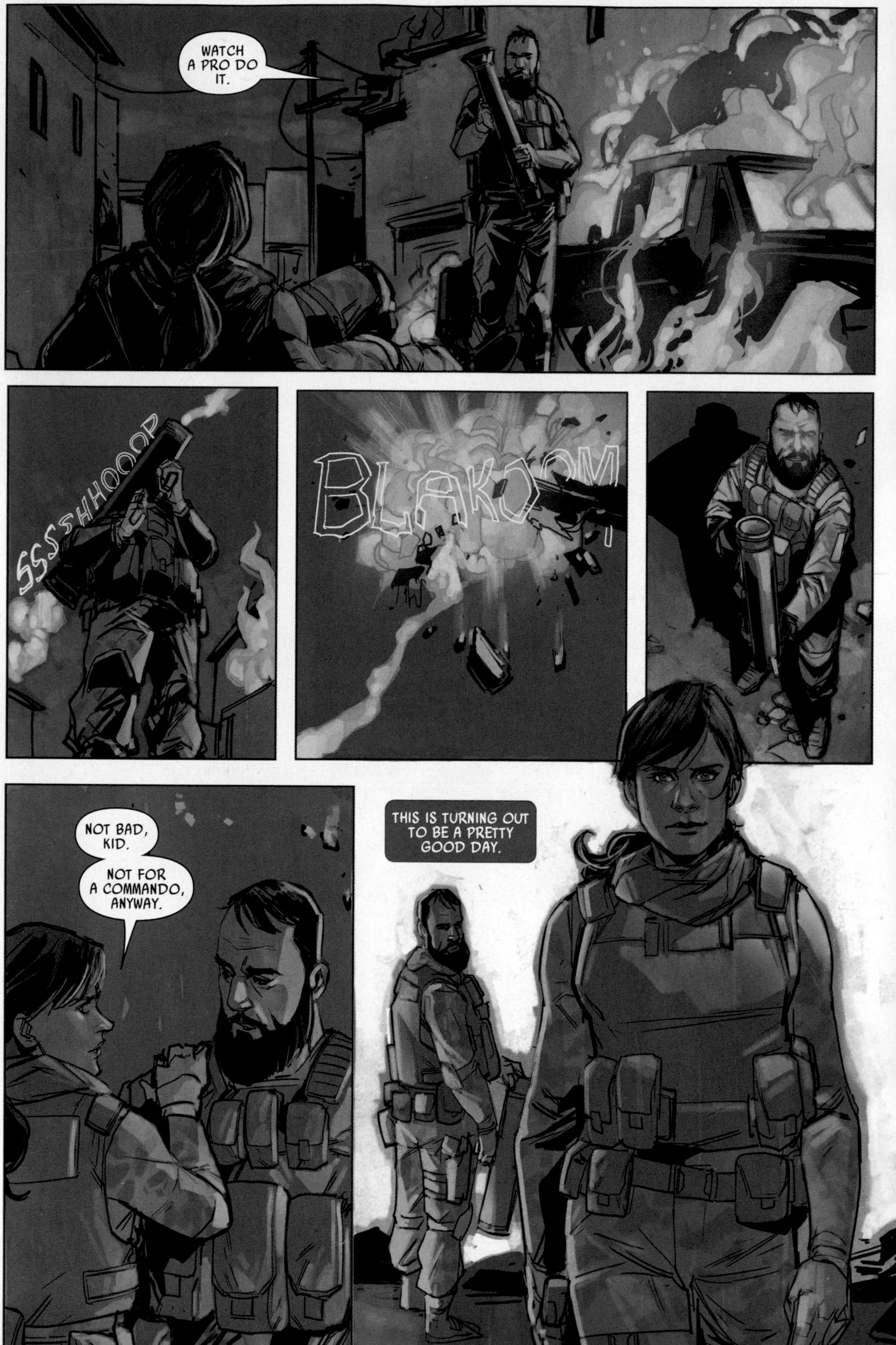
WATCH A PRO DO IT.
SSSSHHOOOP
BLAKOOM
NOT BAD, KID.
NOT FOR A COMMANDO, ANYWAY.
THIS IS TURNING OUT TO BE A PRETTY GOOD DAY.

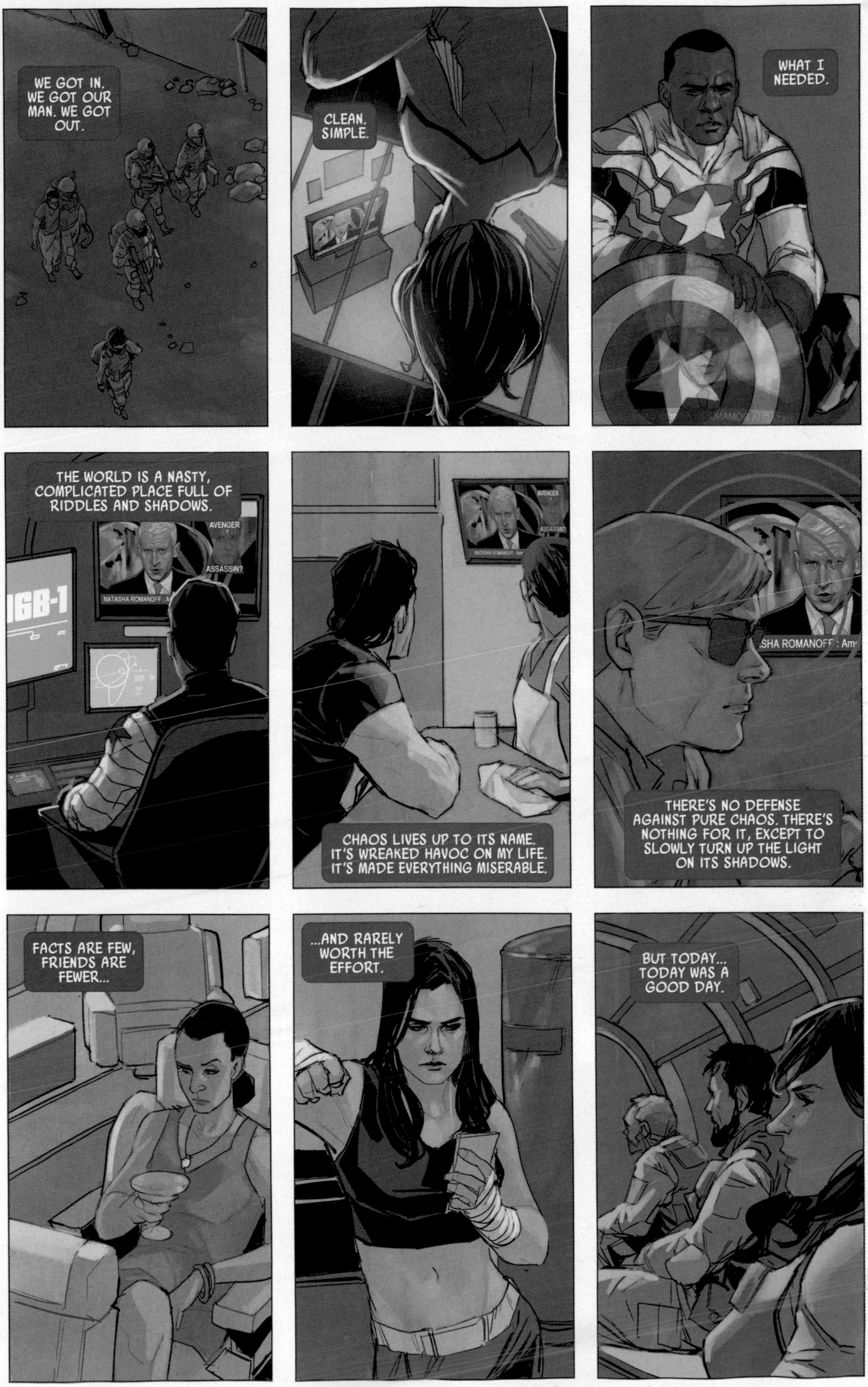
WE GOT IN. WE GOT OUR MAN. WE GOT OUT.
CLEAN. SIMPLE.
WHAT I NEEDED.
THE WORLD IS A NASTY, COMPLICATED PLACE FULL OF RIDDLES AND SHADOWS.
AVENGER
ASSASSIN?
NATASHA ROMANOFF
CHAOS LIVES UP TO ITS NAME. IT'S WREAKED HAVOC ON MY LIFE. IT'S MADE EVERYTHING MISERABLE.
THERE'S NO DEFENSE AGAINST PURE CHAOS. THERE'S NOTHING FOR IT, EXCEPT TO SLOWLY TURN UP THE LIGHT ON ITS SHADOWS.
FACTS ARE FEW, FRIENDS ARE FEWER...
...AND RARELY WORTH THE EFFORT.
BUT TODAY... TODAY WAS A GOOD DAY.

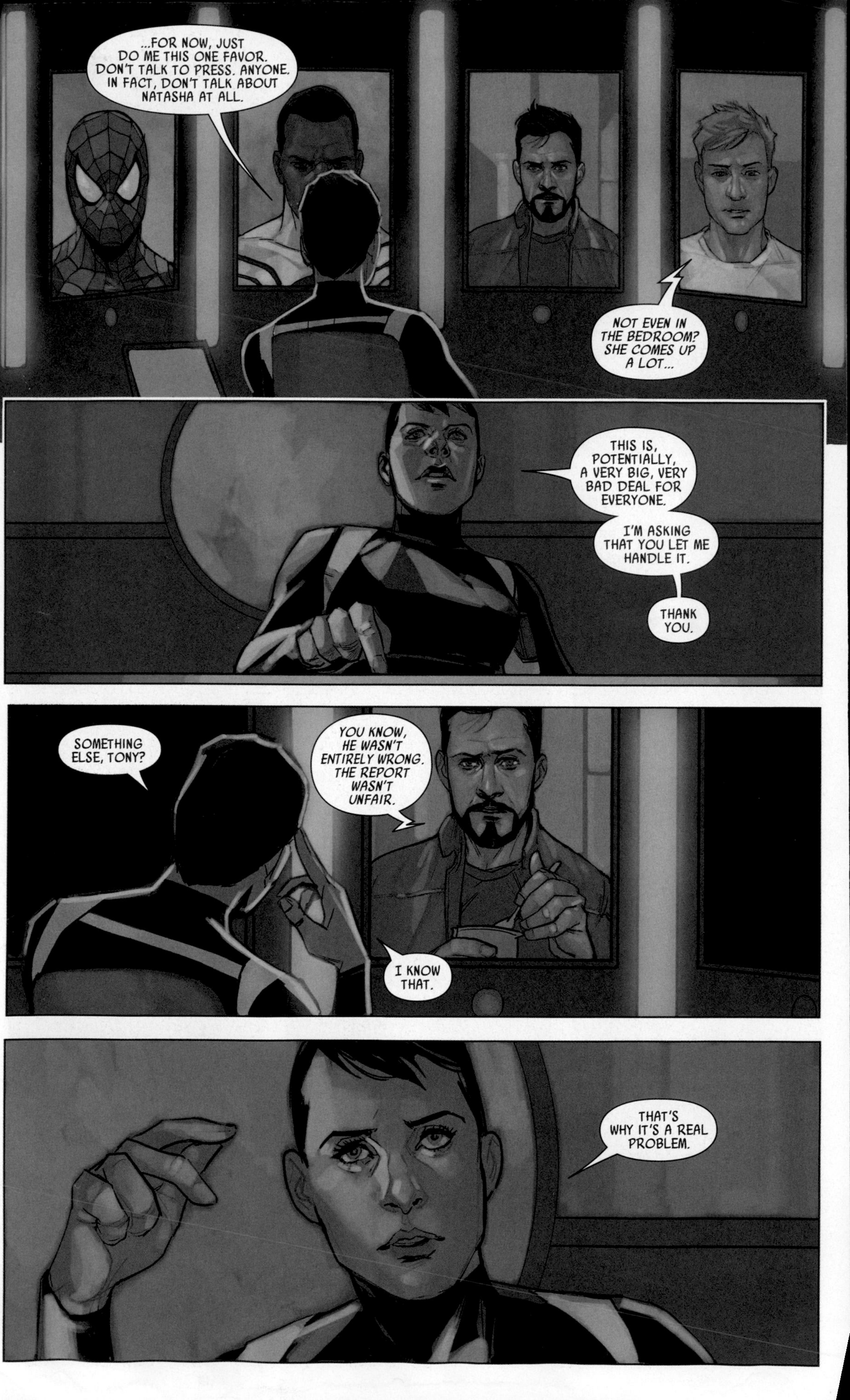
...FOR NOW, JUST DO ME THIS ONE FAVOR. DON'T TALK TO PRESS. ANYONE. IN FACT, DON'T TALK ABOUT NATASHA AT ALL.
NOT EVEN IN THE BEDROOM? SHE COMES UP A LOT...
THIS IS, POTENTIALLY, A VERY BIG, VERY BAD DEAL FOR EVERYONE.
I'M ASKING THAT YOU LET ME HANDLE IT.
THANK YOU.
SOMETHING ELSE, TONY?
YOU KNOW, HE WASN'T ENTIRELY WRONG. THE REPORT WASN'T UNFAIR.
I KNOW THAT.
THAT'S WHY IT'S A REAL PROBLEM.

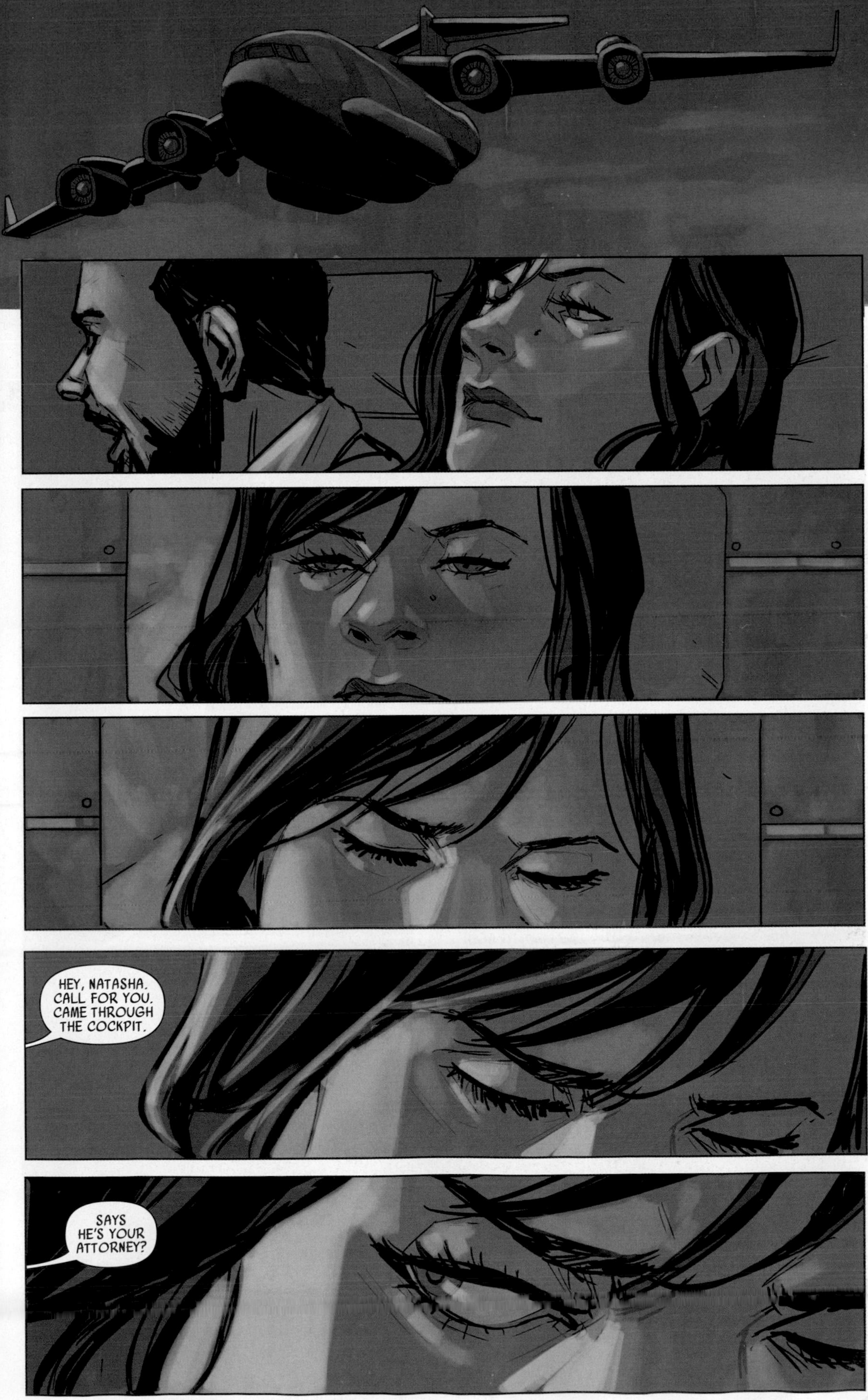
HEY, NATASHA. CALL FOR YOU. CAME THROUGH THE COCKPIT.
SAYS HE'S YOUR ATTORNEY?

...IT'S NOT THAT BAD, NAT. I JUST WANTED YOU TO KNOW BEFORE YOU LANDED. I EVEN DVR'D IT SO YOU CAN WATCH.

IT ACTUALLY HAS A FEW GREAT SHOTS OF YOU.

...YES, CONGRESSWOMAN, BUT THIS IS JOURNALISM. I'M A JOURNALIST, NOT A PREACHER. I'M JUST ASKING THE QUESTION:

CAN WE TRUST THE BLACK WIDOW? CAN THE PUBLIC THAT SHE'S SUPPOSED TO PROTECT?

...A FEW NOT SO GOOD ONES, TOO.

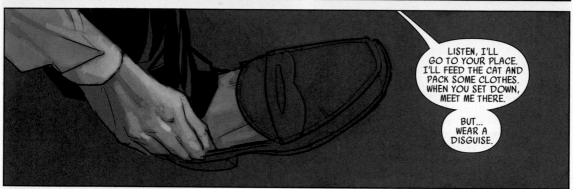

LISTEN, I'LL GO TO YOUR PLACE. I'LL FEED THE CAT AND PACK SOME CLOTHES. WHEN YOU SET DOWN, MEET ME THERE.

BUT... WEAR A DISGUISE.

DON'T WORRY, OKAY? I'M HERE FOR YOU.

...WE WANT TO HEAR FROM YOU ON TWITTER, "#WHOISBLACKWIDOW."

TELL US: DO YOU THINK WE SHOULD TRUST HER?

RUSTED? #WHOISBLACKWIDOW

WE HAVE TO.

CLIK

I'VE ONLY EVER BEEN GOOD AT ONE THING.

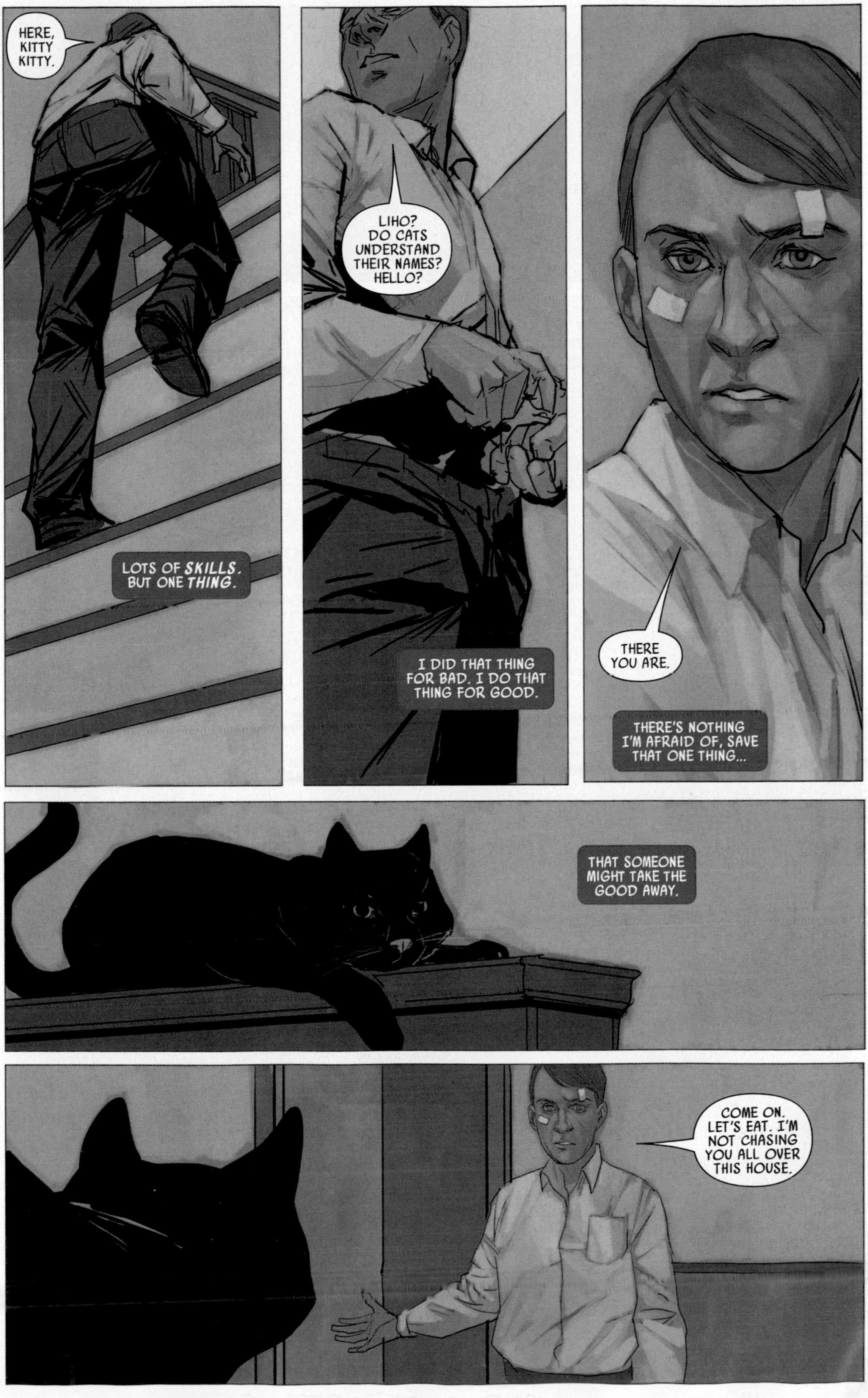
HERE, KITTY KITTY.
LOTS OF SKILLS. BUT ONE THING.
LIHO? DO CATS UNDERSTAND THEIR NAMES? HELLO?
I DID THAT THING FOR BAD. I DO THAT THING FOR GOOD.
THERE YOU ARE.
THERE'S NOTHING I'M AFRAID OF, SAVE THAT ONE THING...
THAT SOMEONE MIGHT TAKE THE GOOD AWAY.
COME ON. LET'S EAT. I'M NOT CHASING YOU ALL OVER THIS HOUSE.

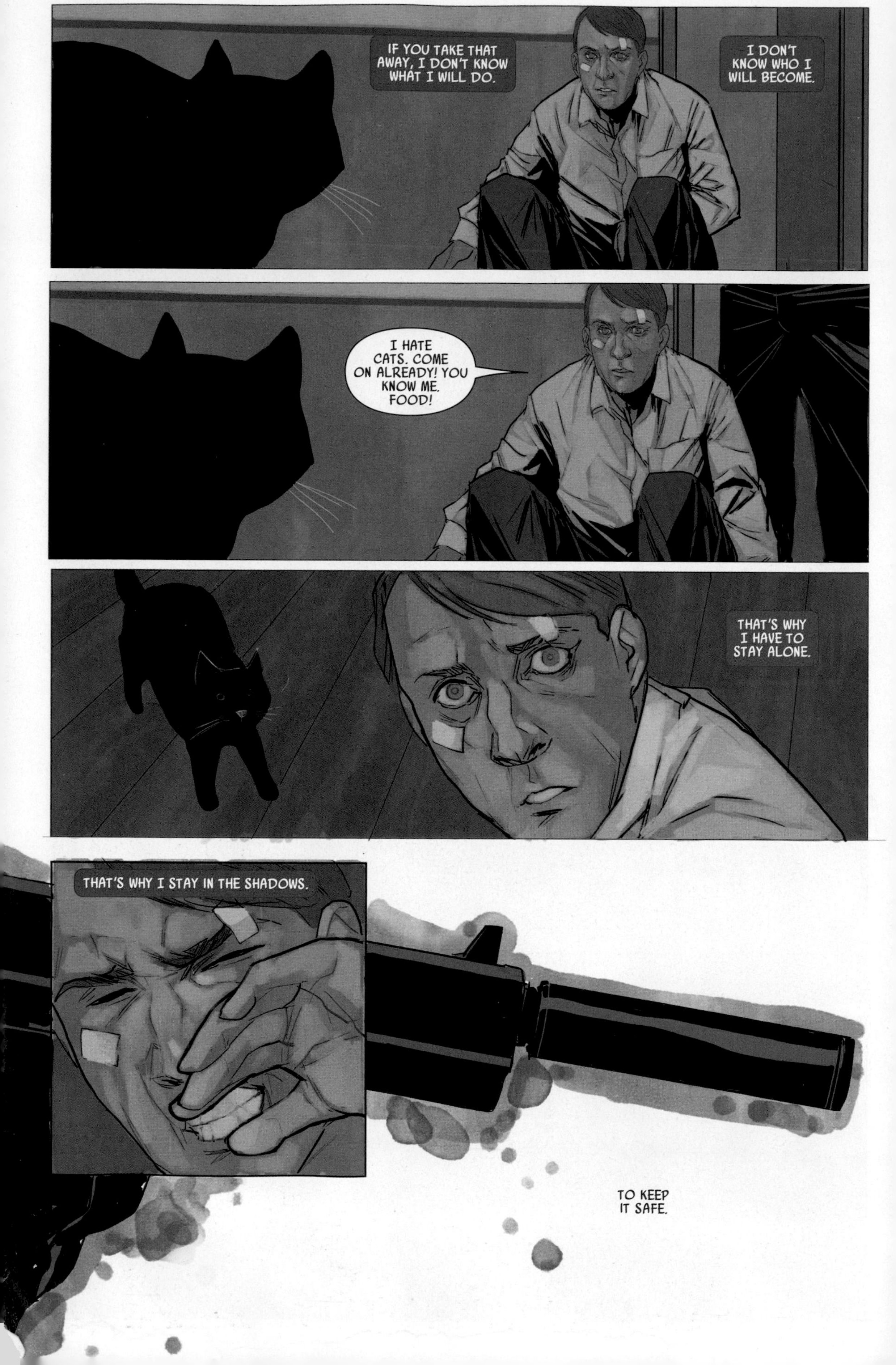
IF YOU TAKE THAT AWAY, I DON'T KNOW WHAT I WILL DO.
I DON'T KNOW WHO I WILL BECOME.
I HATE CATS. COME ON ALREADY! YOU KNOW ME. FOOD!
THAT'S WHY I HAVE TO STAY ALONE.
THAT'S WHY I STAY IN THE SHADOWS.
TO KEEP IT SAFE.

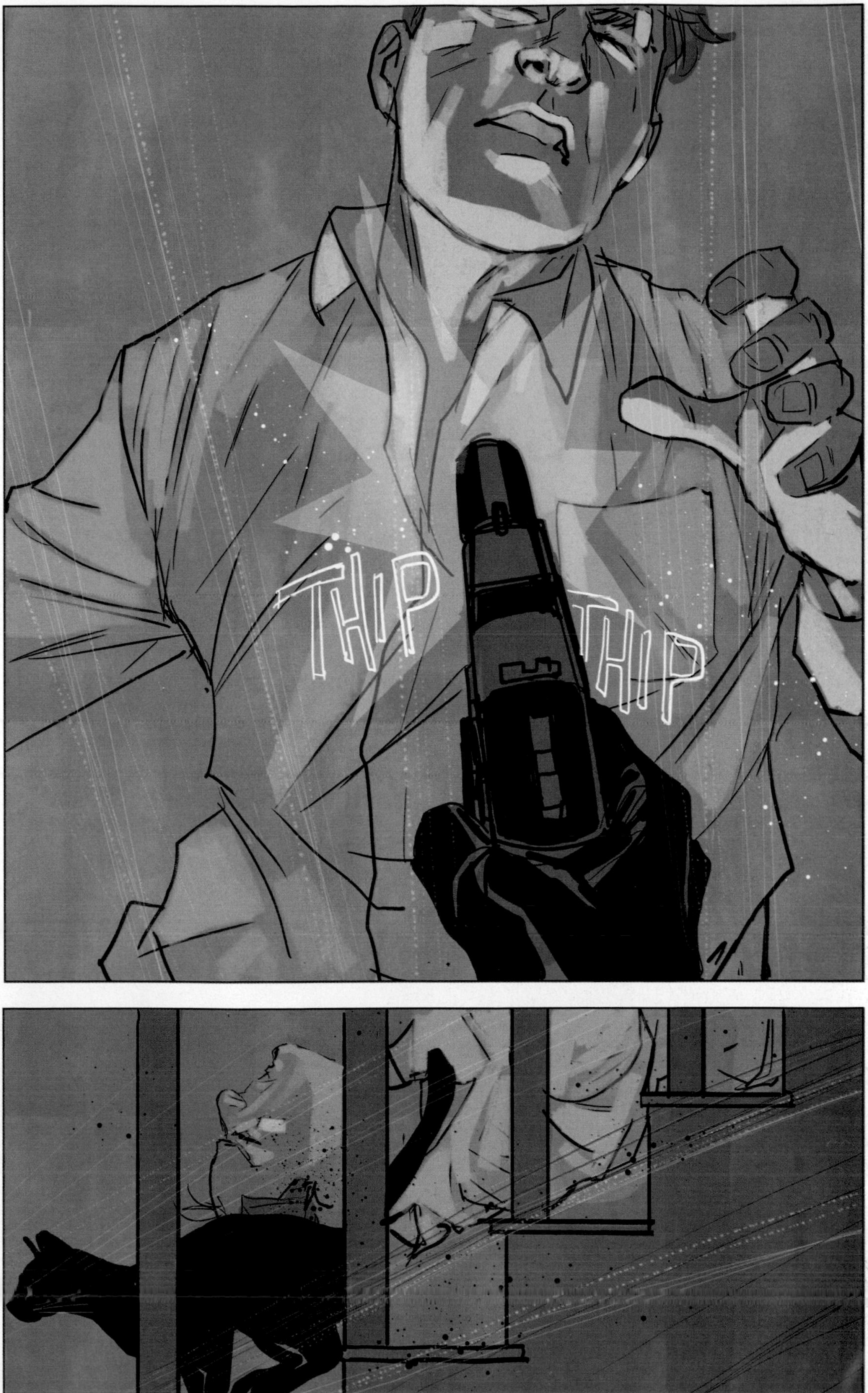
THIP
THIP

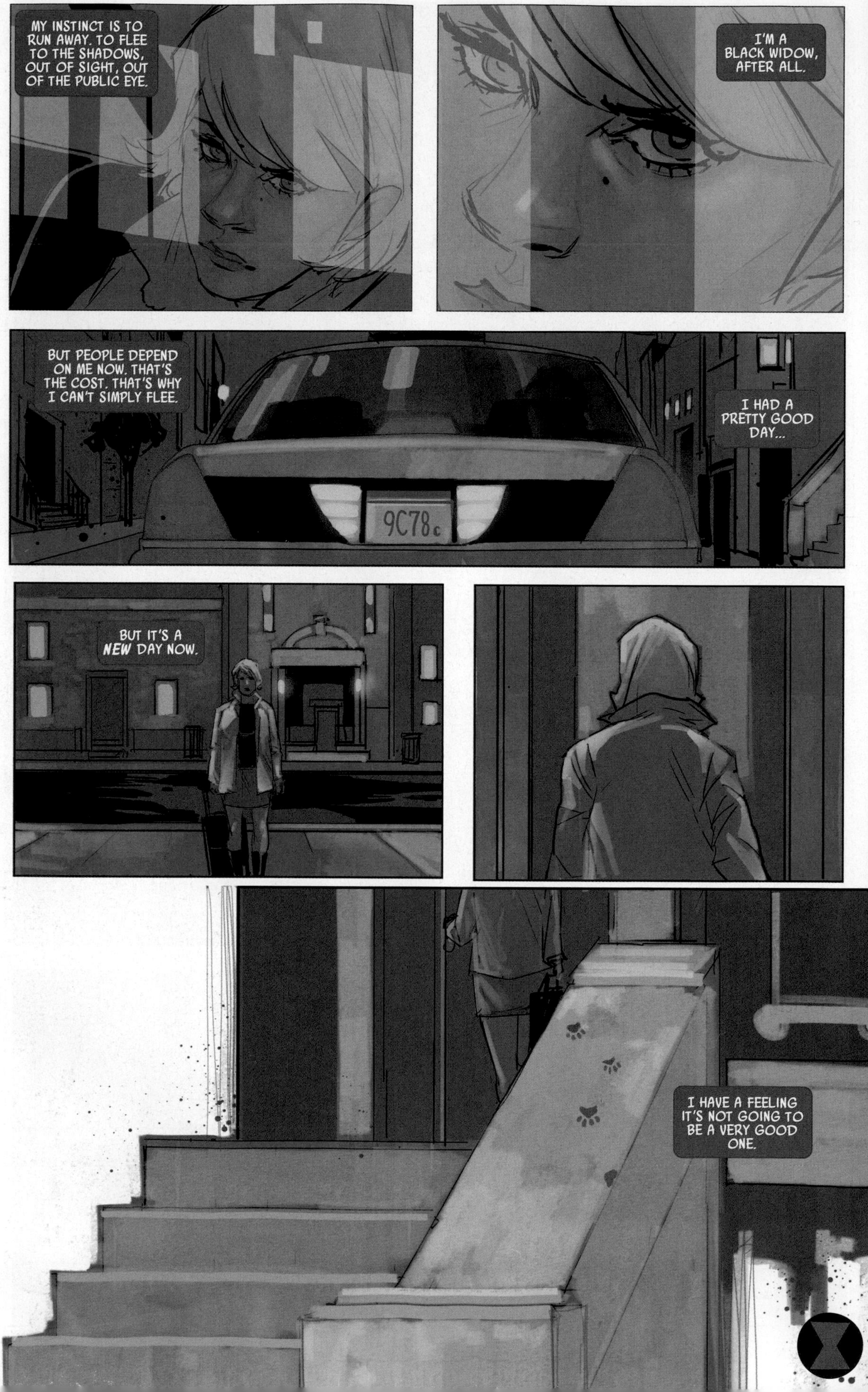
MY INSTINCT IS TO RUN AWAY. TO FLEE TO THE SHADOWS, OUT OF SIGHT, OUT OF THE PUBLIC EYE.
I'M A BLACK WIDOW, AFTER ALL.
BUT PEOPLE DEPEND ON ME NOW. THAT'S THE COST. THAT'S WHY I CAN'T SIMPLY FLEE.
9C78c
I HAD A PRETTY GOOD DAY...
BUT IT'S A NEW DAY NOW.
I HAVE A FEELING IT'S NOT GOING TO BE A VERY GOOD ONE.

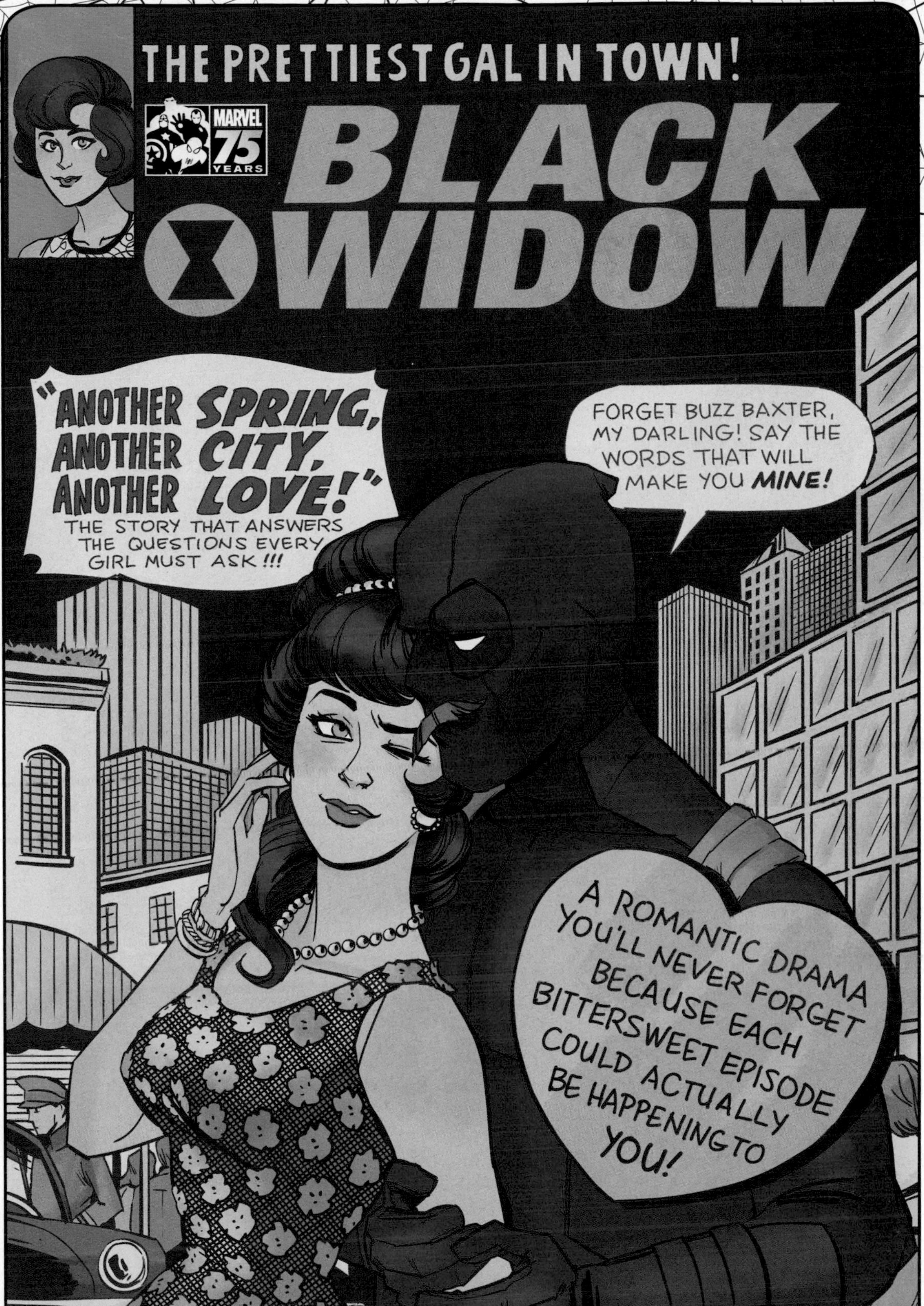
THE PRETTIEST GAL IN TOWN!
MARVEL 75 YEARS
BLACK WIDOW
"ANOTHER SPRING, ANOTHER CITY, ANOTHER LOVE!"
THE STORY THAT ANSWERS THE QUESTIONS EVERY GIRL MUST ASK!!!
FORGET BUZZ BAXTER, MY DARLING! SAY THE WORDS THAT WILL MAKE YOU MINE!
A ROMANTIC DRAMA YOU'LL NEVER FORGET BECAUSE EACH BITTERSWEET EPISODE COULD ACTUALLY BE HAPPENING TO YOU!

#11 DEADPOOL 75TH ANNIVERSARY VARIANT BY ANNIE WU

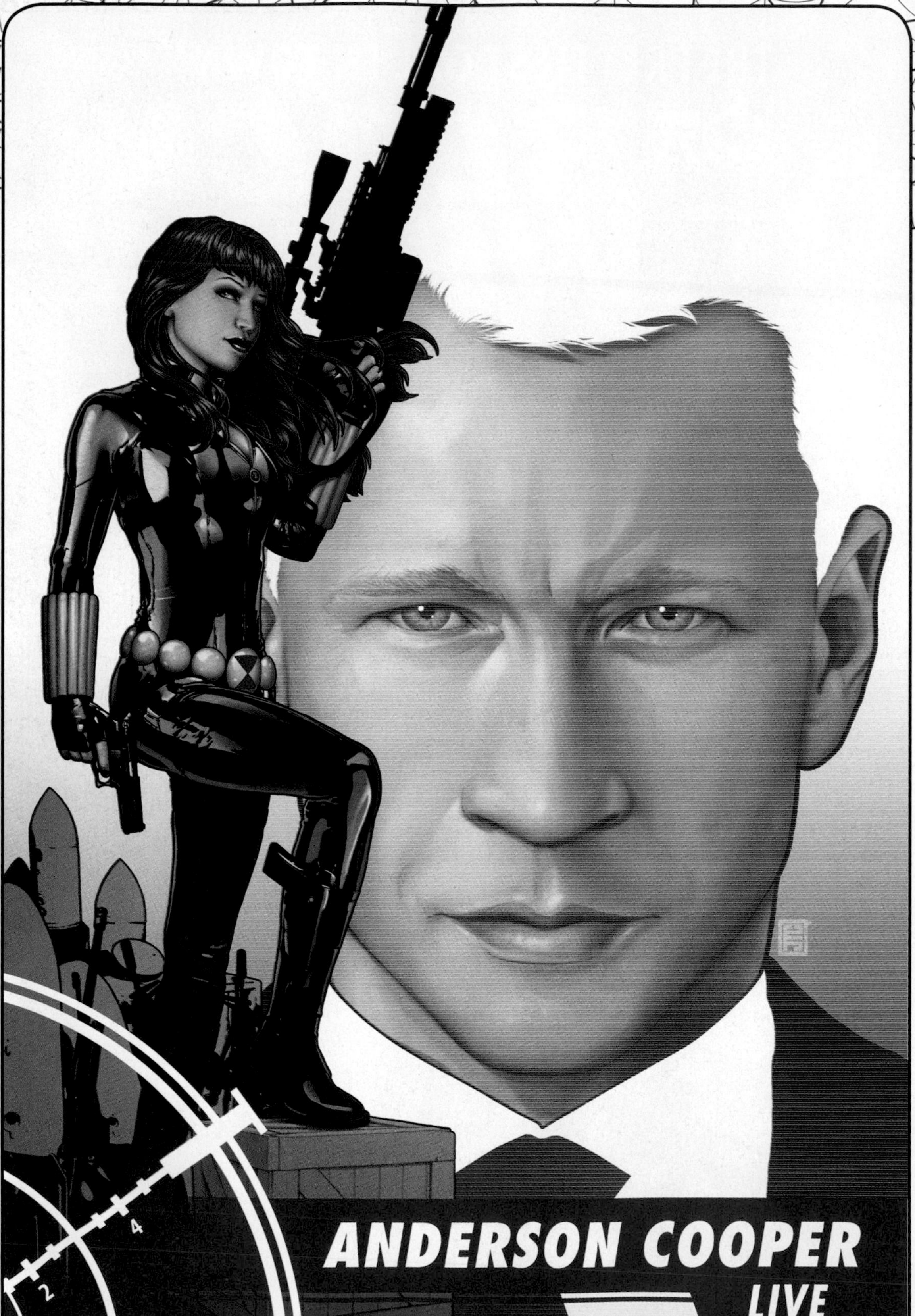

4
2
ANDERSON COOPER
LIVE

#12 VARIANT BY JOHN TYLER CHRISTOPHER

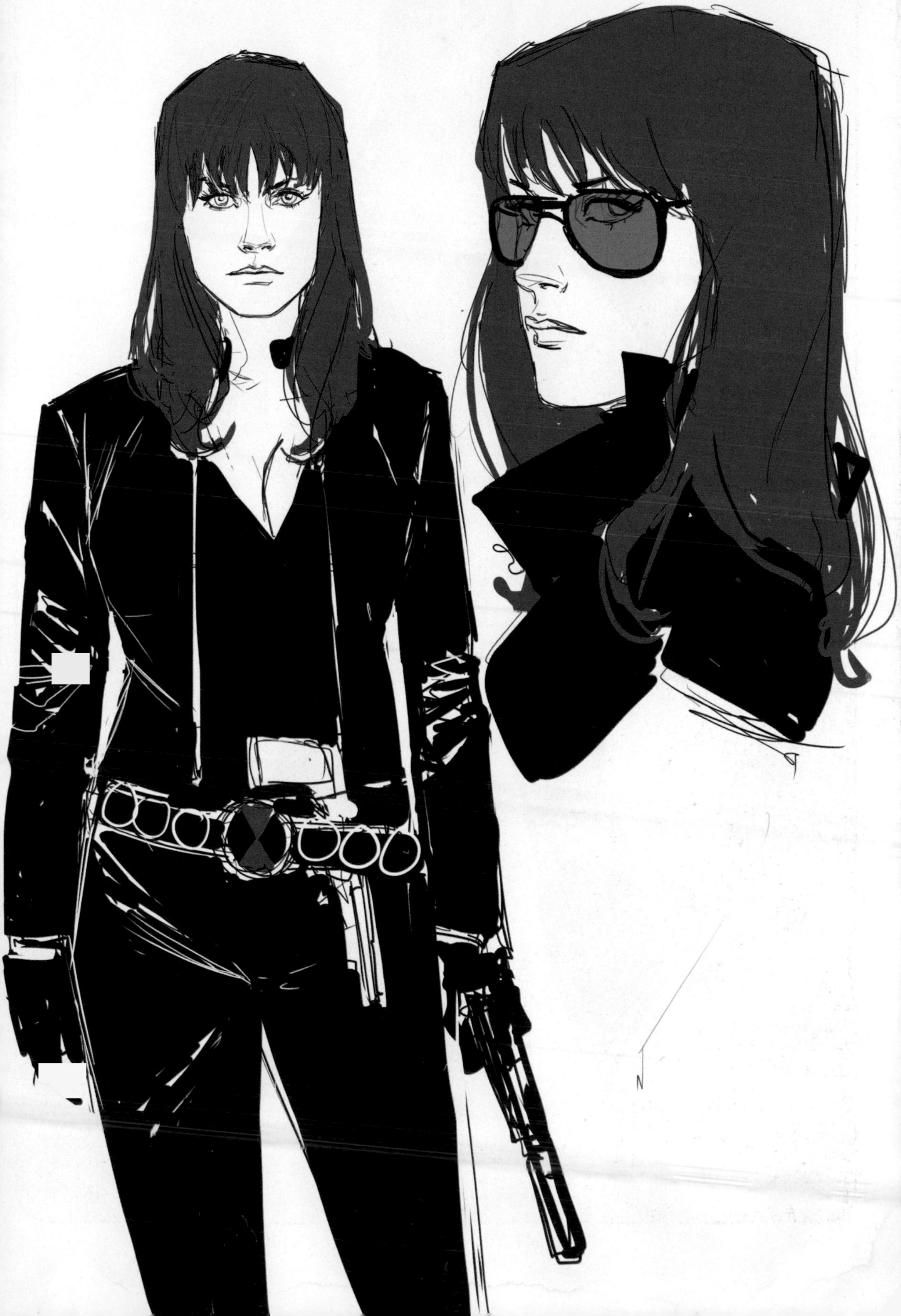

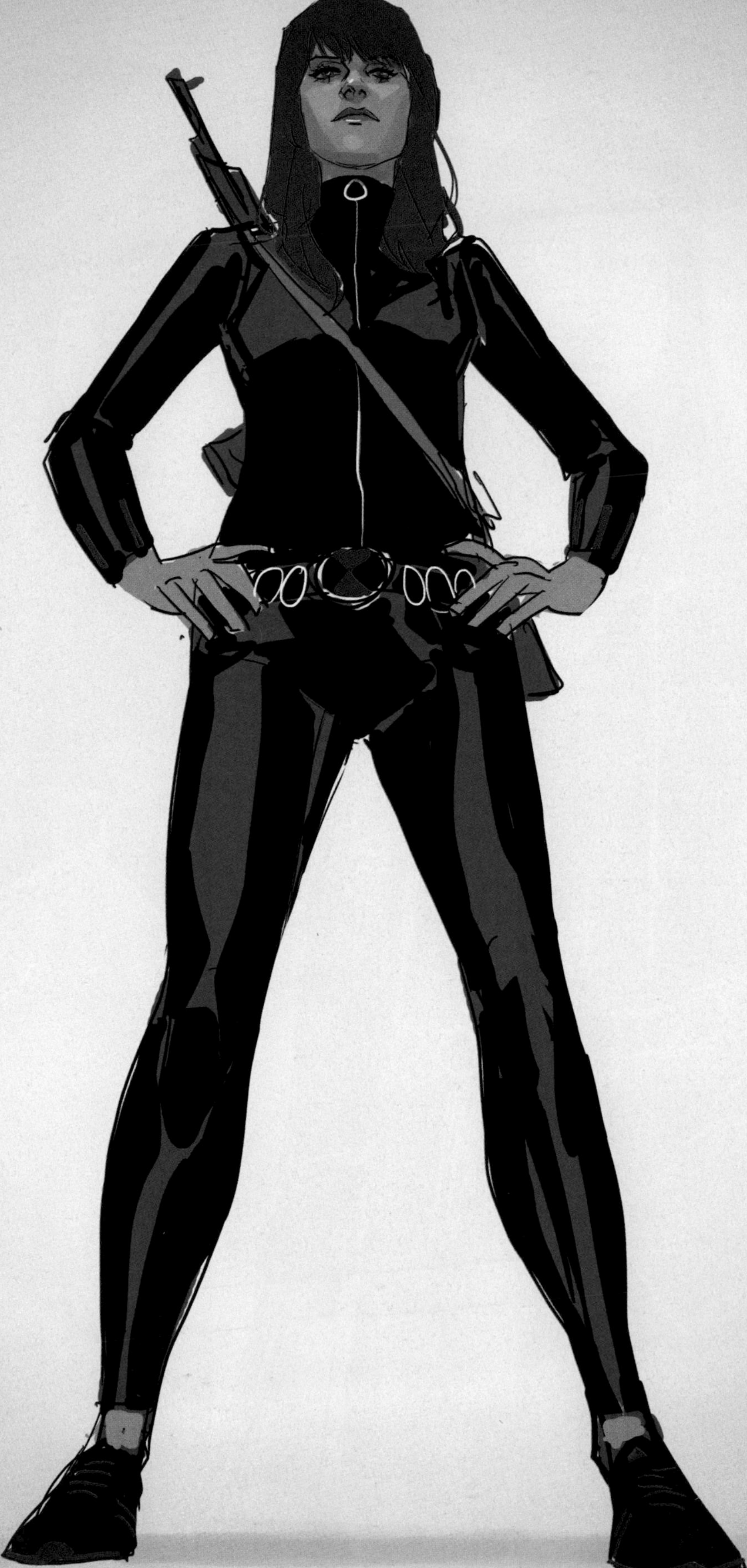

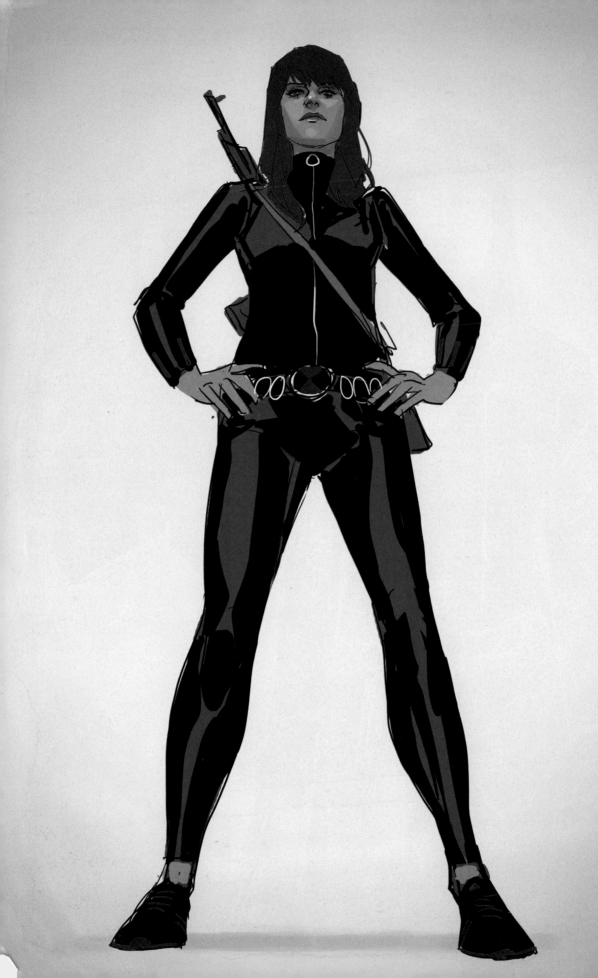

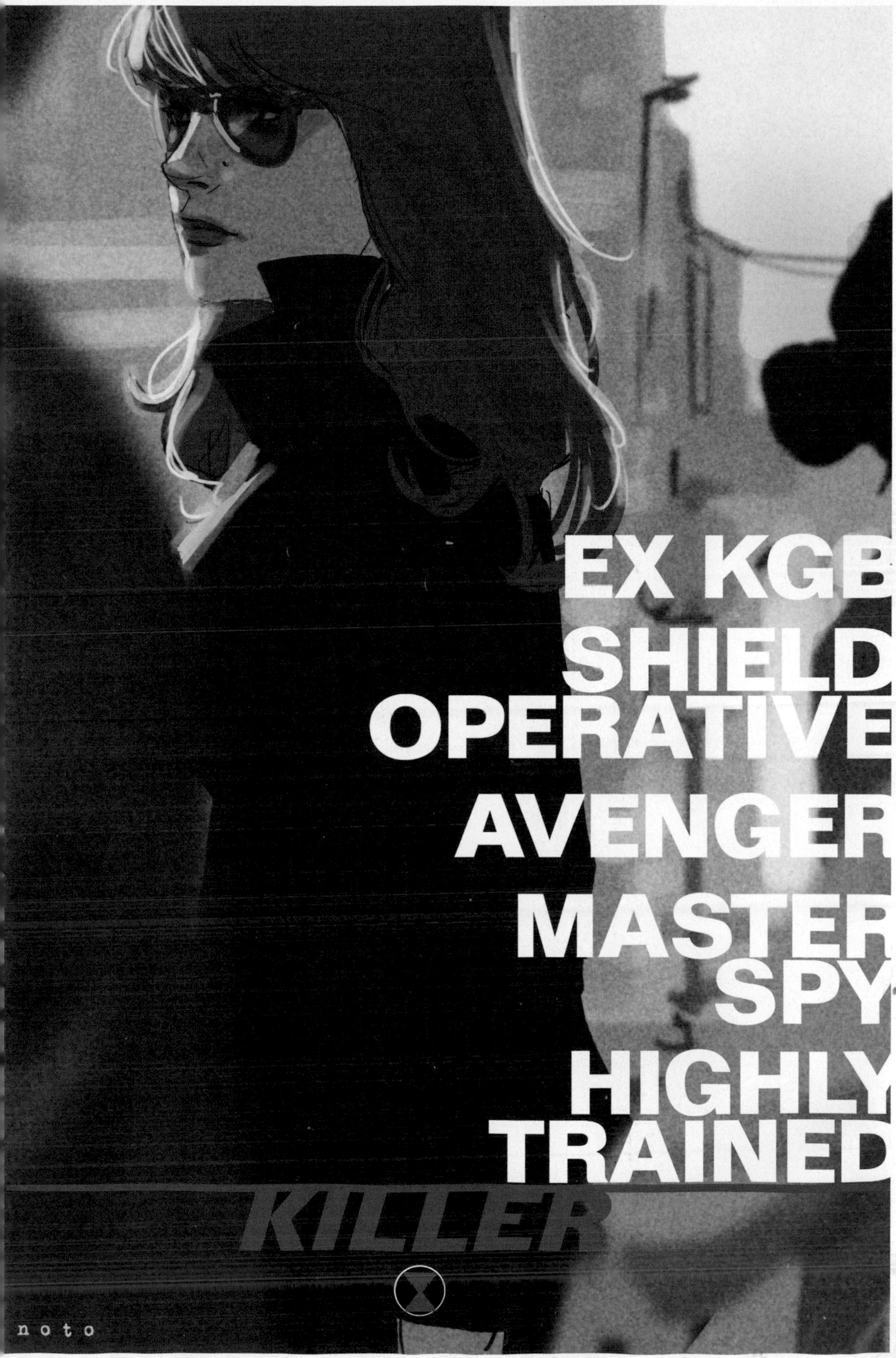
EX KGB
SHIELD
OPERATIVE
AVENGER
MASTER
SPY
HIGHLY
TRAINED
KILLER
noto

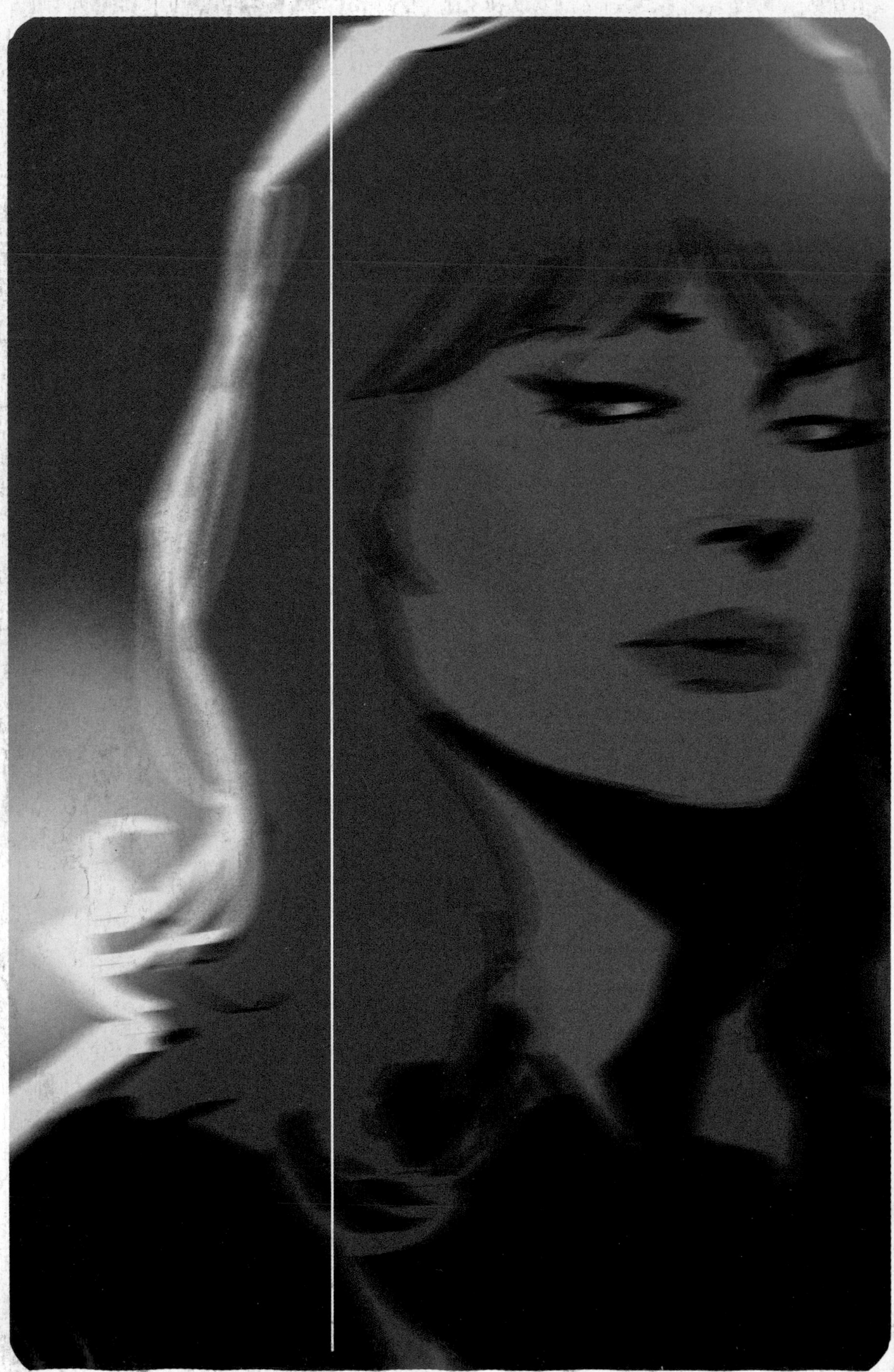

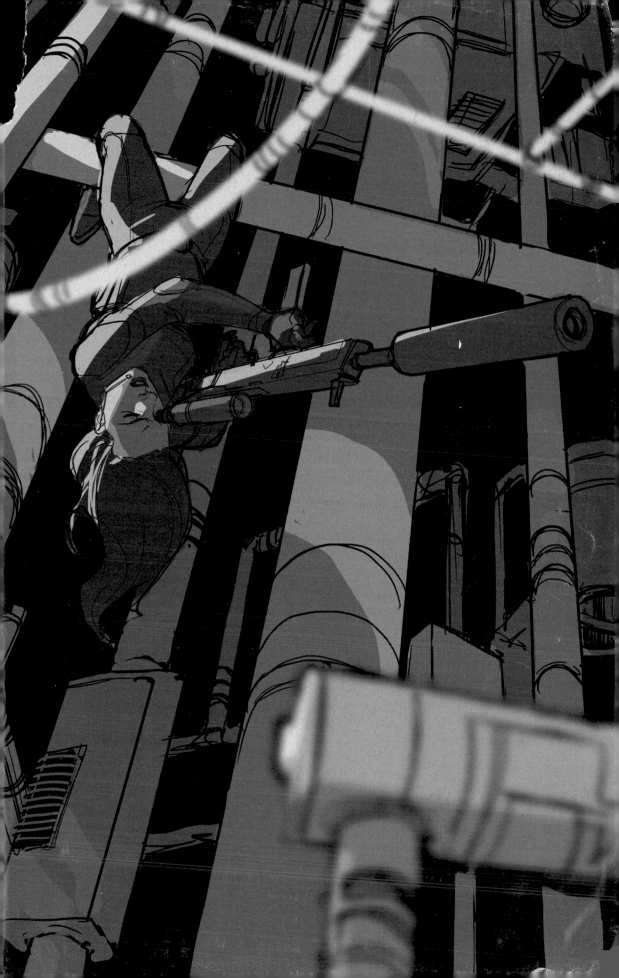

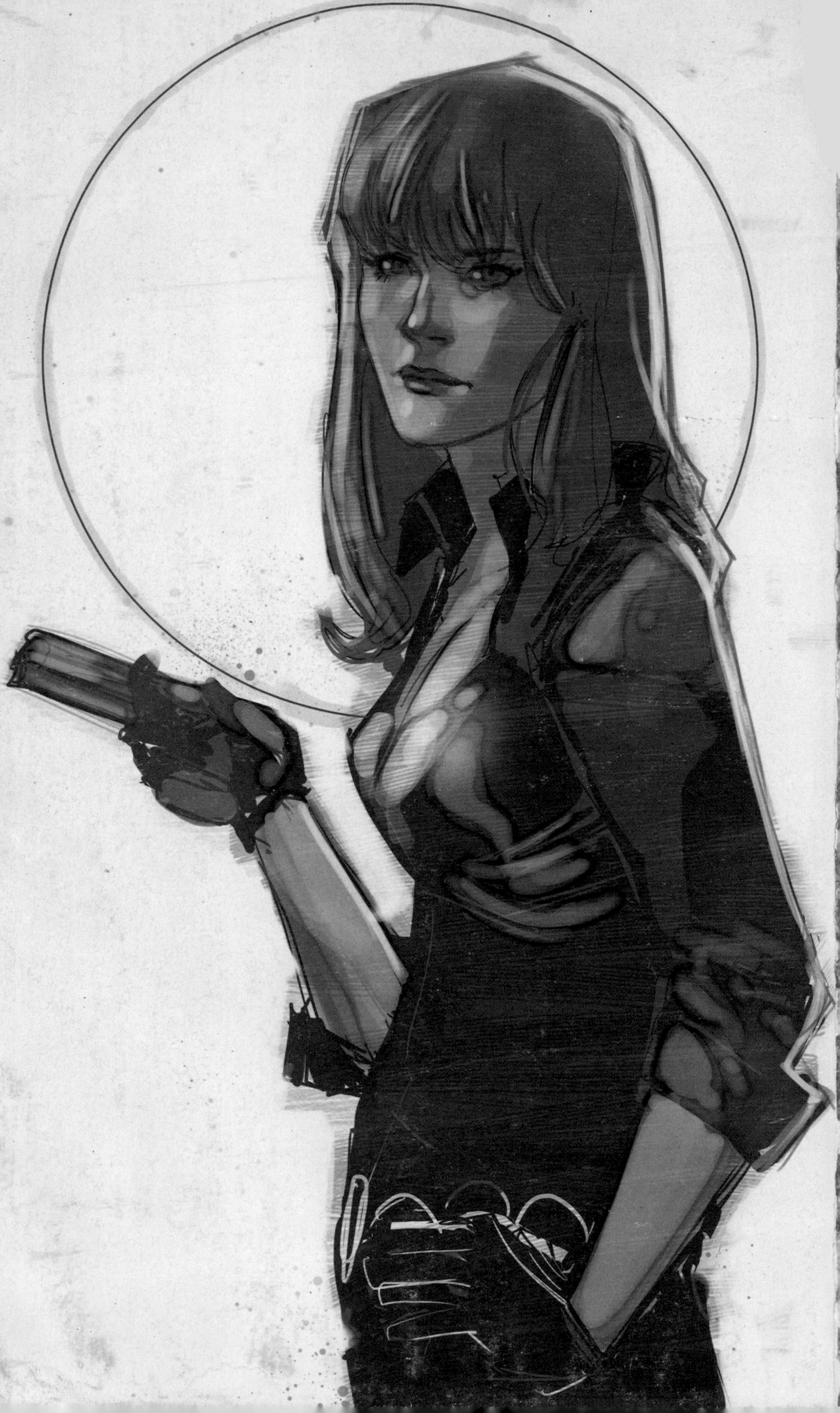